NEW DIRECTIONS IN SOVIET LITERATURE

SELECTED PAPERS FROM THE FOURTH WORLD CONGRESS FOR
SOVIET AND EAST EUROPEAN STUDIES, HARROGATE, 1990

*Edited for the International Council for Soviet and East European Studies by
Stephen White, Professor of Politics, University of Glasgow*

From the same publishers:

Roy Allison (*editor*)
RADICAL REFORM IN SOVIET DEFENCE POLICY

Ben Eklof (*editor*)
SCHOOL AND SOCIETY IN TSARIST AND SOVIET RUSSIA

John Elsworth (*editor*)
THE SILVER AGE IN RUSSIAN LITERATURE

John Garrard and Carol Garrard (*editors*)
WORLD WAR 2 AND THE SOVIET PEOPLE

Zvi Gitelman (*editor*)
THE POLITICS OF NATIONALITY AND THE EROSION OF THE USSR

Sheelagh Duffin Graham (*editor*)
NEW DIRECTIONS IN SOVIET LITERATURE

Celia Hawkesworth (*editor*)
LITERATURE AND POLITICS IN EASTERN EUROPE

Lindsey Hughes (*editor*)
NEW PERSPECTIVES ON MUSCOVITE HISTORY

Walter Joyce (*editor*)
SOCIAL CHANGE AND SOCIAL ISSUES IN THE FORMER USSR

Bohdan Krawchenko (*editor*)
UKRAINIAN PAST, UKRAINIAN PRESENT

Paul G. Lewis (*editor*)
DEMOCRACY AND CIVIL SOCIETY IN EASTERN EUROPE

Robert B. McKean (*editor*)
NEW PERSPECTIVES IN MODERN RUSSIAN HISTORY

John Morison (*editor*)
THE CZECH AND SLOVAK EXPERIENCE
EASTERN EUROPE AND THE WEST

John O. Norman (*editor*)
NEW PERSPECTIVES ON RUSSIAN AND SOVIET ARTISTIC CULTURE

Derek Offord (*editor*)
THE GOLDEN AGE OF RUSSIAN LITERATURE AND THOUGHT

Michael E. Urban (*editor*)
IDEOLOGY AND SYSTEM CHANGE IN THE USSR AND EAST EUROPE

New Directions in Soviet Literature

Selected Papers from the Fourth World Congress for Soviet and East European Studies, Harrogate, 1990

Edited by

Sheelagh Duffin Graham
Senior Lecturer in Russian Studies
University of Strathclyde

St. Martin's Press

© International Council for Soviet and East European Studies,
and Sheelagh Duffin Graham, 1992
General Editor's Introduction © Stephen White 1992

All rights reserved. No reproduction, copy or transmission of this publication may be made without written permission.

No paragraph of this publication may be reproduced, copied or transmitted save with written permission or in accordance with the provisions of the Copyright, Designs and Patents Act 1988, or under the terms of any licence permitting limited copying issued by the Copyright Licensing Agency, 90 Tottenham Court Road, London W1P 9HE.

Any person who does any unauthorised act in relation to this publication may be liable to criminal prosecution and civil claims for damages.

First published in Great Britain 1992 by
THE MACMILLAN PRESS LTD
Houndmills, Basingstoke, Hampshire RG21 2XS
and London
Companies and representatives
throughout the world

This book is published in association with the International Council for Soviet and East European Studies.

A catalogue record for this book is available from the British Library.

ISBN 0-333-55732-8

Printed in Great Britain by Antony Rowe Ltd, Chippenham, Wiltshire

---

First published in the United States of America 1992 by
Scholarly and Reference Division,
ST. MARTIN'S PRESS, INC.,
175 Fifth Avenue,
New York, N.Y. 10010

ISBN 0-312-07990-7

Library of Congress Cataloging-in-Publication Data
World Congress for Soviet and East European Studies (4th: 1990:
Harrogate, England)
New directions in Soviet literature: selected papers from the
Fourth World Congress for Soviet and East European Studies,
Harrogate, 1990 / edited by Sheelagh Duffin Graham.
p. cm.
Includes index.
ISBN 0-312-07990-7
1. Soviet literature—History and criticism—Congresses.
2. Soviet Union—Literatures—History and criticism—Congresses.
3. Russian literature—20th century—History and criticism-
-Congresses. I. Graham, Sheelagh Duffin. II. International
Council for Soviet and East European Studies. III. Title.
PN849.R9W67   1992
891.709—dc20   92-3436
                                                        CIP

Contents

General Editor's Introduction		vii
Preface		xi
Notes on the Contributors		xv
1	The Crisis of Soviet Artistic Mentality in the 1960s and 1970s *Galina Belaia*	1
2	The Left *Avant-garde* Theatre in the Late 1920s *Katerina Clark*	18
3	Tolstaian Times: Traversals and Transfers *Helena Goscilo*	36
4	Myth in the Works of Chingiz Aitmatov *Nina Kolesnikoff*	63
5	The Naturalistic Tendency in Contemporary Soviet Fiction: Thematics, Poetics, Functions *Konstantin Kustanovich*	75
6	Reassessing the Past: Images of Stalin and Stalinism in Contemporary Russian Literature *Rosalind Marsh*	89
7	Village Prose: Chauvinism, Nationalism or Nostalgia? *Kathleen Parthé*	106
8	Brodsky's Poetic Self-portrait *Valentina Polukhina*	122
9	A Matter of (Dis)course: Metafiction in the Works of Daniil Kharms *Graham Roberts*	138
10	Pilate and Pilatism in Recent Russian Literature *Margaret Ziolkowski*	164
Index of Names		183

General Editor's Introduction

The Fourth World Congress for Soviet and East European Studies took place in Harrogate, Yorkshire, in July 1990. It was an unusual congress in many ways. It was the first of its kind to take place in Britain, and the first to take place since the launching of Gorbachev's programme of *perestroika* and the revolutions in Eastern Europe (indeed so rapid was the pace of change in the countries with which we were concerned that the final programme had to incorporate over 600 amendments). It was the largest and most complex congress of Soviet and East European studies that has yet taken place, with twenty-seven panels spread over fourteen sessions on six days. It was also the most representative congress of its kind, with over 2000 participants including – for the first time – about 300 from the USSR and Eastern Europe. Most were scholars, some were activists, and a few were the new kind of academic turned part-time deputy: whatever their status, it was probably this Soviet and East European presence that contributed most directly to making this a very different congress from the ones that had preceded it in the 1970s and 1980s.

No series of volumes, however numerous, could hope to convey the full flavour of this extraordinary occasion. The formal panels alone incorporated a thousand papers. There were three further plenary sessions; there were many more unattached papers; and the subjects that were treated ranged from medieval Novgorod to computational linguistics, from the problems of the handicapped in the USSR to Serbian art at the time of the battle of Kosovo. Nor, it was decided at an early stage, would it even be desirable to attempt a fully comprehensive 'congress proceedings', including all the papers in their original form. My aim as General Editor, with the strong support of the International Council for Soviet and East European Studies (who cosponsored the congress with the British Association for Soviet, Slavonic and East European Studies), has rather been to generate a series of volumes which will have some thematic coherence, and to bring them out as quickly as possible while their (often topical) contents are still current.

A strategy of this kind imposes a cost, in that many authors have had to find other outlets for what would in different circumstances have been very publishable papers. The gain, however, seems much greater: a series of real books on properly defined subjects, edited by scholars of experience and standing in their respective fields, and placed promptly before the academic community. These, I am glad to say, were the same as the objectives of the publishers who expressed an interest in various aspects of the congress proceedings, and it has led to a series of volumes as well as of special issues of journals covering a wide range of interests.

There are volumes on art and architecture, on history and literature, on law and economics, on society and education. There are further volumes on nationality issues and the Ukraine, on the environment, on international relations and on defence. There are Soviet volumes, and others that deal more specifically with Eastern (or perhaps more properly, East Central) Europe. There are interdisciplinary volumes on women in Russia and the USSR, the Soviet experience in the Second World War, and ideology and system change. There are special issues of some of the journals that publish in our field, dealing with religion and Slovene studies, émigrés and East European economics, publishing and politics, linguistics and the Russian revolution. Altogether nearly forty separate publications will stem from the Harrogate congress: more than twice as many as from any previous congress of its kind, and a rich and enduring record of its deliberations.

Most of these volumes will be published in the United Kingdom by Macmillan. It is my pleasant duty to acknowledge Macmillan's early interest in the scholarly output of the congress, and the swift and professional attention that has been given to all of these volumes since their inception. A full list of the Macmillan Harrogate series appears elsewhere in the Macmillan edition of this volume; it can give only an impression of the commitment and support I have enjoyed from Tim Farmiloe, Clare Wace and others at all stages of our proceedings. I should also take this opportunity to thank John Morison and his colleagues on the International Council for Soviet and East European Studies for entrusting me with this responsible task in the first place, and the various sponsors – the Erasmus Prize Fund of Amsterdam, the Ford Foundation in New York, the British Foreign and Commonwealth Office, the British Council, the Stefan Batory Trust and others – whose generous support helped to make the congress a reality.

The next congress will be held in 1995, and (it is hoped) at a location in Eastern Europe. Its proceedings can hardly hope to improve upon the vigour and imagination that is so abundantly displayed on the pages of these splendid volumes.

University of Glasgow   STEPHEN WHITE

Preface

The Fourth World Congress for Soviet and East European Studies took place in July 1990 against the background of continuing tumultuous change in the Soviet Union. It is perhaps not surprising that most of the papers given at the Soviet literature panels dealt with the recent period; this was true of both Western and Soviet speakers (for the first time at an ICSEES Congress there were gratifyingly large numbers of the latter).

Under the title 'New Directions in Soviet Literature' our selection of Congress papers examines new trends in both early and recent Russian literature in the Soviet period.

Katerina Clark's chapter on TRAM uses the rise and fall of that movement in Soviet theatre 'to question our assumptions about the dynamic of Soviet cultural history' in the critical year 1929, showing how its aesthetic stance could not survive in the new orthodoxy about to be imposed on Soviet art. Graham Roberts demonstrates how a writer as shockingly modern as Daniil Kharms, subverting 'the language of authority' and foregrounding 'the authority of language', was bound to be rejected by the Stalinist state as 'ideologically intolerable'.

Judging by the papers on offer, however, Western Slavists' fascination with the Russian *avant-garde* of the 1920s appears to have waned, temporarily, at least, giving way to an interest in newer writing which is very different from the prose of the previous fifty years but which reminds us in some ways of 1920s Modernist prose. It includes strands examined in two chapters in this book: 'cruel realism' *(zhestokii realizm)*, exponents of which are the subject of Konstantin Kustanovich's chapter, and 'the other prose' *(drugaia proza)*, one of whose brightest stars is Tat'iana Tolstaia (see Helena Goscilo's chapter).

Perhaps this concentration on Russian prose (papers on poetry were scarce) of the last twenty or thirty years springs from a desire to discover some of the seeds of *glasnost'* – maybe even to gain an insight into present and future developments in Russian life and politics, such as the rise of nationalism.

Glasnost' has made possible the publication of works by Russian writers past and present, old and young, which would have been unthinkable before Gorbachev. It has also hastened a polarisation of attitudes among Russian writers which to some extent reflects the worrying and even dangerous polarisation visible on the streets. Thus the Great-Russian chauvinist attitudes of some of the village-prose writers *(derevenshchiki)*, detectable even in their pre-*glasnost'* works, have come to the surface, as they flirt with occasionally unpleasant forms of nationalism. Two of our essays examine the evolution of village prose; Kathleen Parthé takes a cool look, from the outside, so to speak, and concludes that the roots of the present upsurge of xenophobia in Russia do not lie in village prose: some *derevenshchiki* did jump on Pamyat's bandwagon, but did so years after it started rolling; rather, the concerns of certain village-prose writers were exploited by some literary critics and others for their own reactionary purposes. The Soviet scholar Galina Belaia's view is from within, her essay betraying a Russian intellectual's anguish at the coarseness and intolerance displayed by some *derevenshchiki* who in the 1960s and 1970s had seemed the voice of conscience. Her view is that under the deforming influence of 'the period of stagnation', 'yesterday's opponents of the regime' have become 'reactionary ideologists blocking the way out of the abyss' the Soviet people find themselves in.

Where does Russian literature go from here?

The problem of identity is one that Soviet citizens individually and collectively will have to face in the moral vacuum left after the collapse of communist certainties and the disclosures of the nation's corruption by terror.

The one essay in this collection dealing with poetry takes as its subject Joseph Brodsky, a Russian poet in exile whose work shows an increasing concern with the question of identity. Valentina Polukhina quotes Brodsky's words about that master of the self-portrait, Rembrandt: 'He was so impudent as to strive to know himself. No more and no less than to know himself.'

The question of national identity has an important place in nineteenth- and twentieth-century Russian literature. It seems to play no role, however, in the work of the new 'naturalists' analysed by Konstantin Kustanovich. They are producing a radically different kind of prose which shocks some readers comfortably used to the didacticism – whether crude agitprop or nobly idealistic – of mainstream Russian literature. Such readers might gloomily conclude that this prose, too, is realism, a 'cruel' realism reflecting the true state of affairs behind the hollow rhetoric which for decades accompanied the self-congratulation of Soviet propaganda, and now all too distressingly on the surface.

Another explanation for this new direction (and others) in Soviet prose is that Russian literature is taking up the threads of Modernism brutally torn in the early 1930s; writers like Petrushevskaia, for instance, who declines to supply the reader with a moral standpoint, are perhaps the heirs of writers like Pil'niak or Kharms.

The didactic tradition nevertheless remains strong in Russian literature. Margaret Ziolkowski shows how Russian writers from Bulgakov to Shalamov and Dombrovskii deploy the story of Pontius Pilate to examine the moral dilemmas faced by Russians in the Stalin era. For Chingiz Aitmatov, as Nina Kolesnikoff demonstrates, myth serves the author's moral ends. Rosalind Marsh describes how in the early days of Gorbachev's regime Russia's dramatists and prose writers began the second stage of telling the truth about Stalinism (begun under Khrushchev), forcing the pace of *glasnost'*. The reassessment of Stalin of the last few years, she contends, bringing her account up to the year 1990, has 'unleashed forces which undermine the legitimacy of the regime and threaten to sweep it away'. The events of August 1991 have proved her right.

Literature continues to be a force to be reckoned with in Russian intellectual and political life. Will this still be the case if a market economy becomes established in the republics that used to be part of the Soviet Union and, for the artist, 'anything goes'?

As the *fin de siècle* approaches, one awaits future developments with interest.

SHEELAGH DUFFIN GRAHAM

University of Strathclyde

The editor gratefully acknowledges the help of colleagues who gave generously of their time and expertise to act as readers and referees.

Notes on the Contributors

Galina Belaia is a professor at Moscow State University and also holds a post at the Institute of World Literature (IMLI) in Moscow. She is the author of numerous books and articles on Russian literature and society.

Katerina Clark is an Associate Professor of Comparative Literature and of Slavic at Yale University. Her publications include *The Soviet Novel: History as Ritual* and, with Michael Holquist, *Mikhail Bakhtin*.

Helena Goscilo is a Professor of Slavic Languages and Literatures at the University of Pittsburgh. She is a specialist in early nineteenth-century prose, Romanticism, contemporary Soviet fiction, Russian women's writing, and comparative literature. Her books include *Russian and Polish Women's Fiction, Balancing Acts* and *Glasnost: An Anthology of Russian Literature under Gorbachev* Vol. I.

Nina Kolesnikoff is an Associate Professor in the Department of Modern Languages at McMaster University. She holds a PhD degree in Comparative Literature. She is the author of *Bruno Jasienski: His Evolution from Futurism to Socialist Realism* and *Yury Trifonov: A Critical Study*.

Konstantin Kustanovich is an Assistant Professor of Slavic Languages and Literatures at Vanderbilt University, Nashville, USA. He specializes in contemporary Russian literature and has published articles on Aksenov, Pasternak, Solzhenitsyn, Trifonov and other twentieth-century Russian writers.

Rosalind Marsh is Professor of Russian Studies at the University of Bath; her previous post was as Director of the Centre for Russian, Soviet and East European Studies at the University of Exeter. She is the author of *Soviet Fiction since Stalin: Science, Politics and Literature* and *Images of Dictatorship: Portraits of Stalin in Literature*.

Kathleen Parthé is an Associate Professor of Russian at the University of Rochester, NY. She has published articles on contemporary

Russian literature and on the works of Lev Tolstoy. Her book *The Radiant Past: Russian Village Prose from Ovechkin to Rasputin* will shortly be published by Princeton University Press. She is the founding editor of the *Tolstoy Studies Journal*.

Valentina Polukhina is a Lecturer in Russian literature at the University of Keele. She has published articles on Akhmatova, Brodsky, Khlebnikov, Pasternak and other Russian poets, and is the author of *Joseph Brodsky: A Poet for our Time* and editor of *Brodsky's Poetics and Aesthetics* to which she also contributed.

Graham Roberts of New College, Oxford, is currently completing a D.Phil. thesis on the prose and dramatic works of Daniil Kharms, Aleksandr Vvedenskii and Konstantin Vaginov. His paper on Vvedenskii's *Nekotoroe kolichestvo razgovorov* is soon to be published, as is his translation of Vladimir Zazubrin's novella *Shchepka* ('The Chip').

Margaret Ziolkowski is Associate Professor of Russian at Miami University in Ohio. She is the author of *Hagiography and Modern Russian Literature* and various articles on recent Soviet literature. She is now writing a book on recurrent motifs in post-Stalinist literature about the Stalin era.

1 The Crisis of Soviet Artistic Mentality in the 1960s and 1970s
Galina Belaia

In recent years we have seen an attempt to make differentiations within Soviet literature, to separate the 'clean' from the 'unclean'. In the main, non-conformist writers are numbered among the ranks of the 'clean': Anna Akhmatova, Mikhail Bulgakov, Boris Pasternak and a few others. Such an approach is socio-political rather than scholarly. The truth is that the artistic intelligentsia of Russia on the whole accepted the revolution, for a variety of reasons, including traditional historical ones stemming from the mentality of the Russian intelligentsia, a mentality that prepared it to accept the idea of coercion, sacrifice, historical guilt before the people, and retribution. None the less the time came when the apparent monolith of Soviet literature began to self-destruct. In this chapter we are concerned with the process of *self*-destruction within the Soviet artistic mentality and not the destruction caused in the period of *perestroika* by the external pressure of incontrovertible facts about the bloody Stalinist past.

Of course, breaches in a totalitarian world-view, in its system of concepts and criteria, are always made individually and have everything to do with the intellectual potential of the individual personality. But alongside this we cannot help noticing that there are several general processes at work: the destruction of the artistic mentality that is taking place before our eyes is a lengthy and extensive process. It is hard to discern in it precise forms, precise moments. We need to find an explanation for those processes which seem paradoxical and which in the last analysis can only be explained by reference to the self-destruction of Soviet mentality as a whole and of the artistic mentality in particular.

For the sake of simplicity, we shall begin by looking at the acute polemic between the 'Russophiles' and the 'Russophobes'. It should be noted that we are talking here about writers who for a long time co-existed peacefully in what was known as 'Soviet literature': Viktor Astafyev, Valentin Rasputin and Vasilii Belov, on the one hand, and on the other, such writers as Vasilii Grossman whom they regard with especial antipathy. Remembering the 1960s we must admit that in those years the writers of 'village prose' were recognised by the critics and by public opinion as a particular branch of Soviet literature, unorthodox and distinguished by their integrity; Vasilii Grossman, not then known as the author of the novel *Zhizn' i sud'ba* (Life and Fate), also stood in opposition to the regime. But the fact is, Grossman's novel was seized and confiscated, while the works of the village prose writers were published. There was therefore something that was different in principle in their positions as writers.

At first sight both currents of literature – both the works that were written by the village prose school, and published, and those which, like Grossman's novel, were written 'for the desk drawer' – had the same range of interests: the Revolution, the people *(narod)*, the people's tragic fate, its disasters. The interests were indeed common to both; but in the course of time it became clear that the depth of insight differed. However, let us not be in too much of a hurry.

In order to explore the hidden drama of the processes taking place in Soviet literature one must choose some conventional starting-point for analysis. I suggest the middle of the 1950s, the XXth Party Congress which opened the door a little way to historical truth. 1956 is the year of the really great breakthrough, the year of the 'Thaw', the take-off point for soaring romantic hopes – and their sudden crash when the Soviet army suppressed the Hungarian revolutionary uprising. The end of the 1950s became the period of reinterpretation of many over-simplified concepts of the human personality. The exposure of the Stalin cult, the return of the victims of repression, the bottomless pit of 'excesses' that had virtually destroyed the peasantry – all this came as a profound shock and led many honest people to an intense spiritual crisis. The complex of day-to-day assumptions and moral values which had dominated in the years of Stalinist ideology was subjected to reassessment. Of course the degree of advance, or rather the extent of the breach in the totalitarian world-view, was different in each case, depending on individual experience. But a massive breach had been made.

In the case of Vasilii Grossman, in all probability it was to his advantage that he was interested not in history 'in general' but in the real, concrete history of his country. Refusing to limit himself to a depiction of the *events* of the war and prewar years, this writer, a witness of and participant in the war between Germany and the USSR, interpreted that war as the clash of two totalitarian states and created his own historiosophy. He thereby broke out of the vicious circle of deluded consciousness. For Grossman the exposure of Soviet imperialism meant a critique of the Soviet mentality, an escape from its fetters. His historiosophy went beyond such abstractions as 'patriotism', 'the nation' and 'Russian history' and concentrated on bringing together the eternal qualities of humankind, the historical qualities of the Russian national character and the psychology of *homo sovieticus*. All this made him a target for the 'Russophiles', who saw in him the classic type of the 'Russophobe'. But this is a theme requiring separate treatment.

The aim of the present chapter is to analyse the historiosophy of the village prose writers; this may help us to comprehend the tragic paradox of Russian culture today – the degeneration of yesterday's opponents of the regime into reactionary ideologists blocking the nation's way out of the abyss.

In the 1960s and 1970s a vanguard of writers appeared who were endowed with a great new spiritual energy. Rich experience, achieved through suffering, was evident in the early, as yet imperfect, works of Viktor Astafyev and Vasilii Shukshin, Fedor Abramov and Sergei Zalygin and other writers who formed the core of village prose. This augured well.

The thoroughness and originality of their approach to reality left no doubts as to their potential.

As is well known, the depiction in earlier Soviet literature of the people – the people proclaimed as the centre of the system of socialist realism – had suffered from obvious inadequacies: strangely, writers avoided the main mass of the people – both those who had won the war and those who had become the victims of all sorts of repressions. After the mid-1950s this became clear, as did the fact that it was no longer possible to write in the old way, and that the right to speak about the people belonged only to someone who knew and could artistically assimilate the soul of the people. The concept of the people, the theme of the people – all this had been profaned in literature. That is why village prose began with a polemical refutation of officially approved artistic postulates. When the artist's eye moved from the epicentre of historical upheavals to the periphery, this was a rejection of the concentration writers had previously afforded to the centre, the *avant-garde* of the actively revolutionary section of the population. When the predominant interest moved to the departing generation, to the characters of old men and old women, this too was polemical, because the writers found it important not so much to study new types as to create 'a living bridge, linking the present with the past' (V. Pertsovskii).[1] In some ways these heroes were, or course, reminiscent of their literary relatives – but distant, not near ones. They recalled not the heroes of Aleksandr Fadeev but those of Nikolai Leskov and Gleb Uspensky, Lev Tolstoy and Anton Chekhov. But here too there was a polemic, subtly defined by Boris Mozhaev: '...our classics, which valued so highly the authenticity of the character of the common people, presented them accurately, but none the less from the outside, whereas our new writers, highly educated and coming in the main from the ranks of these same common people, have been able to open up the inner world and communal inter-relationships of our tillers of the soil... These works have considerably enriched our ideas about the Russian people.'[2]

The new quality and new range of such an approach to reality should not be undervalued. In essence, in the 1960s and 1970s all of them together – Valentin Rasputin and Vasilii Belov, Vasilii Shukshin and Viktor Astafyev, Chingiz Aitmatov and Ales' Adamovich, Vasil' Bykov and Yuri Trifonov, Bulat Okudzhava and Fazil' Iskander and many who followed in their footsteps – all created a single anti-world: a tense spiritual climate in which there was no place for conventional attitudes, demagogy and falsehood. They knew precisely what they did not want. They did not want stagnation in social life, contempt for the people hiding behind demagogic appeals to that same people, the triumph of boors and hagglers, a ban on themes that the literary bureaucrats considered forbidden territory. They did not want lies and untruth about humankind and society and they did not conceal this.

The historical interests of the village prose writers were directed at the distant past – at the 'roots' and 'sources' that lay far beyond the boundary of 1917. But even this was not the most important thing: history became an 'idea', tradition was legitimised in the public consciousness. This had to be defended, affirmed, strengthened in the consciousness of several generations who had grown up in the conviction that before 1917 history did not exist.

Presented at first sight naively and artlessly – as an awareness of the link between the hero and those people who lived before us – the idea of the historical link between different times ceased to be an abstraction: it manifested itself as the natural and organic world-view of what Valentin Rasputin called 'ancient old women' *(starinnykh starukh)* and of old men who had with dignity lived a righteous life and who in their declining years were able to find the words to express their ideas about life and death.

In essence this was a projection of the problems of everyday life into the depths of the human psyche. The link between man and history in the works of Vasilii Belov, Grant Matevosian, Chingiz Aitmatov and Viktor Astafyev was thus explored on an existential level. The personality of the heroes proved strong enough to bear this burden. The artistic complexity of the hero's depiction led to a rehabilitation and a renewal of human self-esteem both for the individual personality and for the people.

The material to be assimilated, which became the object of depiction, possessed a particular persuasiveness, for it was the writer's 'own' material, familiar in every last detail since childhood. It was rooted in every cell of his own life and, more important, his psychology. The artistic world that was portrayed, however, was in the main correlated to contemporary reality through some means of mediation: the heroes had first and foremost to embody everlasting ideas, common to the whole people, of honour and dignity, morality and duty. And that was what they did – Ivan Afrikanovich, the old woman Dar'ia, the old woman Anna, Tanabai and Evgenii Nosov's 'helmetwearers of Usviaty'; a high order of spiritual organisation in their personality made them truly an 'ethical norm' and an 'unattainable model' for contemporary men and women.

But this romanticised world was fraught with hidden dangers. This was a method also born out of polemics – the portrayal of the real 'from the contrary'. Today's demagogues were counterposed to philosophising 'ancient old women', today's boors to 'righteous men', today's disorganisation, which, as Mikhail Bulgakov long ago observed, is a state of society in which people do every job but their own, was counterposed to the ideal order of the old village, which had in historical fact never existed.

Finally, the past as a whole was counterposed to the present, but the present was also assimilated only as a whole, 'in general'; it was not assimilated in concrete historical detail, or, as Aleksei Losev put it, 'intimately'. And when the old material was exhausted, when, in Dmitrii Urnov's words, literature was invaded by a rush of 'the raw material of life',[3] then indeed new attitudes to the contemporary emerged in this literature.

In one of his articles explaining the phenomenon of the unity of Latin-American prose the Paraguayan author Augusto Roa Bastos quoted the words of a colleague: 'In order for literature to exist it is not enough just to have good or successful works. Literature appears only when the most varied works and aesthetic trends are forged into a single harmonious structure which answers the needs of a given society, with a characteristic intensity, continuous artistic tension and orientation towards the future.'[4] Developing this idea, Augusto Roa Bastos writes that for literature to exist it is also necessary to have 'a feeling of the inner link', which cannot appear 'without a common core of essential conceptions'[5] and a particular, internally united world-vision.

Village prose existed for a long time as a 'native heath' *(rodovoe lono)*. The 'common core of essential conceptions' of the world, humankind and history bred a sense of inner link, which we saw in the aspirations and the works of the writers mentioned above and which they themselves felt and feel as a quality that sets them apart and unites them. The unity of the concept 'the national' *(natsional'nyi)* world and humankind' revealed itself in the similarity of plot situations, the way the heroes resembled each other and the stylisation of the language in the form of folk speech. The writers, not fearing any loss of individuality, easily entered a defined line-up, widening the area of their artistic investigations, cultivating their 'native heath'. As they saw it, the individuality of one did not dim or cramp the individuality of another. In their public pronouncements each spoke more of what united than of what divided them. That is how it was.

This unity allowed the critics to speak of the appearance of a new literary style.

At the beginning of the 1970s the critic Lev Arutiunov wrote an article entitled 'The national world and man'. Analysing books of the preceding half-century – works as varied as Faulkner's trilogy, *One Hundred Years of Solitude* by Gabriel Garcia Marquez, *Bremia nashei dobroty* (The Burden of Our Kindness) by Ion Drutse, Chingiz Aitmatov's *Belyi parokhod* (The White Steamer) and *My i nashi gory* (We and Our Mountains) by Grant Matevosian – the critic drew what seemed then to be a surprising conclusion. He considered that all these works shared a common underlying principle, namely this: the artist within the bounds of a 'small' object of portrayal strives to embrace the national existence as a whole, the 'microcosm' becomes an analogy for the 'macrocosm', 'a focus for the problems of humankind'. Arutiunov made it clear that the 'small world' does not signify 'spiritual limitation, isolation from the "large world". It is a question of a new artistic distance between man and the world, of an artistic narrative in which the national world itself, taken in the "usual" perspective of its customary existence, contains the idea of a "common" world, becomes a collective hero and a representative of contemporary life. That is why within its limits man acquires freedom of self-expression, and an autonomous world becomes an analogy of existence.'[6]

When *Proshchanie s Materoi* (Farewell to Matera) appeared in 1976, we read it as the artistic saga of a 'national farewell to a peasant Atlantis' which was sinking under the waves 'everywhere in the world, not only in our country...'. Ales' Adamovich was the first to note this resemblance to a saga, this particular epic tone in Rasputin's *povest'*.

But soon it became clear that *Proshchanie s Materoi* was both the highest point in the development of village prose and at the same time a signal that the path went no further. That, at least, is how it was to look a few years later.

There were critics who saw Vasilii Belov's novel *Vse vperedi* (Everything is Ahead, 1987) as a failure, and these critics were subjected to strong attack, but the truth could not be concealed: the arguments of the novel's defenders were based on the artistic discoveries made by Belov many years before, in *Privychnoe delo* (That's How It Is, 1966) and *Plotnitskie rasskazy* (A Carpenter's Tales, 1968).

We recognised the deep pain and despair that reverberated through Viktor Astafyev's *Pechal'nyi detektiv* (A Sad Detective Story, 1988), but there is no doubt that in his latest works he is moving along a different path and that they are inferior to his earlier works.

So is Nikolai Anastas'ev right in saying that today the moment has arrived 'when the boundaries of the "plot of land", however spacious it may be, have begun to be felt all the same as boundaries'?[7] Perhaps that is why, to use Igor' Zolotusskii's words, 'the novel does not come easily' to contemporary prose?

Returning to the idea of the microcosm/macrocosm, the idea expressed by Faulkner in terms of the 'postage stamp' that can become a metaphor of the 'cosmos', one sees that it was not an artistic principle that had become obsolete: what had become obsolete was a concept of the world which had previously allowed extrapolation from the processes taking place on the 'plot of land' to phenomena of existence as a whole.

The orientation towards tradition, towards olden times, which was the world-view that underlay the works of Rasputin, Matevosian, Belov, Astafyev and many other writers, was appropriate when the writers were coming to grips with the question of man's destiny and were defending the idea that tradition plays an important role in the status of the personality and society. But sooner or later it was bound to become clear that the question of the paths of world history could not be solved by means of a retrospective interpretation of the problems of contemporary society. The romantic idealisation of history was fine as long as it was an artistic-philosophical metaphor. But when it became a programme its lack of historicity became obvious and we saw that we were simply being called backwards in time, being offered 'the commune' (see, for example, Rasputin's *Pozhar* [The Fire]) and a structure based on the commune *(obshchina)* as an ideal of possible 'order' and renaissance – whether in morality, in society or in public life.

In the work of many writers, for example in Vasilii Belov's *Lad* (Harmony, 1978–81), historical method was reduced to the level of ethnography. Ethnography gradually began to replace the question of the paths and means of historical development, and the question was thereby simply removed from the agenda. The future began to be equated with the concept of 'progress', and the word 'progress' itself acquired a noticeably pejorative edge. The cycle of stories *Vospitanie po doktoru Spoku* (Childrearing According to Dr Spock, 1978) betrayed Belov's claims to be offering a system of views on historical and social questions; but the book itself, and then later the novel *Vse vperedi*, revealed that these claims lacked foundation.

The new attitudes to contemporary life which have become the main characteristic of the prose now being written by Rasputin, Belov and Astafyev arose not because these writers had previously been ignorant of contemporary life: that was what they wrote about, after all. But their earlier works had a different projection.

When Astafyev's *Pechal'nyi detektiv* appeared, we saw it was but one step from romanticisation of the people *(narod)* to its equally total and undifferentiated deromanticisation.

No sooner had the prose of the sixties begun to make its way in the world than it once more found itself in a complex historical situation, for which we today have a ready label: the 'stagnation' of the 1970s and 1980s. This prose gave voice to the depths of the people's life at a moment when public life began to be deformed yet again: this prose presented a feeling of personal dignity as the highest value in a period when the rights of the personality were being trampled on time and time again. The cry of Vasilii Shukshin before his death, 'What is happening to us?', his insulted human dignity which burst out in the article-story *Kliauza* (Slander) revealed the tragic depth of the problem raised by the prose of those years, and the stoicism of its authors.

In essence, the prose of the 1960s and 1970s developed not thanks to social and historical circumstances, but in spite of them. And this fact exerted upon it an enduring and not always beneficial influence.

The recoil from the truth which had been revealed at the XXth congress, followed by the reanimation of ideas that in the light of that truth had seemed obsolete, the falsification of our country's history which again took hold from the end of the 1960s – all this had a profound effect upon the psychology of writers. Nowadays we triumphantly boast that 'Manuscripts do not burn.' In actual fact these words of Mikhail Bulgakov's deny a tragic and irreversible reality: manuscripts do burn, and burn away for ever. The variants of *Master i Margarita* (The Master and Margarita) that were burned by Bulgakov cannot be restored, nor can the lost archive of Vasilii Grossman; many texts of poems by Anna Akhmatova, Osip Mandelstam and other writers are unlikely ever to be found.

Village prose received powerful stimulus from 'war prose', but the attacks on Vasil' Bykov for *Mertvym ne bol'no* (The Dead Feel No Pain) were attacks on village prose as well. Its practitioners took their measure from Aleksandr Tvardovsky, the author of *Vasilii Terkin* and the editor of *Novyi mir*, but he was crucified before their eyes. For many prose writers and poets of the 1960s Boris Pasternak was a distant figure; but, independently of poetic taste, his fate made the heart of every decent person tremble.

We have not yet fully evaluated how all this could have broken the spirit of writers who were at the start of their career. Knowledge of the tragic fate of writers who had died in the 1930s, the spectacle of contemporary writers being publicly hounded – all this was bound to deform the creativity of a writer, no matter how great his inner steadfastness. In the clash with personal experience rushing to express itself, a comprehension of the tragedy of the situation bred an inconceivable psychological strain.

There were the prohibitions as well – on themes, on problems. They seemed unexpected in the face of that truth about the past which had been brought to light by the XXth Party congress. The pressure of these bans must not be forgotten when, for example, we talk of Vasilii Belov, author of a novel about the post-Revolution village, *Kanuny* (The Eve, 1972–76). This novel revealed its author's intention of exploring those general human values that had been recklessly obliterated in the zeal for the class conflict which, in Stalin's words, 'sharpened' at the end of the 1920s. The critic L. Emel'ianov, who read the novel in depth and revealed its hidden truth, was immediately anathematised in many critical articles, removed from his job and banished from the front ranks of literary studies. The second part of *Kanuny* did not appear when it was due.

The development of literature was complicated also by the fact that it had no cultural soil to grow in. Initiation into literature in the 1960s took place in difficult conditions, in snatches. Gaps in education were filled by arbitrary names. School killed the living images of Vladimir Maiakovsky and Maksim Gorky; Lev Tolstoy was forgiven but not understood; Fedor Dostoevsky still remained 'in exile' – in the shadow of *dostoevshchina*. The majority of people, and that includes writers, discovered Mikhail Bulgakov only in the 1960s and until very recently his prose of the 1920s, *Zapiski na manzhetakh* (Notes on Shirt-cuffs), *Rokovye iaitsa* (The Fatal Eggs) and *D'iavoliada* (Diaboliada) languished in the repositories of old libraries while *Sobach'e serdtse* (Heart of a Dog) was not published at all in the Soviet Union until 1987. The true heir of Mikhail Zoshchenko, Vasilii Shukshin, began his literary career in ignorance of Zoshchenko; when Eduard Uspenskii was accused of imitating Kharms he had to admit that he had not read him 'either in childhood or in youth. Kharms was banned.'[8] Only in the 1970s – and even then as though he were some exotic creature – was Andrei Bely allowed to return to our literature. Boris Pasternak was slandered, and many people who because of a lack of culture could not understand 'early' Pasternak were deprived of the opportunity to read his 'late' works; as for Osip Mandelstam, the only people to talk of him were his contemporaries. The inertia of the old evaluations was very great and their influence continues to the present day, because the decree on the journals *Zvezda* and *Leningrad* is still being studied in our schools and institutes of higher education, and lecture halls still resound to the word 'scum' *(podonki)*, which Zhdanov threw at Akhmatova and Zoshchenko in 1946.

The artist's spiritual development was also impeded by the fact that for a long time there existed an unwritten register of feelings that could be talked about and feelings that could not. On the banned list was the study of man's inner world on an existential level. And only in the war years, when, as Iosif Utkin has put it, it was discovered that such important ideas as love for a woman or love for one's country had slipped into the 'list of abstractions' and become 'mentionable only in code', were writers faced with the necessity of overcoming the inertia of this approach to human beings.

Even such a concept as humanism had been put in doubt. What meaning did it have in the Soviet mentality? 'Arguments about socialist humanism', wrote the critics in the 1920s and 1930s, 'are heard today from several writers from the intelligentsia who are sincerely striving to move forward in step with us. They admit the class struggle, but they speak not of class hatred, they speak of humanism instead.... They come to us with propaganda for humanism, as if there is anything in the world more truly humane than the class hatred of the proletariat.'[9]

This taboo on certain themes, ideas, names and words, this deformation of concepts had effects that must never be underestimated. Let us recall one of Yuri Trifonov's last stories of how in the 1960s the short story *Vechnye temy* (Eternal Themes) was returned to him with a disdainful assessment. (And that happened at *Novyi mir* in Tvardovsky's time!) Recounting this episode in 1974, Trifonov recalled that a member of the editorial board 'was deeply convinced of the fact that eternal themes were the lot of some other literature – perhaps also necessary, but in some sense irresponsible and lower in rank than the literature that he was editing'.[10]

As late as 1982 Lidiia Ginzburg, mentioning existential themes, still had to be careful: 'The concept "existential" ', she said in concealed polemic with the hidden editor or the future critics of her book, 'must not be confused with "existentialist", that is, representing "existentialist philosphy".' Existential themes, explained Ginzburg, were 'themes of life and death, the meaning of life, love, eternity and swift-flowing time, nature and the city, labour, creativity, the fate and position of the poet, art, culture and the historical past, communication with the divinity and unbelief, friendship and solitude, dream and disappointment. Also social and civic themes: freedom, the state, war, justice and injustice.' In other words these were themes which 'touch on fundamental aspects of human existence and its basic values'.[11] All this had to be defended, fought for, pushed through.

Despite the circumstances, the village prose writers had begun to introduce existential problems into literature. They began by destroying the most serious ban – the ban on the question of general human values. For years on end we had been subjected to a vulgarised interpretation of the contrast between class principles and general human principles and it is only very recently that this contrast has been publicly disowned. Mikhail Gorbachev at a meeting in Moscow with the 'Issyk-Kul Forum' reminded us that 'as long ago as the beginning of the century V.I. Lenin expressed a thought of colossal depth: about the priority of general human values over the tasks of one or another class.'[12]

That reminder was made in October 1986. It is thanks to literature – not philosophy or history or social studies, but literature – that the ground had already been prepared for these words. Writers, knowing that they were taking serious risks, had consciously striven to overcome narrow class concepts. Faith in the beneficial strength of human community, in the constructiveness of moral tradition and in the accumulated centuries-long experience of toiling humanity, formed the basis of their perception of the world; this note of faith singled them out in contemporary literature and emerged in their works as a particular philosophical-artistic position.

But talk of 'eternal' laws of human nature was seditious in those Brezhnev years. And that is why Vasilii Shukshin could not make a film version of his novel *Ia prishel dat' vam voliu* (I Have Come To Give You Freedom). He was interested in the question of the nature of power in general, but that question did not exist in the Soviet mentality. The thrust of what he wrote was that unenlightened and undeveloped consciousness is by definition not ready for power; such an attitude was seditious and the state would not give money for a film like that.

In 1979, five years after the death of Shukshin, I wrote an article entitled 'How to live, how to die...' and a young final-year student, S. Aseev, on his own initiative took it to Viktor Astafyev. On the back of the last page Astafyev recorded his approval of the idea that themes of 'life and death' in village prose are not a 'limitation':

> This idea is a very timely and necessary one, because in our country every attempt is made to hem in, efface and generally remove the theme of common human values, to single us and our society out as something exceptional, and this is not simply a bad thing but also an impoverishment. In the first place it contradicts the tasks of that society itself, which considers itself not simply humane, but the only humane society in the contemporary world, no less, not understanding that exclusivity leads to a holier-than-thou attitude, which in turn leads to separation from other people and the rest of the world and, moreover, to a consciousness that the majority can do anything it pleases, that everything is allowed... to hew, hack, quarrel, rob one's neighbour, to laud some and revile others.
>
> And all this happened, is still happening, but should not go on happening. How simple everything is! When shall we live to see this simplicity comprehended? Not soon, I fear! For everything is being done the wrong way round – simplicity is turned into complexity and complexity is simplified into banalities.

However strange it may seem, the cohort of honest and intelligent writers about whom we are talking did not appreciate and develop their own virtues. Astafyev, Belov and Aitmatov are all organic, God-given writers. Their first books unintentionally confirmed the thought expressed by the American author John Gardner: 'Art is as original and important as it is,' he wrote, 'precisely because it does *not* start out with clear knowledge of what it means to say. Out of the artist's imagination, as out of nature's inexhaustible well, pours one thing after another. The artist composes, writes or paints just as he dreams, seizing whatever swims close to his net. This, not the world seen directly, is his raw material.'[13]

That was how they began. They portrayed the world, not eschewing artistry, but standing on that platform from which real literature has always begun its conquest of the world: keeping true to the materiality of the image. Later came the time of diagram and thesis.

This was the point at which it became clear that a literature which had developed in the conditions of a deformed and deforming public life, which voluntarily took upon itself the role of opposing the stagnation of consciousness, suffered from serious and ever-deepening contradictions. It had not become 'a single harmonious structure', because the intensity of its development was not equal to its 'orientation towards the future', and the future presented itself as indistinct and uncertain. And the paths of the writers began to diverge.

As a result Astafyev, for example, is today reconsidering his views of the 1960s and 1970s and in doing so is revising his previous evaluations. The edge of his criticism is directed not against particular social strata and formations 'but against society as a whole, and the people *(narod)* in Astafyev's work does not divide into town and country dwellers, it is one people', writes Igor' Zolotusskii.[14]

But, in the first place, the nation *is* divided. Or if it does not divide, then this is because, as Zolotusskii has remarked, Astafyev considers that the town has already so spoiled the country that as a result of assimilation 'the pure peasant no longer exists, there are agricultural workers, there is a new kind of person' whose 'language and thoughts and behaviour are different from those of the traditional inhabitant of the peasant hut'.[15] In the second place, why is it good if Viktor Astafyev is again describing 'society as a whole', the people as 'one people'? And why must it be depicted 'without mercy'? And can we without protest accept Astafyev's aesthetic crudeness, which shows no mercy for humankind? Should we silently attribute everything to the pain and despair of the writer at the sight of the disintegration of morals in contemporary society? Astafyev asks 'What has happened to us?' and piles upon us *descriptions* of horrors and miseries in contemporary life, oppressing the reader both with their quantity and their import. That is all. Is it enough?

When at the end of his life Vasilii Shukshin exclaimed, 'What is happening to us?', he was not just shuddering emotionally; perhaps alone among the village prose writers Shukshin in the 1960s and 1970s painted a gallery of various national *types*. He showed us not only 'crackpots', as the legends that are forming about his name would have us believe, and not only such 'strange people' as Kozulin in the story *Daesh' serdtse* (There Goes the Heart), who shoots off a salvo at night as a sign of joy that a heart transplant has been carried out in Cape Town; in *Srezal* (Gleb Cuts Them Down To Size) Shukshin showed also the ruinous force of ignorance, aggressiveness, insufficient education; in *Krepkii muzhik* (A Strong-Willed Fellow) he saw the destructive power unleashed by the expropriation of the past, the triumph of a boor whose psychology was formed in the epoch of lawlessness and desecration.

Shukshin did not write his stories in order to *describe* this painfully familiar event. He was interested in the disintegration of a centuries-old psychology, for which there was now nothing sacred, and its substitution by the psychology of a destructive demagogue. 'At the start Shurygin handled this business as he did any other, with shouting and swearing', wrote Shukshin. 'But when people began to gather round, when they began to sigh and exclaim and feel sorry for the church, Shurygin suddenly felt himself to be an important figure with unlimited authority. He stopped swearing and did not look at people, as if he could not hear or see them.' And when his friends asked him, ' "Kolya, why are you doing this?", Shurygin flew into a rage, the blood drained from his face and he shouted, "Clear off, you drunken lout!" '

Shukshin's heroes were even then expressing surprise: 'What's got into him?' And the writer sketched in more 'features of the portrait' of a man with no education or spiritual world who has become the recipient of power. The destruction of the sacred object was his means of self-definition. Lev Anninskii many years ago appreciated this discovery by Shukshin.

Vasilii Shukshin never repeated that much-quoted Chekhovian idea that we should all squeeze the slave out of ourselves drop by drop. But he showed how much of the slave remains in contemporary man, he drew out the other side of slavehood: the absence of the very idea that 'freedom' might be possible. He spoke of people's unreadiness for freedom, their lack of a sense of personal dignity. This was a tragic and alarming theme, and the approach to it was a concrete historical one. It opposed idealisation of any kind, including idealisation of the great and indestructible imperial consciousness.

The philosopher Merab Mamardashvili had observed that in a situation of divorce from reality and deprived of the culture of abstract thought 'primary human feelings and sufferings acquire a charge of negative, vicious energy'. In recent years this negative vicious charge has entered the 'national' idea. The formation of the idea took place in difficult circumstances and its development was distorted from the outset; in today's public pronouncements by the village prose writers it has taken on a vulgar aspect that fits in perfectly with the primitive phase of Soviet civilisation today. 'In human terms I can understand the wrath of Viktor Astafyev', writes Mamardashvili. 'I can see that he is pacing round and round his own real feelings as an honest and profound man, but *somehow he can't untangle them, comprehend their true source*.'[16] Russian writers, for example Rasputin and Astafyev, writes Mamardashvili, are trying to renew life

> by struggling against all foreign and modernist 'escapades' and summoning by incantation the traditional spirituality of the folk life and its structures. But behind all these words they are performing that same old vanishing trick with reality. And I sincerely do not understand and would like to say to these people personally: the initial pain is the same for the Russian people as for others, perhaps even stronger, and it is absolutely comprehensible to me, it accords with my own feelings, but can they really not hear that these moralising slogans, all this put-on awareness and grandeur, is the old song of 'Tatar' or 'alien' invaders? How can this go unperceived by their intellectual and moral ear? It is with precisely this language and through this language that all the destructive processes invaded morality, spirituality and ecological harmony, and there is no point here in blaming industry, for there is no industry, as there is no world power and no reality. It is characteristic of Russia to have all the disadvantages of contemporary phenomena without having their advantages, that is, the phenomena themselves. She has suffered all the vicious consequences and defects of industrialisation without having had industrialisation itself (if we discount factories that are simply large and have a large gross output). Russia is not industrialised in the European sense of this word. She has all the negative consequences of urbanisation, but no city; the phenomenon of the 'city' is absent.[17]

Time has shown that the village prose writers possessed wide-ranging and organic experience of life, but a low level of philosophical and intellectual culture. At the beginning they created a serious and important artistic metaphor, in which old Russia was counterposed to Soviet Russia with its orgy of bureaucracy, officialdom and hypocrisy. But the idealisation of old Russia absolutely does not work as a philosophy of history, which is the category to which they elevated it. And they turned out naive and intellectually feeble, because the idea of returning to old Russia is being advanced by them in all seriousness. They think that we can return to the commune, that yesterday's peasantry and today's are one river in which we can bathe twice.

Their claims to historical-philosophical forecasts are doomed to failure and this makes them aggressive, leading them into primitive chauvinism, insulting to people of other nationalities.

It is probable that the breach with the totalitarian mentality requires more intellectual effort than they were capable of. 'Russophobes' in their usage are yesterday's 'enemies of the people' from the arsenal of Stalinist ideology. Their appeal to 'world power' bears witness to the tenacity of the 'imperial consciousness', the central link in the Soviet mentality. The victory that in their time they won over 'Sovietism' and the system was thus revealed to be only a relative one. But the phenomenon of village prose itself is important not only for historians of literature but also for future historians of the mythological consciousness and its tenacity in the art of totalitarian countries in the twentieth century.

Translated by Lesley Milne, who gratefully acknowledges the help of Sergei Belov and Irina Ninova.

Notes

1. *Zvezda*, 9, 1969, p. 209.
2. *Literaturnaia gazeta*, 31 October 1979.
3. *Voprosy literatury*, 3, 1987, p.19.
4. *Pisateli Latinskoi Ameriki o literature* (Moscow, 1982), p.71.
5. Ibid., p. 78.
6. L.N. Arutiunov, 'Natsional'nyi mir i chelovek' in *Izobrazhenie cheloveka*

(Sovetskaia literatura i mirovoi literaturnyi protsess) (Moscow, 1972), p. 174.
7. *Voprosy literatury*, 3, 1987, p. 10.
8. *Moskovskie novosti*, 8 February 1987.
9. *Na literaturnom postu,* 21–22, 1929, p. 12.
10. *Voprosy literatury* 8, 1974, p. 188.
11. Lidiia Ginzburg, *O starom i novom* (Leningrad, 1982), p. 17.
12. *Literaturnaia gazeta*, 22 October 1986.
13. *Pisateli SShA o literature*, Vol. 2 (Moscow, 1982), p. 35. The source of the quotation is John Gardner, *On Moral Fiction* (New York, 1978), p. 13.
14. *Znamia*, 1, 1987, pp. 223–4.
15. Ibid..
16. *Teatr*, 3, 1989, p. 96.
17. *Zaria vostoka* (newspaper, Tbilisi), 25 June 1989.

2 The Left *Avant-Garde* Theatre in the 1920s
Katerina Clark

1929 has become fixed in our imagination as an infamous year in the Soviet Union. If we are to believe much recent Soviet literature, it is the year all those Marxist Judases with large noses stormed over the countryside destroying Russian culture – a process we used to know as collectivisation. It is also the year countless cultural institutions were purged; the year of the campaign against the non-Party writers Zamiatin and Pilniak; the year Bulgakov's plays were removed from the stage; the year Lunacharsky was removed from office as Minister of Education and Culture, etc. In short, 1929 was one of the darkest of the dark years of Soviet cultural history.

In this chapter, I want to focus on an incident of that year and on the cultural body most closely involved in it. Both are now largely forgotten, but I bring them back to our attention not so much to suggest their intrinsic value as to question our assumptions about the dynamic of Soviet cultural history in this critical year.

The body I have chosen to focus on for this case study is TRAM, the Leningrad Theatre of Worker Youth *(Teatr rabochei molodezhi)*.[1] The incident is a moment in late 1929 when TRAM formed an alliance with several other leftist and agitational theatres known as the Revolutionary Front in the theatre, or Revfront. This front comprised, besides TRAM which led it, the Red Theatre, the Agitational Theatre, and the Leningrad Worker Theatre of the Proletcult.[2] These four theatres met on 3 November at the TRAM headquarters (together with invited guests from the Party, press and government) and drew up and signed a 'revolutionary contract' *(dogovor)* according to which Revfront took upon itself the task of eradicating from Soviet culture all vestiges of the traditional theatre, leaving the stage free for a truly revolutionary, proletarian, mass-agitational theatre such as those they represented. In practice, this demand meant eradicating primarily the former Imperial theatres, by then renamed academic theatres, that is to say places such as the Bolshoi and the Mariinsky (since renamed the Kirov) and also establishment drama theatres such as the Maly in Moscow and the State (or former Alexandrinsky) in Leningrad. But the Front wanted to eradicate above all its absolute *bête noire*, MKhAT (the Moscow Arts Theatre), allegedly the quintessential bourgeois theatre. After signing their 'contract' in an atmosphere of elation, those present at the meeting streamed out of the hall to form columns and march to Ostrovsky Square in front of the State Theatre where with loudspeakers mounted upon trucks they staged a confrontational protest against 'academic art', chanting their slogan 'The Liquidation of MKhAT as a Class' *(Likvidatsiia MKhATa kak klassa)*.[3]

TRAM was in a position to take this stance because of its proletarian revolutionary purism. Its director Misha Sokolovskii (1901–41), one of those Komsomol activist firebrands who refused to ever wear a tie and insisted on being called by the most informal version of his name – 'Misha' – had from the theatre's very inception in 1925[4] zealously guarded TRAM's profile as strictly worker youth with Komsomol (or Party) affiliation. Of the original 64 members, 30 per cent were Party members and 65 per cent Komsomol (only two were neither),[5] and it was stipulated that any further recruits should be no older than 23.[6]

From the very beginning Sokolovskii counterposed the sort of theatre his young workers would be producing with conventional theatre. Unlike the latter, it would take subjects from the everyday lives of the workers, both on the factory floor and in their homes. One of the plays even attempted a realistic simulation of a factory shop on the stage with actual production processes.[7] The aim was to air the problems encountered both in attempting to improve levels of production and as the working class attempted to move from a bourgeois-capitalist to a socialist consciousness. The ambitious Sokolovskii claimed that what TRAM did was not really art at all but something much more important, 'the means of organisation of young people's everyday lives'. Originally, the theatre was conceived as being strictly amateur and using only full-time workers. On *his* stage, 'the working lad plays himself', and hence in a sense both acts out and even realises his own transformation even as he helps transform his peers.[8]

The plays were *by* the workers and Komsomols, *of* the workers and Komsomols and *for* the workers and Komsomols (at every performance there would be a huge block of cheap seats made over to Komsomol organisations). The young authors who wrote TRAM's plays, such as Arkadii Gorbenko, Nikolai L'vov and Pavel Marinchik – names you will not find in any literary encyclopedia – allegedly all came from a worker milieu and were completely inexperienced as writers. But, if that were not sufficient guarantee that the plays were *by* workers, these writers were not to be regarded as god-authors and their texts would be worked on by the theatre collective so that their own experience was brought to bear on their plays in a very immediate way.

Worthy as this enterprise might seem, for its first few years TRAM had received little material encouragement or political sponsorship though it had a favourable press. The periodic calls from its supporters that the theatre get some premises of its own or that its performers be better paid went unheeded.

In 1927–8 a series of events served to alter radically TRAM's standing in Soviet cultural life. For instance, in May 1927 Agitprop held a major national conference about theatrical policy, a conference whose resolutions functioned as guide-lines for all of Soviet culture for the next few years. By comparison with the Party's last major pronouncement on culture, the Resolution on Literature of 1925, the Agitprop resolutions reflected a shift to giving proletarian culture and proletarian cultural organisations a greater role in Soviet culture – a shift that could only improve the status of TRAM. For instance, the conference resolved that theatre be accessible to the masses, and take as many subjects as possible from their own lives or relevant to them.[9] The following year (1928) the First Five-Year Plan was launched and rapid industrialisation accompanied by a 'cultural revolution' became the cornerstone of official policy. The 'proletarianisation' and 'bolshevisation' of all areas of Soviet life became central items on the agenda, and many of the purges of Soviet institutions were conducted under these rubrics.

TRAM was in many respects the theatre of this new historical moment. During the late twenties, as never before or since, the Komsomol played a leading role in guiding Soviet culture and TRAM was riding the crest of its wave. Also, at this time, it was official policy that priority be given in culture to the efforts of the young; indeed a special national organisation had been set up for this purpose, the Society For the Encouragement of Youthful Talent.[10] In a sense, a Komsomol Theatre of Worker Youth could not miss.

Actually, by the late twenties there was no shortage of Komsomol and worker theatres to claim this historical moment as theirs. TRAM proved one of the few truly viable ones in that it seemed to have found the formula for turning agitational dramas about factory life into pithy, rollicking and enormously popular productions (no mean feat). Again and again – especially while on tour – the spillover crowd had to be chased away as it threatened to break down the doors of the theatre and get in, or the run of a particular play had to be extended by popular demand. In June 1928 the theatre went on a highly successful tour to

Moscow where its performances impressed the heads of both the Central Administration for Political Enlightenment (Glavpolitprosvet) and of its parent body, the Department of Education and Culture or Narkompros (i.e. Pel'she and Lunacharsky) and hence its standing in the theatrical world began to increase even more dramatically.[11]

By 1929 TRAM had emerged from its modest beginnings to become a major force in the Soviet theatre. Even before the Moscow tour of 1928 it had begun to sprout branches in cities like Moscow and Baku, but after it the theatre took off in a big way, expanding to 70 branches by 1929,[12] and 300 by 1932.[13] It also expanded its empire into the other arts, sponsoring IZORAM in the fine arts in 1928, followed shortly by KINORAM (or KRAM) in film, MUZORAM in music and BALETRAM in ballet.[14]

The importance of TRAM did not derive from the number of organisations in its empire, however, but from its increasing status as a viable version of the way forward for the Soviet theatre. As, in the course of the next three years, theoreticians, bureaucrats and directors argued over what this way forward might be, they began to identify three possible approaches, each crystallised in a particular theatre; that of MKhAT, that of the Meierhold theatre TIM (Teatr imeni Meierkhol'da), and that of TRAM. MKhAT was of course TRAM's declared anathema, but even TIM was feeling the pressure of the new rival. Indeed, the enthusiastic endorsement of TRAM by Lunacharsky and other Soviet authorities may have had something to do with the fact that they had long sought an alternative to TIM as the mainstay of Soviet revolutionary theatre. Some of them began to suggest that the young upstarts of TRAM had begun to outstrip those old role models,[15] or even that Meierhold should start to learn from TRAM.[16] Meierhold himself had begun to pay lip-service to this view.[17]

As TRAM gained power and prestige, it began to advance ever more inflated claims about the role it would play in forging the new man and the new society, insisting that it be seen not as just a theatre but rather as an entire social movement of youth, so called 'tramism' *(tramizm)*.[18] This position was prominent in the speeches made at a regional meeting of TRAM theatre organisations held at the Smolny in April 1929 where 'tramizm' was defined in terms of the theatre's new slogan 'TRAM is the Agitprop of the Komsomol'.[19] By this it meant that TRAM was not only to be important as a propaganda medium, but was allegedly to be instrumental in helping raise productivity and reeducate the workers. To such ends, cells of TRAM, or *Tramiadra*, were established in all the major factories.[20] When, five months later, the Revolutionary Front was formed, its 'revolutionary contract' contended that the theatrical circles – hitherto the mainstay of agitational work in the factories and Komsomol – had to be replaced by 'agitational-propagandistic brigades'.[21]

When, consequently, on 3 November 1929, virtually on the eve of the Revolution anniversary, the members of the four theatres in the Revolutionary Front led by TRAM lined up on Ostrovsky Square facing the State Theatre and insistently chanted their demand, 'The Liquidation of MKhAT as a Class', this incident had all the makings of a black day in that black year. From TRAM's very inception in 1925, it had taken as its slogan the famous lines from 'The Internationale', 'We shall build a new world – our world. He who was nought shall be all'.[22] Now, with their new slogan 'The Liquidation of MKhAT as a Class' they were essentially implying that the institutions such as MKhAT which had previously enjoyed the status in the cultural sphere analogous to that of the kulak in the village, those who had been 'all' by virtue of their purported monopoly over that currency called culture, should now be 'nought'. Potentially, this incident has all the signs of being yet another onslaught by the underprivileged on the position of the educated and professional classes, yet another purge of an intellectual institution as part of a twin campaign for 'proletarianisation' and Party/Komsomol hegemony, and hence comparable with the purges at this time in the Academy of Sciences, the conservatoria, publishing houses, the Formalists' institute (the State Institute for the History of the Arts), and countless others. At the same time, TRAM's claim for hegemony might seem to have been informed by a crudely mechanistic sense of the function of culture, culture's only utility seemingly being what it might achieve as a form of agitation or as a means of raising economic yields. Thus we seem to have a scenario here where Kulture's very existence is threatened by the primitive agitational drama.

All these conclusions are valid, but they do not tell the whole story. In many senses, the campaign by Revfront with TRAM at its head was not a moment when the Great Unwashed confronted the cultural élite, or when Soviet power attempted to rape the fair maiden Kulture, but more a matter of internecine warfare within the leftist intelligentsia. For a start, although TRAM was originally founded as an amateur theatre, in the 1927–8 season a decision had been taken to go professional and its members had been given extensive theatrical training, but TRAM seems to have become more militant vis-à-vis the established theatres in proportion as it became more professional and, in consequence, more directly those theatres' rival.[23] One of the major motives in the Revfront demonstration seems to have been its four theatres' frustration at seeing little improvement in the chronic paucity of material support they received from the cultural bureaucracy in a year when official rhetoric would seem to suggest that *they* were the theatres of the hour; in the immediately preceding months their subsidies had even been cut.[24]

Also, TRAM was far from exclusively a worker theatre. While histories of TRAM allege that its authors were untutored workers who came to the theatre straight from the factory floor, further examination reveals that many of them were quite well-educated and had already established themselves as career Komsomol cultural workers – as had their director, Sokolovskii.[25] Others in the theatre did not even fit the mould of the Komsomol activist. For instance, the acknowledged 'godfather' of TRAM, technically head of the Literary Artistic Section but in practice its chief theoretician and mastermind – *and* its chief spokesman on Ostrovsky Square – was no raw worker youth but Adrian Piotrovskii, the son (albeit illegitimate) of Faddei Zelinskii, a famous professor of classics at Petersburg University.[26] Piotrovskii was himself a respected classicist and translator from Greek, Latin and German, a sometime member of OPOIAZ (the Formalist circle), a former disciple of Meierhold and an experienced director and author in the professional theatre and even film. He was not the only exception to this rule of the pure working-class TRAM member; the Musical Section of TRAM was headed by the young Dmitrii Shostakovich (likewise from a background in the professional classes and with higher education – in this case the Conservatorium); Shostakovich wrote the musical score for many of the TRAM productions and also went on to direct MUZORAM.[27] Even Filonov, a mystical 'analytical artist' who has returned to prominence in recent years as one of the glaring omissions or 'blank spaces' in Soviet cultural history, was close to Revfront (closer actually to the Red Theatre than to TRAM). But lest we see these figures as somehow chance and unwitting members of this militantly proletarian cultural movement we must remember that Piotrovskii in 1921 went off as a volunteer to fight in Kronstadt while Filonov was so vehemently opposed to NEP that he would not let a Nepman cross the threshold of his apartment.[28]

Thus our canonical map of the cultural life in 1929 which has it divided up into heroes (such as Eisenstein, Filonov and Shostakovich) and villains (such as the leaders of RAPP, a militantly proletarian writers' organisation which tried to purge from Soviet literature all those who were not 'proletarian' in the sense of workers or Party members) does not discriminate very well what are in fact fine shadings in a complex topography. Some of this complexity derives from the singularity and extremism of the times.

The year 1929 was declared by the Party to be the year of the *bol'shoi perelom*. Generally translated as the Great Breakthrough, *bol'shoi perelom* actually has for many the somewhat sinister connotations of a major breaking of the bones; as Mandelshtam might have had it (as in his 'The Age' *[Vek]* of 1923), 'your spine [will be] shattered,/ My beautiful, pitiful age'.[29] At the time, however, large sections of the intelligentsia welcomed the *bol'shoi perelom* as a meaningful concept; for them, it promised a 'great breakthough' which might finally liberate society from a stultifying conformism and that special bugbear *meshchanstvo* (philistinism, the commercialisation of culture, the taste of the 'boulevards', etc.); it might realise a post-bourgeois culture. *Of course* the various ways they conceived this post-bourgeois culture did not correspond exactly to the Party's conception of cultural life after the *bol'shoi perelom*, but in the name of the new culture they welcomed wholeheartedly many of the extremist policies designed to smash the backbone of that 'beautiful, pitiful age'.

Purging is endemic to all utopias, and at this time large sections of the intelligentsia were in the grip of utopian fantasies. TRAM was no exception. Indeed the whole enterprise was in a sense an exercise in that ultimate utopianism of intellectuals that took too literally the words 'He who was nought shall be all'. It is perfectly consistent that in this year many of the branches of TRAM, together with those of their allied organisations such as IZORAM, should form into 'communes *(bytovye kommuny)* where members lived and ate together, pooled their earnings, shared the household tasks and, in a spirit which must have warmed poor Chernyshevsky in his grave, gathered together in their scarce leisure-time for improving lectures and discussion sessions.[30]

Thus when Revfront stood on Ostrovsky Square, rather as when the Decembrists in 1825 had stood on the Senate Square nearby, they stood for something larger than can be contained in better budgets or buildings. Though they agitated for a status reversal of the sort promised in that couplet from 'The Internationale' long used by them as a slogan – 'He who was nought shall be all' – what they wanted ultimately was outlined in the *other* part of the slogan, in that couplet's preceding line: 'We shall build a new world, our world'.

TRAM's leadership had ambitions for their theatre far greater than that of mere agitprop for the Komsomol. Piotrovskii, Shostakovich and Sokolovskii were all spear carriers of a pan-European movement for theatrical reform which had begun around the turn of this century and did not originally, or necessarily, have much connection with political revolution, let alone Bolshevism. In their view, their old mentor Meierhold with his 'theatrical October' had taken the baton of this movement quite some distance into the Bolshevik revolution, but not far enough. What TRAM promised was the ultimate marriage of the movement for theatrical reform with the Bolshevik proletarian revolution. The reason why intellectuals like Piotrovskii, Sokolovskii and Shostakovich were attracted to this kind of theatre was precisely because it promised to create a truly proletarian revolutionary culture. By 'proletarian', however, they meant not so much those who worked in industry or those who were underprivileged (although they certainly valued those qualities in TRAM's members) as they meant the native speakers of urban slang.

In the most recent phase of the movement for theatrical reform (approximately the late twenties), many theatre activists in both Russia and Germany had focused on urban slang and the urban underclass as the royal road to a post-revolutionary culture. They had fastened in particular on that somewhat unlikely genre, the opera, and contended that the reform of the opera, the storming of that bastion of high culture, would be the crucial act for the Great Breakthrough. For some decades the opera had essentially been dominated by the Wagnerian ideal of the *Gesamtkunstwerk* in which all the arts were integrated or 'synthesized' by the shaping force of the music. In reacting against this ideal, the theatre reformers sought in particular a different relationship between word and music so that the text should no longer be subordinated to the demands of the melody. Moreover, in discussing the libretto, they stressed the importance of using actual, conversational speech and preserving its intonations, rather than the artificial, bookish language of conventional opera.[31] At the same time, the opera began to incorporate subjects from the life of the proletariat or underclass, and also to use non-canonical forms and instruments, such as jazz and the accordion.

Piotrovskii, Shostakovich and others who worked with TRAM were local leaders of the movement for opera reform, and their theories informed most of the TRAM productions in the late twenties. There were no actual operas produced at TRAM, but then the movement for opera reform was much broader in its implications than opera alone (one can discuss it in terms, for instance, of shifts in linguistics made at about this time, and also in terms of the kind of *skaz* used by Zoshchenko and other popular Soviet authors of the late twenties). Music played a central role in all of the TRAM productions, which were typically satirical comedies or melodramas interlarded with musical numbers, or outright musicals. In addition, its two principal composers, Shostakovich and V. Deshevov, were also working on experimental operas at this time. Indeed Shostakovich's opera *The Nose (Nos)*, which had its première in 1929, was hailed by the champions of the new opera as an exemplum.

In the writings of TRAM's theorists (principally Sokolovskii and Piotrovskii) the Wagnerian opera and other such highly formalised theatrical modes were rejected in the name of a 'dialectical materialist' art.[32] This term was far from unique to TRAM but was used at this time by many groups who wanted to claim that their art best met the needs of the new Soviet society. TRAM's invocation of 'dialectical materialism' should not blind us to the fact that in many respects its aims have to be seen as a development of the general ideas held by the Russian *avant-garde* as it emerged even before the Revolution in the Futurist movement. TRAM aimed to deliver a version of that much-vaunted 'Slap in the Face of Public Taste' (the title of the Futurists' manifesto of 1912), to wake up a public lulled into complacency by a pernicious and overly-commercialised bourgeois culture, and thereby transform not just their behavioural patterns, but their habits of mind *(vnutrennii byt)* as well. Like the Futurists, TRAM would shock its audience into a new awareness by presenting them with all manner of contradictions, incongruities, radical displacements and shifts; in articles by the theorists of TRAM they sometimes used the key Futurist term *sdvig* (displacement) or Eisenstein's favourite 'montage' *(montazh)*.

Eisenstein, another heir to the Meierhold and Futurist traditions, had in his articles of the late twenties begun to call his method of montage 'dialectical materialist', too. In his account, much of the dialectic was to be derived, likewise, from clashes and contradictions. However, the shock was to be induced largely by visual and formal contractions in a film. In his films, characters and plot developments tend to be perfectly sustained and even somewhat conventional; in *The Battleship Potemkin* (1925), for instance, he structured what is essentially a simple tale in accordance with the model for Greek tragedy.[33] He sought to achieve his 'dialectic' largely through radical cutting and by introducing contrasts and clashes both within the composition of an individual frame or shot and in their juxtaposition with others – clashes of camera angle, graphic directions, volumes, depth, length of shot, light and shade, and so on.[34] This visual dialectic, he claimed, would (as it were, *qua* dialectic) bring about a revolution within the consciousness of his viewer so that the aesthetic dialectic and political-cum-class dialectic structuring the revolutionary plot on the screen would be 'in sync' and the revolution in consciousness wrought in the viewer would give him a new, dialectical-materialist consciousness.

The early TRAM productions had been less ambitious. But beginning with *The Days are Melting (Plaviatsia dni*, 1928) which was premièred in the spring of 1928 (a month before the triumphal tour of Moscow) the theoreticians-*cum*-directors of TRAM attempted to pioneer a rather more radical version of dialectical-materialist art where the dialectic was built on clashes, incongruities and contrasts not just in visual imagery and in the pacing of the work (montage), but extending to every aspect, including even character and plot.

TRAM aimed to present a 'conflicted' and 'multi-layered' account of reality so that no single and coherent version of anything would be projected; always its opposite would be there, and frequently its opposite would be presented simultaneously. This was achieved in a variety of ways; most typically, while one account of events was acted out on centre stage, a contrary reality was presented on the rear stage or in inserted film clips projected somewhere else, or a particular actor's account of reality was parodied in light or sound effects. Together with this insistence that *nothing* be presented as coherent and integrated, went the abolition of the linear, teleological plot and of the conventions for representing time on stage; playwrights were not to feel bound by chronological sequence in any way. Perhaps the most radical break with conventional dramaturgy came with the stipulation that no character be given an 'integrated psychic image' or stable identity. In glaring contrast to the conventional agitational play, the characters of a TRAM production were not to be presented as black and white and conflicting accounts of their moral/political identity should be represented.

In time, the directors of TRAM also sought to break down the identification between actor and character that was so central to Stanislavsky's system and introduce 'contradictions' there, too.[35] If, in the early productions, TRAM actors had played themselves (the young workers of the day), starting with *The Days are Melting* they began to construct a critique of their roles even as they were acting them, and each actor was instructed to convey to the audience not merely his character's thoughts and actions, but also his own 'attitude' *(otnoshenie)* to the character he was representing (clearly this principle is close to Brecht's concept of alienation).

Theorists of TRAM did not rest with this indeterminacy of character, but added further that a TRAM script should avoid conforming to any generic model, that it never be considered to have a final version and even that it should present no conclusions to the audience. In other words, no overriding system from the conventions of the theatre should control events on stage, rather as, according to the theorists of the new opera, the system of music was no longer to control what happened on stage in an opera.

One must ask: if characters were not to be represented as black and white or even have a consistent identity, and if there was to be no explicit message, how could TRAM's plays be of much use as propaganda, which both the Soviet cultural bureaucracy and TRAM itself identified as their central purpose? Likewise, how could such complex and confusing plays meet Agitprop's central demand of 1927 that plays be readily accessible to the masses?

The answer given by the theoreticians of TRAM was that their theatre was truly radical because the synthesis of the manifold contradictions inherent in its productions was to be made not on stage, but in the minds of the audience. The audience should be assaulted by the dialectic, confront it, and resolve its conflicts for themselves. Such things as emotions, thinking-through a situation, and even the time-honoured struggle between good and evil which conventions have led us to expect to see on the stage should now be transposed to the audience. It is within their consciousnesses that the making-whole was to take place, not on stage.

Thus TRAM's primitive and pedestrian melodramas and comedies of the factory floor had, willy-nilly, to become the agents of epistemological revolution. This is very weighty baggage for such a medium to bear. Yet TRAM's productions of the late twenties appear to have been no less successful with their audiences than their earlier, less ambitious works. In terms of its popularity, indeed, the theatre has to be compared once more with that of Brecht; his *Threepenny Opera*, written in the distinctly *non comme il faut* language of the street, became an overnight sensation, propelling him to prominence as a major dramatist and director of the twentieth century. Such, unfortunately, was not to be the fate of Piotrovskii or Sokolovskii.

My gentle reader may have noticed that at the beginning of this article I placed Revfront on Ostrovsky Square confronting the State Theatre with the chant 'The Liquidation of MKhAT as a Class', but somehow over all the intervening pages I have not managed to make my heroes take one further step. The reason for this is not just because I wanted to leave the reader in suspense, but also because the dénouement was a fizzle. In the event, Revfront was unable to storm the citadel of High Culture because that citadel had in *some* senses already fallen, or more specifically it had heeded the call of the Agitprop Conference of 1927 and other suasive events (such as the firing of the old director in 1928) and had added to its repertoire several plays on contemporary working-class or revolutionary themes. The Front appears to have miscalculated somewhat, because the production they were picketing that day happened to be the première of one of these, Furmanov's Civil War drama *The Revolt (Miatezh)*. For that production the director of the State Theatre, N. V. Petrov, had military units and an orchestra of wind instruments appear on stage and then march out through the audience. On hearing the approaching demonstrators, he instructed the soldiers to march out of the hall to confront the group on Ostrovsky Square, while the orchestra was sent to the balcony overlooking the square to drown out the speeches of protest with 'The Internationale' – TRAM's own signature song... . According to his account, he then simply conferred with the demonstration's leaders and they were able to agree in a comradely manner on future collaboration.[36]

Whatever reality lay behind this account, such a dénouement is not as unfeasible as it might seem, because Piotrovskii, Sokolovskii and Petrov were in a general sense from the same camp of the theatrical intelligentsia, that is, heirs of the Meierhold tradition who had worked throughout the twenties for theatrical reform and a more revolutionary theatre. Indeed, as recently as 1927 they had all collaborated in directing the mass spectacle staged on the Neva River to mark the tenth anniversary of October.[37] However, this was probably not all the 'dénouement'.

The reason why Revfront picketed the State Theatre was not just because it was the nearest bastion of 'academic art'. That theatre had been chosen as the stage for the première of *The Heights (Vysoty)*, a play by Yuri Libedinsky, one of the leaders of RAPP. RAPP, the Russian Association of Proletarian Writers, was the single most powerful leftist organisation in Soviet culture during the Plan years, and in many respects a direct rival to TRAM: both groups had emerged from Komsomol sponsorship and were riding the same wave of Komsomol influence in Soviet culture; both claimed to represent the proletariat; [38] and both expanded drastically during the Plan years, forming a network of branches throughout the country, and amalgamating with other organisations which were then subordinated to their leadership (e.g. in Revfront). Of the two, RAPP was by far the more powerful, but TRAM with its meteoric rise to prominence since 1928 represented RAPP's major challenge.

Before the Agitprop Conference of 1927 the challenge had not been very direct because the two organisations operated in different spheres – theatre and literature. However, thereafter each began to encroach on the territory of the other. In the resolutions of the Agitprop conference, theatre had reemerged as the central medium for Party agitational work, so the ambitious RAPP expanded its horizons to include theatre (as is evident in the fact that Libedinsky, one of their leading prose writers, produced a play). In so doing, it chose to identify its activities with MKhAT, no doubt a major factor in TRAM's singling out that theatre in its slogan.[39] At the same time, TRAM began to expand its sphere of influence in the arts. It organised at its headquarters a forum at which would be discussed the 'methods and forms of socialist art' in general.[40] And in 1930 it incorporated in Revfront a major faction in RAPP known as Litfront (the Literary Front) which was at the time challenging the RAPP leadership.[41] During 1930 the struggle between the two intensified, and although TRAM had some powerful patrons, RAPP was generally able to take its revenge on the masterminds of TRAM for their hubris in challenging MKhAT, RAPP's own chosen vessel for proletarian theatre.[42]

The clash between the two organisations was not merely a naked power struggle, but was conducted over the issue of what direction Soviet culture should take. Both RAPP and TRAM called their art proletarian and revolutionary, but the two had diametrically opposed conceptions of what this might mean: RAPP favoured realistic depiction and psychological studies, TRAM a 'monumental', poster-style art which rejected all attempts at psychological portraiture. The two also held diametrically opposed attitudes toward Western *avant-gardisme* and the cultural heritage of the past. While TRAM was closely allied to the proletarian theatres and avant-garde music of contemporary Germany, RAPP's orientation was to the classics of Russian literature. But time proved, for the time being, to be on RAPP's side.

During 1930 many prominent figures such as Eisenstein, Meierhold and Shostakovich were attacked for what was called 'Formalism' but what essentially represented pan-European *avant-gardisme*. Piotrovskii was included in this company, and the attacks on him were so intense that by the joint meeting *(slet)* of the 70 TRAM organisations in February of that year, TRAM were already renouncing their 'godfather'.[43] Piotrovskii did not leave TRAM, and the theatre continued to win official praise and honours, but its meteoric rise had peaked and by the second half of 1931 it had receded dramatically in prominence.

Ultimately, as we know, the 'academic theatre' (i.e. those theatres most identified with pre-revolutionary Russian theatrical traditions) prevailed in the battle for the new theatre which had focused on the oppositions TIM versus TRAM versus MKhAT. In the thirties, MKhAT's Stanislavsky was installed as the absolute authority figure for theatre. In some senses, this dénouement was foreshadowed all along; indeed, in trying to account for the fact that throughout TRAM's history the cultural bureaucracy so frequently dragged its feet or looked away when called on to support this theatre which more than most met their official criteria for the new culture, the most plausible explanation has to be that at heart most of those in power favoured more traditional cultural bodies. It might also have been said, however, that the TRAM of 1929, as a marriage between *avant-garde* experimentalists bent on transforming the landscape of culture, on the one hand, and theatrically-gifted workers, on the other, was bound to come unstuck since the partners were ill-matched in so many ways. Shostakovich, for instance, had to work overtime on his fellow communards of TRAM to persuade them that the new music was more truly 'proletarian' than the more melodious and schmaltzy revamped Tchaikovsky and Beethoven peddled as 'revolutionary music' by RAPP's counterpart in music RAPM (the Russian Association of Proletarian Musicians).[44] In a sense, 1930 represents the year the marriage came unstuck.

But our story does not end there. TRAM was essentially the theatre of the hour for the years of the First Five-Year Plan and the cultural revolution, but it did not wear well as the country entered the thirties. By then, the country was finding worker mores a less compelling subject for its theatre and hence TRAM had lost much of its original purpose. By the mid-thirties it was attracting only small audiences and in 1936 and 1938 the main TRAMs in Moscow and Leningrad (respectively) were combined with others to form the Theatres of the Leninist Komsomol (the Leningrad TRAM was actually merged with its fellow member of Revfront, the Red Theatre). However, TRAM's problems in the thirties were really at a more fundamental level than unpopular themes; its aesthetic stance was at odds with the new direction of Soviet culture and its clumsy attempts at adjusting were pronounced pedestrian and boring.

Starting in 1932, as we know, a major shift occurred in Soviet culture when all independent organisations were abolished and single unions set up in each field (the Writers' Union, the Composers' Union, and so on). However, in a sense a more fundamental change had been begun the previous year when Maxim Gorky, on his return from exile to head

Soviet literature, launched a campaign for language reform. Starting with his essay 'On work with language', he continued his campaign in a heated exchange over the language of Panferov's novel of collectivisation, *Brusski;* this exchange went on until 1934 when Party officials pronounced in favour of Gorky's position. Throughout it, Gorky insisted that folkisms, regionalisms, sub-standard locutions and slang be excised from Soviet literature.[45] What Gorky was really arguing for – and what was adopted – was the mandating of a single, spare and standardised – 'classical' – language for Soviet literature. In other words, the ideal of a new culture based on the actual language of urban youth was killed forever – or at any rate until the late fifties when Vasilii Aksenov and others revived it in a new school of 'youth prose'.

Notes

1. For a fuller account of the history of TRAM see Pavel Marinchik, *Rozhdenie komsomol'skogo teatra* (Moscow–Leningrad, 1963); B. Mironova, *TRAM. Agitatsionno-molodezhnyi teatr 1920–1930-kh godov* (Leningrad, 1977); A. Piotrovskii, 'TRAM (stranitsa teatral'noi sovremennosti)', *Zvezda,* 1929, no. 4, pp. 142–52; N. A. Radiants, *Teatr molodykh* (Leningrad, 1965), and 'Teatry rozhdennye revoliutsiei', in *Teatr i zhizn'* (Moscow–Leningrad, 1957), pp. 307–40; and V. Rafalovich, *Vesna teatral'naia* (Leningrad, 1971).
2. *Krasnyi teatr, Agitatsionnyi teatr* (sometimes called the *Dom derevenskogo aktera* because it was used to provide agitation for collectivisation) and *Leningradskii rabochii teatr Proletkul'ta.*
3. 'Edinyi front revoliutsionnykh teatrov', *Krasnaia gazeta,* 5 November 1929, p.6. See also the account by N. V. Petrov, then director of the State Theatre, in his *50 i 500* (Moscow, 1960), pp. 288–93.
4. TRAM emerged out of a theatre studio Sokolovskii had been running since 1922 at the Gleron House for the Communist Education of Youth *(Dom kommunisticheskogo vospitaniia molodezhi),* a Komsomol institution. In 1925 the Komsomol decided to upgrade its status to a fully fledged theatre.
5. D. Tolmachev, 'Teatr rabochei molodezhi', *Rabochii i teatr,* 1925, no. 40 (6 October), p.4.
6. 'Teatr rabochei molodezhi', *Rabochii i teatr,* 1926, no. 33 (15 August).
7. D. Tolmachev, 'Zovi Fabkom', *Zhizn' iskusstva,* 1928, no. 3 (17 January), p. 10; 'TRAM', *Rabochii i teatr,* 1926, no. 7 (16 February), p. 17.
8. *Sovremennyi teatr,* 1929, no. 28–29, pp. 396–7.
9. 'Rezoliutsiia po dokladu V. G. Knorina "Ocherednie zadachi teatral'noi

politiki" ', in Agitprop TsKRKP(b), *Puti razvitiia teatra* (Moscow, 1927), pp. 475–91.
10. 'Moskva. Organizatsiia Obshchestva sodeistviia molodym darovaniiam', *Zhizn' iskusstva*, 1929, no. 4 (27 January), p.20.
11. Mikh.D., 'Idut novye liudi (na dispute o Teatre rabochei molodezhi)', *Komsomol'skaia pravda*, 16 June 1928, p. 5; A. V. Lunacharskii, 'Tram', *Pravda*, 8 July 1928; Boris Filipov, *Kak ia stal domovym* (Moscow, 1974), p. 99; 'Moskva', *Zhizn' iskusstva*, 1929, no. 8 (21 February), p. 20; 'Leningrad', *Zhizn' iskusstva*, 1928, no. 17 (24 April), p.21.
12. 'Za druzhnuiu stroiku komsomol'skogo teatra!', *Krasnaia gazeta*, 1929, no. 91 (20 April), p. 4.
13. V. Mironova, *TRAM. Agitatsionno-molodezhnyi teatr 1920-1930-kh godov*, p. 6.
14. S. R., 'Tram na zavtra', *Rabochii i teatr*, 1930, no. 11 (26 February), p. 4.
15. E.g. R. A. Pel'she, the head of Glavpolitprosvet, cited in Mikh. D., 'Idut novye liudi (Na dispute o teatre rabochei molodezhi'), p. 5.
16. 'Moskva. Krizis teatra im. Meierkhol'da', *Zhizn' iskusstva*, 1928, no. 34 (19 August), p. 14.
17. 'Novye boi na teatral'nom fronte i pozitsiia Meierkhol'da', *Zhizn' iskusstva*, 1929, no. 3 (13 January), p. 12; S. Mokul'skii, 'Vystuplenie Meierkhol'da v Leningrade', op. cit., p. 10.
18. See also M. Sokolovskii's speech to the First All-Union Conference of TRAMs in 1929 in which he described TRAM as a 'socio-political organisation. It represents that part of the Komsomol *aktiv* which strives toward the building of socialism...'. 'I-aia vsesoiuznaia konferentsiia TRAMov', *Pechat' i revoliutsiia*, 1929, no. 8, p. 120.
19. 'Za druzhnuiu stroiku komsomol'skogo teatra!,' p. 4; V. G-v, 'V bor'be za tramovskoe dvizhenie', *Zhizn' iskusstva*, 1929, no. 19 (12 May), p. 11.
20. 'V nogu s zhizn'iu!', *Krasnaia gazeta*, 1929, no. 224 (29 September), p. 6.
21. *Zhizn' iskusstva*, 1929, no. 46, p. 12; Adrian Piotrovskii, 'Puti i pereput'ia samodeiatel'nogo teatra', *Rabochii i teatr*, 1930, no. 39 (15 July), pp. 4–5.
22. Mironova, *TRAM. Agitatsionno-molodezhnyi teatr 1920-1930-kh godov*, p. 6.
23. In September 1928 TRAM was finally given new premises, Glaviskusstvo tried to get it the same tax-breaks as the academic theatres, and intensive training was set up for its members with such famous theatrical directors and pedagogues as S. Radlov and V. Solov'ev, and yet it was also beginning to take a more aggressive stance; see 'TRAM gotov k nastupleniiu', and 'Leningrad', *Zhizn' iskusstva*, 1928, no. 38 (16 September), pp. 11, 14.
24. See, for example 'Pod znakom peregruppirovki', *Zhizn' iskusstva*, 1929, no. 20 (19 May), p. 1; Veg, 'Revoliutsionnyi-proletarskii front teatra pod ugrozoi', *Zhizn' iskusstva*, 1929, no. 38 (22 September), p. 2; 'Za edinyi khudozhestvennyi tsentr. (Otkrytoe pis'mo sovetskoi obshchestvennosti Leningrada)', op. cit., p. 3; 'V Leningradskom proletkul'te', *Zhizn' iskusstva*, 1929, no. 40 (6 October).
25. Pavel Marinchik, *Rozhdenie komsomol'skogo teatra*, p. 35.
26. B. Filipov, *Kak ia stal domovym*, p. 91.

27. 'Novosti iskusstva. TRAM', *Rabochii i teatr*, 1930, no. 15 (16 March), p. 15.
28. Gennadii Gor, 'Zamedlenie vremeni', *Zvezda*, 1968, no. 6, p. 179.
29. Stanza IV, lines 3–4: 'No razbit tvoi pozvonochnik,/Moi prekrasnyi zhalkii vek.'
30. S. Romm, 'Iskusstvo v bytovykh kommunakh', *Rabochii i teatr*, 1930, no. 8 (February), p. 3; S. M. Khentova, *Shostakovich v Petrograde-Leningrade* (Leningrad, 1979), p. 71. I am of course alluding here to the communal models provided in N. Chernyshevsky's *What Is To Be Done?* (1863).
31. I. Sollertinskii, 'Problemy "opernogo naslediia" ', *Zhizn' iskusstva*, 1929, no. 18 (1 May), p. 10; I. Sollertinskii, 'Vozmozhnye printsipy sovetskoi opery', *Zhizn' iskusstva*, 1929, no. 31 (4 August), p. 3.
32. My account of 'dialectical materialist' art as defined by the theorists of TRAM is derived from Adrian Piotrovskii, 'Kinofikatsiia teatra (neskol'ko obobshchenii)', *Zhizn' iskusstva*, 1927, no. 47 (22 November), p. 4; *Dialekticheskii materializm – osnova raboty TRAM. Leningradskii TRAM v Moskve* (Leningrad, 1928); 'TRAM', *Zvezda*, 1929, no. 4, pp. 142–52, 'Rekonstruktsiia dramy', *Zhizn' iskusstva*, 1929, no. 10 (8 March), p. 2, ' "Klesh zadumchivyi" i problemy komsomol'skogo teatre', *Zhizn' iskusstva*, 1929, no. 22 (2 June), pp. 5–6, 'Aktery v TRAMe', *Rabochii i teatr*, 1930, no. 43 (4 August), pp. 2–3; S. Mokul'skii, ' "Klesh zadumchivyi" v Lngr. Tram', *Zhizn' iskusstva*, 1929, no. 20 (19 May), p. 6; M. Sokolovskii, *Za novyi byt* (Moscow–Leningrad, 1927).
33. See his essay 'The Structure of the Film' in *Film Form. Essays in Film Theory*, ed. and trans. Jay Leyda (New York, 1949), esp. pp. 162–6.
34. See S. Eisenstein, 'The Cinematographic Principle and the Ideogram' and 'A Dialectic Approach to Film Form' in ibid., pp. 28–63.
35. I am, of course, referring to Constantine Stanislavsky, the founder and chief theoretician of MKhAT (the Moscow Arts Theatre).
36. N. V. Petrov, *50 i 500*, pp. 288–93.
37. 'Leningrad. Massovoe prazdnestvo', *Zhizn' iskusstva*, 1927, no. 45 (6 November), p. 38.
38. This claim was even less well-founded in the case of RAPP than for TRAM. However, in 1930 RAPP conducted a drive to recruit 'shock-workers' *(udarniki,* highly productive workers) into its ranks, swelling its numbers from 1500 to 10 000 of which 80 per cent were 'shock-workers': 'Prizyv udarnikov v literaturu – vnimanie!', *Literaturnaia gazeta*, 1930, no. 48 (21 October); V. Kirshon, 'Pervye itogi prizyva udarnikov v literaturu" (his speech to the Fourth Plenum of the Board of RAPP), *Literaturnaia gazeta,* 1931, no. 49 (10 September).
39. The decision was taken at a RAPP plenum of 1929. See V. B. ' "Vysoty" Iu. Libedinskogo', *Zhizn' iskusstva,* 1929, no. 12 (17 March), p. 6.
40. 'Leningrad. Diskussionnyi klub', *Zhizn' iskusstva*, 1929 no. 16 (14 April), p. 14.
41. 'Konsolidatsiia sil – pervoocherednaia zadacha' (editorial), *Rabochii i teatr*, 1930, no. 54–5 (15 October), p. 1; 'Dogovor revoliutsionnogo fronta', *Rabochii i teatr*, 1930, no. 58–9 (31 October), p. 10.
42. See Amanda Metcalfe, 'RAPP and the Theatre: 1927–1932', a paper

delivered at the Fourth World Congress for Soviet and East European Studies in Harrogate, England, 23 July 1990.
43. S. R. 'Slet 70 TRAMov', *Rabochii i teatr*, 1930, no. 10 (21 February), p.5.
44. Khentova, *Shostakovich v Petrograde-Leningrade*, p. 71.
45. M. Gor'kii, 'O rabote nad iazykom', *Literaturnaia gazeta,* no. 26 (15 May), 1931.

3 Tolstaian Times: Traversals and Transfers
Helena Goscilo

> Time, which is the author of authors...
> Francis Bacon, *Advancement of Learning*
>
> Time travels in divers paces with divers persons.
> William Shakespeare, *As You Like It*

During one of his habitual meditations on history, Yuri Trifonov reportedly stated, 'Time imposes its frame on a man, but it is within a man's power to widen the frame, if only slightly.'[1] In her fiction Tat'iana Tolstaia not only widens the frame, but packs within it an assortment of experiences that insistently push against the restraining contours and, on occasion, actually extend our vision beyond the frame. The multi-layered apperception of time in Tolstaia's fictional universe assimilates manifold temporal concepts, variously designated as folkloric or mythic; 'monumental' (Ricoeur);[2] 'pure' or 'experienced' (Bergson);[3] and 'great' (Bakhtin).[4] Tolstaia's highly complex handling of time originates in her syncretism – her propensity to condense elements from disparate sources into maximally compressed texts that usually narrate metonymical lives illustrative of timeless configurations.

Implicitly conceived by Tolstaia as a collective singular,[5] time, like most phenomena and conditions in her created universe, hinges chiefly on individual perception (Ricoeur's 'soul, mind, consciousness') and derives only secondarily from external data (Ricoeur's 'world').[6] Consequently, temporal categories and one's experience of them vary not only according to changing circumstances, but also, and primarily, in relation to age, cast of mind, and psychological states. Roughly speaking, the three broad phases of inner development determining temporal consciousness in Tolstaia's fictional world coincide with the three stages of human life charted by the Sphinx's famous riddle in Sophocles' *Oedipus the King*: childhood, adulthood (or maturity) and old age.

According to Trifonov, 'Every writer has "an emergency ration" or...a treasure to which he resorts sooner or later: childhood' (147). Tolstaia began sooner than later, excavating her treasure with her first story. ' "Na zolotom kryl'tse sideli..." ' (On the Golden Porch, 1985), which identifies childhood with mythic time: that is, the timelessness of the eternal present. There and in several subsequent works, Tolstaia spatialises childhood time through the chronotope of the Edenic garden: 'In the beginning was the garden. Childhood was a garden. Without end or limit, without boundaries or fences...'.[7]

During this 'innocent' or 'unconscious' phase of life, only seasonal or diurnal markers organise the temporal flow in an iterative pattern. This profoundly cyclic life, as in folklore,[8] consists predominantly of mornings, days, evenings and nights against a background of springs, summers, autumns and winters, with no hours or years (what Bergson calls 'physical' and Ricoeur 'cosmological' time) impinging on a child's mythic sense of her/his surroundings: 'They spent a boring day: they waited for lunch, then waited for dinner. Grandfather ate a hard-boiled egg. At night it started raining again' ('Svidanie s ptitsei' [Rendevous with a Bird], 122).

Numerous autobiographies, including Rousseau's *Confessions,* Mary McCarthy's *Memories of a Catholic Girlhood* and Nabokov's *Speak, Memory,* have conventionalised the garden as a metaphor for childhood or a setting associated with light, fruit, water, abundance, order and, above all, timelessness.[9] Musing on this topos in his own *Autobiography,* Edwin Muir tellingly remarks, 'It was as if, while I lay watching that beam of light, time had not yet begun.'[10] Nabokov similarly remembers 'the harmonious world of a perfect childhood' as a 'veritable Eden of visual and tactile sensations' in a 'free world of timelessness'.[11] A major component in this early idyll of boundless joys, then, is a sense of plenitude and security paradoxically combined with freedom from temporal linearity: that is, from chronology, large-scale cause and effect and teleology.

Years as such have little meaning in a child's universe. Hence children's frequent recourse, in Tolstaia's fiction, to those maximal (or 'otherworldly') formulations discredited by Lev Tolstoi like 'never', 'forever', and 'always'; hence also their penchant for fantastic, inconceivable temporary hyperbole as well as anachronistic conflation of time frames.[12] Characteristically, the child narrator in ' "Na zolotom kryl'tse sideli..." ' alludes to a period, 'when (in a hundred years) we graduate to the eight grade' (41); young Petia in 'Svidanie s ptitsei' has no difficulty believing that Tamila is seven thousand years old (115); and the recalcitrant girl narrator of 'Liubish' – ne liubish' ' (Loves Me,

Loves Me Not) declares of her beloved old nurse Grusha, 'Pushkin also loved her a lot and wrote about her: "My frail little dove". But he didn't write anything about Marivanna' (3).

In its more radical expression this timelessness or the incapacity to conceive of temporal movement as gradual change or progression (instead of cyclic repetition) manifests itself in a rejection of death. Reminiscing about her old governess Zhenechka, the adult narrator in 'Samaia liubimaia' (The Most Beloved) explicitly recalls that in childhood 'to tell the truth, we were convinced of her immortality – and at the same time of our own' (93). Collapsing the distinction between the dead and the living, the narrator of 'Liubish' – ne liubish'' observes, 'High up, in the window, his nose pressed against the dark glass, glimmers the hanged uncle, runs his hands over the glass, and peers out' (12), while her counterpart in ' "Na zolotom kryl'tse sideli..." ' announces: 'Life's eternal. Only birds die' (41). When Petia in 'Svidanie s ptitsei' gains knowledge of mortality through his grandfather's death, he cannot return to the prelapsarian perpetual present of his childhood Eden, but must enter the more problematic and differentiated sphere of maturity.[13]

The loss of timeless harmony and immortality as one falls into the adult world of chaos, pain, death and darkness inevitably marks, for Tolstaia, a new perception of, and relationship to, time.[14] Whereas immersion in the present, in the immediacy of presence, characterises childhood, Tolstaia portrays adulthood contrastively in terms that recall Aristotle's 'before and after'.[15] Aristotle defines time as 'the number of motion in respect of "before" and "after" ', his 'instant' requiring that 'the mind make a break in the continuity of movement, insofar as the latter is countable. This break can be made anywhere. Any instant at all is worthy of being the present. The Augustinian present,[16] however,...is any instant designated by a speaker as the "now" of his utterance.'[17] The connection between movement and time on which Aristotle insists is most palpable during this middle stage of existence, wherein adults experience time primarily as mutability and respond to it in Augustinian terms: with memories of the past and expectations of the future.

The underlying sameness of these modes of temporal perception, despite their ostensibly diametrically opposed impetus, is dramatised in Lewis Carroll's *Through the Looking Glass*, where the White Queen argues for a two-directional memory: 'It's a poor sort of memory that only works backwards.'[18] Memory of the past, in other words, determines expectations of the future and acts, in a sense, as its arbitrary arbiter. Frank Kermode recognises as much, offering two persuasive (if homespun and small-scale) illustrations in his assertion that 'there is...a kind of forward memory, familiar from spoonerisms and typing errors which are caused by anticipation, the mind working on an expected future'.[19] Although antithetically orientated, retrospection (what Genette labels narrative analepsis) and prospection (Genette's narrative prolepsis) may be said to participate in a common mental activity along a single continuum and, narratively, to invoke the same device of anachrony – of reaching into the past or future.[20]

Narratively speaking, for Tolstaia the retrospective stance of adulthood accomplishes a twofold effect. Since it registers the deprivation of an earlier, carefree state born of a transforming uncorrupted vision, its diachronic cast emphasises, *within the narrative itself* (or, to borrow Genette's vocabulary, on the level of *story*), the 'devouring' nature of temporal flow: hence the *'ubi sunt?'* elegiac nature of backward glances.[21] Yet retrospection potentially offers *the reader* (that is, on the level of *narrative*) a synchronic, bifocal view of a given phenomenon in which clinical powers of mature observation are textually juxtaposed with a child's vivid imagination, impervious to time's passage.[22] Here, as elsewhere, Tolstaia relies on a strategy that simultaneously achieves two contradictory ends: on the one hand, it separates temporal units in the participant's biography, while on the other, it narratively draws those phases together for the reader in a proximity that urges analysis. In ' "Na zolotom kryl'tse sideli..." ' only two pages separate a poetic, trope-laden paean to the magical contents of Uncle Pasha's attic as viewed through the child narrator's eyes from the prosaic dismissal of the same phenomena by her adult self, which, however, deliberately engages (for contrast's sake) the earlier, irrevocable perspective (47–8). What the collocation underscores is the unifying or narrative aspect of memory, analogous to the narrative cast of one's reading practices and of one's approach to history.[23]

To establish the seemingly definitive break (creating a 'now') between a golden past and the lacklustre, contingent present, Tolstaia employs developed metaphors that highlight physical spatial barriers (separation), yet are embedded in a context of immediacy (identification). To examine several eloquent examples: in ' "Na zolotom kryl'tse sideli..." ' the adult narrator reminiscences, 'we glanced back once, with perplexed fingers felt *the smoky glass, behind which* our garden waved its handkerchief for the last time before it sank to the bottom' (47); in 'Milaia Shura' (Sweet Shura) 'Thousands of years, thousands of days, thousands of translucent *impenetrable curtains* fell from the skies, thickened, *solidified into thick walls, blocked the roads*, and kept Aleksandra Ernestovna from her beloved, who was lost in time. He remained there, on the other side of the years, alone, at the dusty station... . Time's passing and the *invisible layers of years grow thicker and thicker*, and the rails grow rusty, and the roads become overgrown, and in the ravines the weeds grow more and more luxuriant' (35); in 'Krug' (The Circle) Tolstaia resorts to zeugma to concretise insuperable temporal occlusion through the photographs of the black-market female dwarf in her youth, in which 'the young speculator waved *through the glass, through time, through a lifetime*' (69).[24] Nostalgia for an irretrievable past and yearning for a projected future pull adults away from the present moment – a deflection partly reinforced by their submission to clock (cosmological) time (for example, the adult narrator in ' "Na zolotom kryl'tse sideli..." ' calculates, 'I have five minutes left.' [47]). Soul-time and cosmological or clock-time operate according to different if occasionally intersecting principles. Since clocks represent an effort at physical (external) tabulation of temporal flow, it is no accident that Tolstaia announces the moment of her characters' physical (tangible) deaths through the traditional metaphor of the striking hour (in 'Krug', 'The hour to depart chimed' for Vasilii Mikhailovich [72]; in ' "Na zolotom kryl'tse sideli..." ', one of two figures on a clock who represent 'masters of Time', 'the golden Lady of time, after draining the cup of life, will strike a final midnight on the table for Uncle Pasha' [48]). The present adulthood, then, derives essentially from the past and the future, which jostle against each other in one 'heterochronous' (Bakhtin's 'multi-temporal')[25] Tolstaian story after another that dialogise a multiplicity of chronotopes to convey the diversity of human experience through 'great time'.

In her treatment of memory, Tolstaia, not unlike Husserl, draws a distinction, on the one hand, between retention or primary remembrance, which more or less parallels Kermode's 'immediate memory', defined as 'the registration of impressions we fail to "take in", but can recover a little later by introspection' (53), and, on the other hand, recollection or secondary remembrance, located at a greater remove from the recalled event (Ricoeur, Vol. 3, p.26). Adulthood in Tolstaia's universe feeds off both and relies on both for future projections. With advancing age, however, primary remembrance fades, ceding to recollection, which increasingly dominates.

In old age, according to Tolstaia, the future orientation weakens or disappears entirely, edged out by the impulse to 'sum up', to evaluate the past. Memories rule old age and in a sense return the individual to childhood, with its undifferentiated approach to the world. Facts, fantasies, lived experience, hopes, possibilities and so forth all occupy the same psychic level for Tolstaia's aged characters, for they are all equally distant (or proximate). Stories such as 'Milaia Shura' and 'Samaia liubimaia' dramatise this disregard of boundaries, which Tolstaia's narrative technique intensifies. One might summarise this period of one's life as the Augustinian phase, in which 'soul' time preponderates, while 'world' time recedes to the periphery. In effect, what various critics have singled out as Tolstaia's predilection for portraying childhood and old age can more precisely be explained as her fascination with the dictates of one's inner being, as opposed to the demands of an external, 'objective' reality and its corollary – cosmological time.

The three eras roughly mapped out above in no way mean to imply clear-cut temporal division on the narrative level in Tolstaia's fiction. On the contrary, perhaps the most distinctive feature of Tolstaia's style – and one that lends it a unique rhythm – consists in her proclivity to sabotage temporal distinctions or to render them ambiguous through the violation of traditional boundaries. Admittedly, Tolstaia does refer to seasons, to years and to periods labeled 'before', 'after', but these ostensibly precise signposts dissolve – lose their ability to signify – for lack of grounding in a meaningful context. In 'Samaia liubimaia', for instance, the reader learns that the comment, 'Good tea. Evgeniia Ivanovna. Hot' (101), invariably elicits an emotional reaction from Zhenechka because those words were uttered by the historian who represents the sole love interest ('perhaps for a week, perhaps for her whole life') in her experience: 'That's what she was told during the day, at three o'clock, in February before the war, in a warm country home.' Rather than conveying valuable information, however, the specificity of the hour and month underscores the *lack* of more general temporal indicators (such as the year, the length of their acquaintance, and so on), whose presence would locate the event in some sort of sequence, thereby eliminating the grotesqueness of this excessive precision.

Moreover, Tolstaia often makes it impossible to gauge the correspondence between narrative and narrated time, and on those rare occasions when she does provide conditions for such a calculation, it becomes instantly apparent that the ratio is lop-sided and in any case prone to uncertainty, for those conditions alter. Tolstaia's dazzling succession of mimetic and diegetic, of scenic and summative, of iterative and durative, of chronological and analeptic or proleptic defies any attempt to categorise her narrative mode except by individual sentences – a unit insufficiently comprehensive to lead to meaningful generalisations about Tolstaia's treatment of time. Perhaps the one tenable observation to be made about her temporal orchestration on a larger scale is that she opts for diffusion through uncommon diversity.

Why, one may ask, does Tolstaia load her short stories with multiple, swiftly alternating chronotopes? Because she wishes to compress as much as possible on the horizontal axis of linear time and space and the vertical axis of psychological time and space into a brief narrative. To create the illusion of presenting an entire life (extensive narrated time) within a dozen pages (minimal narrative time) necessitates extraordinary omission and a condensation that can only be achieved by rapid, unorthodox transfers instead of the leisurely or unobtrusive modulations that a longer narrative traditionally permits. Tolstaia's bold trespass across conventional borders in the interests of diffusing time takes several forms: (1) manipulation of verb aspect and tense; (2) purposely enigmatic use of narrative voice; (3) symbiotic interplay between extended metaphor and metonymy; and (4) subjectivisation or humanising of objects.

VERB ASPECT AND TENSE

Analysing Proust's innovative treatment of time, Genette raises the rarely confronted issue of frequency; that is, the relationship of repetition between the narrative and the diegesis. Germane to frequency is the distinction Genette makes between the singulative narrative (whereby a verb indicates a single completed action – equivalent to the Russian perfective) and the iterative (whereby a verb signals a habitual action whose function verges on the descriptive – a feature of the Russian imperfective).[26] Genette concludes that iterative and singulative forms in Proust's *A la recherche du temps perdu* 'are entangled in a way that leaves the verbal aspect in utter irresolution'.[27] That deliberate mixture of aspect so as to disperse time is likewise a major trait of Tolstaia's narratives, which regularly interweave single-action verbs with iteratives that establish economically a way of life. As a result, what is habitual and what is singular becomes equivocal. If one adds to the dimension of frequency that of duration, which in Russian is also carried by the imperfective aspect, then one can appreciate how Tolstaia's alternation of imperfective and perfective raises several unanswerable questions.

To further complicate the picture, Tolstaia has a penchant for showing the past spilling over into the present, which she transmits by a scrambling of tenses. The legitimate and customary use of the present tense in Russian within a narrative passage in the past tense so as to increase the flavour of immediacy expands in Tolstaia's hands into a stratagem for condensing 'all time' into a single time. Furthermore, the ability of the Russian future tense to denote repeated actions in the past or present enables Tolstaia to convince the reader throughout several paragraphs that what is a wish or a waking dream actually took place, and likely more than once. Tolstaia's compression of these devices into a relatively small space manifests itself most effectively in the profoundly retrospective story 'Samaia liubimaia'.

Within the subsuming realm of reminiscences, the narrator of 'Samaia liubimaia' moves back and forth on the temporal axis with a stunning rapidity and ostensible arbitrariness that play havoc with conventional notions of narrative chronology. Characteristically, most of Tolstaia's emphatically precise details work against verifiable facts. As elsewhere (for example, 'Krug'), she takes pains to leave open to conjecture whether the story's heroine is even alive at the point where narrative and narrated intersect. Zhenechka's death is intimated, in a typical Tolstaian paradox, through repeated references to her immortality ('She planned to live forever' [93]; 'And we thought that Zhenechka was immortal' [103]; 'and we believed that Zhenechka was immortal' [108]); recollections of an era, 'long, long ago,...[when] Zhenechka was alive' (93); and the elegiac observation: 'she is no more, she became a shade, and the night wind will scatter her dilapidated dwelling' (109). No clue is provided as to the cause or time of Zhenechka's (probable) death.

The story's extensive time-recording lexicon renders supremely palpable the passage of time, while steadily blocking the reader's access to the story's sequence of events. Countless references to seasons nonetheless give no idea whether these are separated by a few years, a decade, or more. Many of the story's effects are achieved chiefly by Tolstaia's loops and leaps from one period to another, as she sums up an unspecified but undoubtedly long interval through the single summative (perfective) sentence, 'Time passed, and we became adults' (106), yet details in five paragraphs a single episode that could have lasted just a few minutes but *never* occurred; the section opening with 'we'll choose a day...' and the following paragraph, both couched in the future tense, modulate to the present in the third paragraph ('We wade through the grass'), which remains in effect until the close of the fifth paragraph. That ending, however, erases the 'contents' of the entire section with the simple words, 'it's not true, no one will come, there's nobody to come, she is no more, she became a shade' (109). Having just exposed that stretch of narrative as fantasy through the implied confirmation of her heroine's death,[28] in the paragraph that immediately follows, Tolstaia proceeds to resurrect Zhenechka, narratively speaking, as she backpedals with no warning to an imprecisely identified earlier moment when Zhenechka was awaiting a letter. Although the reader can deduce that this moment comes late in Zhenechka's life because the parodistically ludicrous letter that finally arrives expresses misgivings that Zhenechka may die in her relatives' home (presumably of old age), once again the exact temporal relationship of this incident to previous and subsequent ones remains enigmatic.

What renders the treatment of time in this story more complex, perhaps, than customary in Tolstaia's fiction is its extraordinary structure: Tolstaia essentially moves over what is presumably the same general terrain twice, bringing the narration up to the immediate present at least three times.[29] Framed in two lyrical passages that instal the central locus of the family dacha (a rough analogue for Zhenechka's biography: 'our dacha is growing old, is collapsing on its side'[93]), the narrative first sketches out in the present and future tenses (so as to signal iterative actions) Zhenechka's arrival at the dacha and the children's behaviour with her (93–5); it then backtracks to her introduction into the household, tracing her characteristic pattern over the years *via* illustrative incidents (95–9); it moves still further back in time to her youth and her putative love (99–101), after which, in an extended reprisal of the story's opening ('the dacha is quietly growing old and falling apart' [102–3]), it effects a transition to the second portion of the narrative. After its initial temporal regression, that section for the most part observes chronology, though in an uneven rhythm of detailed close-up alternating with a summarising panoramic perspective (104–8; 109–10). The second half of the story approximately retraces the first, not only complementing and paralleling it (often in reverse, for its progress is sequential, whereas that of the first part is predominantly recessive), but also relying on readers' recall of the texture of earlier portions to seduce them into credulity in the subsequent segments. Thus the passage starting with 'We'll choose a day' (109–10) acquires the illusory aura of a refrain accurately designating repetition of a formerly-enacted ritual because its tense, mood and tone deliberately echo the earlier evocations of the dacha (93–4, 102–3). Only with 'it's not true' in the final sentence does the imaginary (exclusively interior) nature of the activities (convincingly exteriorised through physical minutiae) become apparent. In brief, we are cajoled into acceptance on the basis of precedent. Here and elsewhere in Tolstaia, verb aspect and tense tend to supply elusive and misleading clues, enlisted in the interests of obfuscating rather than illuminating temporal demarcations.

VOICE

Part of the complexity of Tolstaia's texts also arises from the reader's inability to anchor the narrative in a single voice or to pinpoint whose voice is speaking at a given moment. Tolstaian stories of childhood proceed chiefly through quasi-direct discourse *(style indirect libre, erlebte Rede)*, but even within that category the voice may be located at any stage of the narrator's life. Tolstaia represents that life with an unpredictably irregular selectivity in which the ratio between narrated time and narrative time (Genette's duration)[30] varies so pronouncedly that a given scene of several minutes may occupy several pages, while a single synoptic sentence may encapsulate whole decades. If, as Genette claims, Proustian narrative 'tends to become increasingly discontinuous, syncopated, built of enormous scenes separated by immense gaps and thus tends to deviate more and more from the hypothetical "norm" of narrative isochrony' (93), Tolstaia's brief, maximally compressed narratives push that discontinuity to its limit. Within such unevenly spotlighted or incarnated segments of an individual biography, one is hard put to determine with any accuracy not only the precise period of a given existence that the text is bringing to life, but also the temporal stand-point from which the narrative emanates; that is, the 'maturity' of the voice. For instance, in ' "Na zolotom kryl'tse sideli..." ', the implied bifocal presentation of material not only becomes explicitly bifocal (with the posterior prevailing, without fully eliminating the anterior), but at several junctures defies differentiation; for example, 'And from there, from behind the distant horizon, the green summer with its ants and daisies was already running, laughing and brandishing a multi-coloured flag' (44). Through a synthesis of what arguably conveys a typical child's focus ('with its ants and daisies') and an adult's tropological formulation ('the green summer... brandishing a multi-coloured flag'), Tolstaia leaves the reader suspended in uncertainty regarding the narrating voice's temporal distance from reported events.

The lack of fixity also characterises the narrative apostrophes scattered throughout Tolstaia's fiction. Close to the conclusion of ' "Na zolotom kryl'tse sideli..." ' a seasonal metaphor (which continues the child's mode of organising time's flow that the first half of the story instals) announces Uncle Pasha's sudden (?) ageing and attendant attenuation of physical powers: 'Autumn came into Uncle Pasha's home and hit him in the face. Autumn, what do you want? Wait, are you really serious?' (47). The apostrophe to autumn, unlike the subsequent one to life ('What stupid jokes you play, life!' [48]), may seem sufficiently ingenuous for us to assign the temporal perspective of this paragraph to the narrator's childhood. Yet within that very paragraph the narrator notes: 'How adult we've become', and in the next paragraph, with no signal of an abrupt break or extended temporal lapse, 'How long it's been since I was here last! How old I am!' If, indeed, the narrator has reached old age, then whom does she apostrophise in the paragraph's opening: 'What are you fussing around for? Do you want to show me your treasures?' Presumably Uncle Pasha, who was 50 years old (42) when the narrator was still a child, but who now may be anywhere between 70 and 100, depending on one's subjective notion of what constitutes 'old age'. Tolstaia subverts efforts to establish at story's end even the approximate age of the narrating 'I' and other central characters through contradictory pseudo-data: at some point during the narrator's childhood Uncle Pasha's first (young, but of unspecified age) wife Veronika dies; roughly in that same period, her younger step-sister Margarita moves in with Uncle Pasha; an unknowable number of years later, when the narrator is (or feels) old, Uncle Pasha ages noticeably; after an equally unspecified interval of days? months? years? he dies. How does one reconcile the narrator's lament at this junction about her senescence with the yellow dog bought to guard Veronika's property, which after her death languished in a trunk with mothballs (44), yet survived to close Uncle Pasha's eyes before departing? (48) – a fantastic, ambulatory advertisement for canine longevity that violates all biological and narrative logic! The now wizened Margarita urges her middle-aged daughter ('pozhilaia' [48]) to bury Uncle Pasha's remains, now reduced to 'dust' ('prakh' [48]) stored in a can in the chicken coop. Unless Uncle Pasha underwent cremation, how many years must have elapsed for his body to have disintegrated into dust? Despite the wealth of Tolstaia's temporal signals, the reader's sense of the duration inscribed in the text – 30 years? 40? 50? – remains purely conjectural.

Various devices at first may distract the reader from the uneven pacing of the narrative, whereby the major portion of the story's narrated timespan is packed into the last two pages of the nine-page narrative, as the past iterative virtually disappears, ceding to the multi-functional present tense and the terse singulative past. The concluding paragraphs differ from the remainder of the story, for they unmistakably register a mature consciousness whose philosophical ruminations and omissive summation sets this coda somewhat apart. This is not to deny that earlier sections of the story absorb aspects of the adult point of view. When the enraptured child narrator exclaims at the contents of Uncle Pasha's attic, 'O room! O childhood *[detskie]* dreams!' (45), the adjective 'detskie' instantly bespeaks a retrospective vantage point, for only an adult awareness could classify those dreams as specifically childlike. But that awareness ousts the child's mentality, which has filtered the majority of experiences and thus determined much of the narrative's discourse, strikingly late in the story. Moreover, that displacement leaves unresolved a host of question about narrative and narrated time.

The startling apostrophe to Uncle Pasha, '... Hey, wake up, Uncle Pasha! Veronika's going to die soon' (44), which belongs to the domain of Genette's (originally Tsvetan Todorov's) ' "predictive" narrative' (216), likewise presents the reader with a number of problems. Cast *in the future tense*, it launches a prophetic glimpse into Uncle Pasha's imminent way of life that acquires the status of exposition.

> You'll wander around the empty house without a single thought, then you'll perk up, bloom, look around you and remember, chase away the memories, then yearn and bring – to help with the housekeeping – Veronika's younger sister Margarita, just as pale, large and beautiful. And she's the one who in June [of what year? HG] will be laughing in the bright window, bending over the rain barrel, passing among the maples on the sunny lake.
>
> *O, how in our declining years...*(44).

This is manifestly not a child's discourse, though the narrated time in question represents a moment in the narrator's childhood. Even ignoring the flagrant inconsistency of proleptic omniscience in a narrator who doubles as narrated participant in the story's diegetic and thus has limited knowledge, the reader cannot assign the passage to a reasonably specific time frame. Nor can s/he be certain that the same voice at the identical stage of development is responsible for the truncated citation from Tiutchev's lyric, which, through its grammatical 'timelessness', enables the story to overtake the narrating in the next paragraph.³¹ If ascription is problematised more nakedly here than in other Tolstaian stories, it merely underscores what may be partially camouflaged elsewhere: Tolstaia's scrambling of temporal categories for the sake of metonymical compression.

METAPHORS AND METONYMIES

Tolstaia's skilful fusion of metaphor and metonymy likewise helps her to manipulate narrative time in a distinctive manner. Contrary to Aristotle and subsequent rhetoricians and critics who regard metonymy and synecdoche as a subspecies of metaphor, Roman Jakobson conceives of them as antithetical because they are generated according to opposite principles. Whereas metaphor belongs to the selection axis of language, metonymy belongs to its combination axis. If one accepts as accurate the structuralist law of language whereby all linguistic units provide context for simpler linguistic units and find their own context from more complex ones, the metonymies become condensations of contexture, produced by deleting one or more items from a natural combination.³² Both Jakobson and recent theorists of narratology such as Peter Brooks characterise prose as 'forwarded essentially by contiguity',³³ thus predominantly metonymical. If metonymy as a trope results from the process of combination and non-logical deletion, the selected details comprising the trope are, as E. B. Greenwood has reasoned, 'surrogates... for the mass of observed detail which would have been there in actuality', but has been deleted.³⁴ In such cases, then, 'the appropriate critical response to the metonymic text would seem to be an attempt to restore the deleted detail, to put the text back into the total context from which it derives'.³⁵ Thus, theoretically at least, metonymy propels narrative along the horizontal axis while concurrently inviting the reader to insert all the material that has been deleted en route. That task of insertion or completion retards movement forward and potentially reorients the reader to the vertical axis, the axis of metaphor.³⁶ It is precisely through the interpenetration of metaphor and metonymy, through a tilting of the two axes and a bold exploitation of hybrids that Tolstaia creates temporal and spatial disjunctions in order to inflate and scramble her fictional time and space.

An exemplary text for analysis in this regard is 'Reka Okkervil'' (Okkervil River). If the narrative driven by contiguity (the preponderantly metonymical mode recording Simeonov's meeting with the singer he has long worshipped) may be represented by a continuous horizontal line, Tolstaia constantly halts, retards or reverses the movement through metaphors. Particularly the matrix metaphor of the river, which swells into a mini-universe representing the emotional state into which Vera Vasil'evna's singing plunges Simeonov, occupies substantial narrative time while, conversely, embodying what is essentially narrated timelessness, for that universe exists outside of time. The lushly poeticised world verbally installed by the metaphor contributes *vertical* content or depth without pushing the narrative along. What 'action' transpires does so in Simeonov's fantasies, that is, along the vertical axis: '[He] listened once again, yearning for the chrysanthemums, pshtpshtpsht, that had long faded in the garden, pshtpshtpsht, where they'd met, and once again, gathering underwater pressure, throwing off dust, laces and years, Vera Vasil'evna would creak and appear as a languid naiad – an unathletic, slightly plump turn-of-the-century naiad – 0, sweet pear, guitar, sloping champagne bottle!' (18).

In Bakhtinian terms, Tolstaia resorts here to the chronotope of the miraculous world, with 'an emotional, subjective distortion of space, which is in part symbolic', a world that is stretched out along the vertical axis so that everything coexists 'in sheer simultaneity' (as in Dante) and 'time is utterly excluded from the action'. These units, in other words, synchronise diachrony.[37] After its first, establishing evocation, Tolstaia metonymically conjures up this atemporal world existing wholly in Simeonov's imagination[38] by simply referring selectively to aspects of it (for instance, the river bank, Vera Vasil'evna's round heels, the chrysanthemums) as the need arises or by extending the metaphor through additional details. In fact, the links that hold her narrative together are located not on the horizontal plane of diegesis, but rather in the echoes between these deflective metaphors that expand into trope-saturated limbos. These limbos enable Tolstaia to move back and forth temporally and spatially without essentially disturbing, but by suspending, the linear narrative activity in which the tenor of her metaphor is embedded. Moreover, by expanding or taking far afield the vehicle of her metaphor[39] Tolstaia achieves two goals: she deflects her readers from the prosaic forward motion, dissuading them from a clear-cut chronology or sequentiality; and through reverberations between her metaphorical structures she is able to provide a sense of coherence (operating largely on a figurative level) that distracts one from the very issue of temporal and spatial markers. In other words, the erection of such a multi-directional framework allows her to move freely along both planes (backwards and forwards, up and down), while the repetition of motifs from those structures of metaphor, judiciously implanted at intervals, establishes a verbal rhythm that creates the illusion of unity. What we have, in a sense, is subversion regularised. An invaluable benefit of such a staggeringly daring disregard for conventional narrative practices is the reader's conviction that s/he has witnessed the key moments, or been privy to the primary aspects, of a given character's life and can deduce the rest; in other words, the reader responds appropriately to the metonymy of a life exposed largely in metaphorical terms. By exploding a standard unfolding of time and space, Tolstaia abstracts the enormous gaps in the narrative of that biography and merely provides several highly-charged details from which to extrapolate and fill in the spaces. Since intensity of impact must compensate for lack of comprehensiveness, those details incline toward dramatic contrast, establishing either poles between which our input may function or a concentration of one or two traits that we may generalise into a recognisable type. That is why some Tolstaian portraits, for instance, in 'Sonia', 'Peters', 'Samaia liubimaia', 'Ogon' i pyl' ' (Fire and Dust) and 'Milaia Shura', smack of caricature if divorced from the metaphors where the revelatory nuances reside.

Of all Tolstaian texts 'Reka Okkervil' ' explores that technique most thoroughly, but it also affects narrated and narrative temporality in such metaphor-laden stories as 'Svidanie s ptitsei', 'Ogon' i pyl'' 'Krug', 'Noch' ' (Night), and 'Somnambula v tumane' (Sleepwalker in a Fog), whose rhythm is regulated by metonymical implantation at various junctions of an overarching metaphor that intimates a miraculous or transcendent world. Although elaborated on a more modest scale, the lost continent of Atlantis ('Svidanie s ptitsei'), the lure of sirens on distant shores ('Ogon' i pyl' '), the voyage ('Krug'), the mysterious dark night ('Noch' ') and fog ('Somnambula v tumane') fulfil a function parallel to that of the river in 'Reka Okkervil' '. In all instances, the rhythmic undulation of motifs from these time-free metaphors serves to disperse time, thereby facilitating quintessentially Tolstaian temporal leaps and transfers that resist measurement.

OBJECTS AND MEMORY

As several commentators have noticed, Tolstaia's stories teem with objects crowded densely into rooms, thoughts and paragraphs. The vivid, indeed, aggressive presence of examples from every conceivable category of material phenomena (furniture, cutlery, flora and fauna, clothing, printed matter, and so forth) asserts itself frequently through colourful, extended metaphors or personifications that transmute inert matter into living beings: fruits and cheeses sleep, dresses tuck up their knees, bathing suits squint in anticipation, a sewing box sleeps belly-up with paws in the air, and so on. Objects in Tolstaia's fictional universe fulfil three functions that, generally speaking, cannot be divorced from the inner life of her characters. In that sense they corroborate Kant's notion of time as the form of our 'inner' and space as the form of our 'outer' experience, and the inescapably symbiotic nature of their intersection, which Bakhtin's concept of the chronotope presupposes.

If one divides Tolsaia's cast of characters rather crudely, as some critics have done, into two contrasting groups – of idealists or spiritual beings on the one hand, and pragmatists on the other – one sees that the latter, such as Rimma in 'Ogon' i pyl' ', and Mar'ia Maksimovna in 'Spi spokoino, synok' (Sweet Dreams, Son), tend to overprize material possessions, dream of additional acquisitions and, within the narrative, appear framed in object-packed settings. At their simplest, these objects exteriorise internal hierarchies – they straightforwardly attest the characters' subordination of spiritual values to material comfort.

Apart from serving as an index of a character's acquisitiveness, objects also function as trappings reflecting characters' tastes, powers of self-presentation, or assumptions about social status. Thus Filin's talent in the story 'Fakir' (The Fakir) for conjuring up delicious food served in exquisite dishes amidst elegant surroundings haloes him with an aura of refinement and uniqueness, even though he objectifies his guests by assimilating them into his artistically arranged backdrop. Since the fraudulent 'social status' implied by the specifics of his *mise-en-scène* has extraordinary significance for him, his current amour Alisa and above all the recording centre of consciousness, Galia, the concrete items reveal the psychological frailties of all three.

From a contemporary stand-point, however, these are rather tired techniques, enervated by regular deployment in nineteenth- and twentieth-century fiction (in, for example, Dickens, Balzac, Flaubert, Fontane, James, Trifonov). More original and complex is Tolstaia's third use of objects: as a means of extending the temporal framework of her narratives and situating that extension in a moral context. Tolstaia's device of linking objects with human history, memory and conscience plays a crucial part in her strategy of temporal displacement. Pushkin, as we know, had a penchant for studding his works, and particularly his narrative poems, with lists (see, for example, *Ruslan and Liudmila, Eugene Onegin, Poltava, Count Nulin)*, and in this regard Tolstaia may be considered his true, if profligate, descendant. Story after Tolstaian story swells entire paragraphs with an inventory of objects that, tellingly, tend to be heaped in an attic (' "Na zolotom kryl'tse sideli..." '), a bazaar, or a market ('Liubish' – ne liubish' ', 'Krug', 'Spi spokoino, synok'), and thus have a past, a history of previous ownership that documents human experience. Objects embedded in such eloquent contexts become so thoroughly integrated into their owners' lives as to appear inseparable from them. Although Tolstaia most frequently presents those items as fallen into desuetude, after they have been wrenched from the original context that conferred meaning upon them,[40] the articles, when recontextualised, acquire what we normally consider human qualities – consciousness, emotions, and so forth. Metonymically they preserve, if only *in potentia* (for those insignia must be acknowledged for the preservation to become actualised), aspects of the lives they formerly inhabited. This susceptibility of objects to participation in human life may be seen in 'Liubish' – ne liubish' ', for instance, where the five-year-old protagonist says of the lampshade that she and her father purchase at the flea market: 'The lampshade is young, easily frightened, it's not used to me yet... . Dad [carries] the lampshade, still dark and silent, but already accepted into the family: it's ours now, it's one of us, we'll come to love it. And it's frozen still, waiting: where are they taking it? It doesn't know yet that time will pass, and it, once the favourite, will be ridiculed, cast down, discarded, exiled, and in its place, amidst rejoicing, will ascend a new favourite: a fashionable white five-panelled "squattie". And then, offended, mutilated and betrayed, it will endure the last mortification: it'll serve as a crinoline in a children's play and will sink forever into garbage oblivion. Sic transit gloria mundi!' (8).[41] In this anthropomorphised image, the item's projected history (Genette's prolepsis) approximates human fate, as the case of the governess Mar'ivanna in 'Liubish' – ne liubish' ' and stories like 'Milaia Shura' and 'Somnambula v tumane' illustrate: in advanced age those who formerly held centre-stage in the human drama become relegated to the prop room and forgotten. For the material world, to which humankind at least partly belongs, is selectively subject to the forces of time – to mutability, dissolution and, ultimately, oblivion. Yet, as the narrator in 'Samaia liubimaia' comments, 'time's meat grinder gladly destroys large, bulky, solid objects – closets, pianos, people – whereas any fragile trifles, whose very appearance was greeted by ridicule and a squint, all these little china dogs, little cups, little vases, little rings, little pictures, little photos, little boxes, little notes, knickknacks, little doodads and doilies – pass through it untouched' (97). Typically for Tolstaia, the tiny, ostensibly insignificant item preserved from the past can prove most revelatory if invested with human experience and can kindle our memory not only of bygone days but also of those beings whose lives overlapped, however briefly, with our own.

In the era of *glasnost'*, remembering has acquired the dimension of a national cause, as Soviets strive to recuperate previously unacknowledged or inaccessible portions of their history. Even before *glasnost'*, however, chroniclers like Solzhenitsyn valorised memory for enabling the holy mission of preserving historical truth.[42] Writers as dissimilar as Varlam Shalamov, Nadezhda Mandelshtam, and Lidiia Chukovskaia likewise have struggled to immortalise a record of human experience that they fear will otherwise escape human memory. Uninitiated into the deconstructionist scepticism of the new historicism, Russians unanimously assume that an 'objective history' lies waiting merely to be reclaimed and shared on a national scale. Little though Tolstaia has in common with these writers, her preoccupation with time's passage and particularly its effect on perception and memory has led at least one critic to conclude: 'Time is T. Tolstaia's main protagonist. She lavishes attention on old age, old women, old letters, old records, and forgotten feelings.'[43] Time in Tolstaia's universe yields somewhat less readily to repossession than in Proust, either involuntarily or through conscious effort. Recollection inevitably entails subjectivity and stresses loss, for the interdependence of a specific moment in time with a given human perspective and set of circumstances makes it impossible for either to be regained completely,[44] as Heraclitus's maxim, 'You cannot step into the same river twice', asserts, and as the narrator in ' "Na zolotom kryl'tse sideli..." ' discovers when she returns to the attic housing the mysterious objects that enthralled her in childhood: 'What, is all this the stuff that enchanted us? All these rags and junk? Dilapidated painted dressers, crude oilcloth paintings, plant stands with uneven legs, worn plush velvet, darned tulle, clumsy fakes bought at the market, cheap beads? And this sang and shimmered, burned and beckoned? What stupid jokes you play, life! Dust, ashes, rot. Surfacing from the magical bottom of childhood..., what, apart from a handful of rough sand, have we brought away with us? Yet just as he did a quarter century ago, Uncle Pasha winds the golden clock with trembling hands. Above the face, in the little glass room, huddle the little inhabitants – the Lady and the Chevalier, masters of Time' (47–8). Yet articles such as those inventoried above stimulate memory (however approximate) or speculation (however inaccurate) about times past, and become potential links in the endless chain of human existence. 'Le présent', as Leibniz observed, 'est chargé du passé, et gros de l'avenir.'[45] In the specific example just cited, the seemingly random *bric-à-brac*, not unlike a grave-marker which, while registering death, brings memories to life, raises to the surface the luminous image of Uncle Pasha sedimented in the narrator's psyche.

Especially objects manifestly associated with temporal continuity, and appearing singly rather than as entries in a catalogue, filter the past into Tolstaia's present. Photographs, portraits, old letters and poems enable Tolstaia's personae to regain and retain memories of bygone days. Worn snapshots in 'Milaia Shura', 'Samaia liubimaia', ' "Na zolotom kryl'tse sideli..." '; portraits of now-dead relatives in 'Peters' and 'Spi spokoino, synok; correspondence yellowed with age in 'Sonia' and 'Milaia Shura'; and poems (composed by authentic and would-be poets now dead) in 'Liubish' – ne liubish'' and 'Krug' all insinuate the past into the present. These visual and verbal *memento mori* not only activate memory, but in a sense resuscitate the dead, whose participation is enlisted in the narrative's present through two favourite Tolstaian devices that dissolve temporal and spatial boundaries. A passage from 'Milaia Shura' offers a superb instance of Tolstaia's technique. During the narrator's visit to the story's eponymous octogenarian protagonist (surrounded, significantly, by 'knick-knacks, oval frames, dried flowers'[30]), in the midst of the latter's excursus into the past, the narrator discerns a young version of the old woman in the photographs on the wall. Instead of referring to the photographs, Tolstaia by-passes mention of mediating representation so as to evoke the young Shura's presence in the room directly: 'on the peeling wallpaper a ravishing beauty is smiling, looking thoughtful, acting capricious – sweet Shura, Aleksandra Ernestovna. Yes, yes, that's me! With a hat, and without...'(30). Since no formal punctuation marks set off the old Shura's confirmation of her younger identity, the two merge and, moreover, ease the transition to talk of Ivan Nikolaevich, her lover of sixty years ago, whose image, like Shura's, remains intact: 'he's squeezed in the album, spread-eagled in four slits in the cardboard, squashed by a lady in a bustle, crushed by some shortlived little white dogs who died before the war with Japan' (30). Because Aleksandra Ernestovna's memories of Ivan Nikolaevich and her ancient decision not to run away with him have not diminished in relevance or vitality over six decades, and, with the aid of photographs, become shared by the narrator in the present, Tolstaia recreates the moment of decision also in the present, oscillating unobtrusively not only between external and internal discourse, but also, as one can in Russian, between past tense and the dramatic present: 'She's already made up her mind. There he is – right beside you, within arm's reach! Here, take him in your hands, hold him, there he is, flat, cold, glossy, with a gold border, slightly yellowed – Ivan Nikolaevich! Hey, you hear? – she's made up her mind, yes, she's coming, meet her, that's it, she won't hesitate again, meet her, where are you, yoo-hoo!' (35). Here, Ivan Nikolaevich, like Shura, exists concurrently in several forms and dimensions: as young in the photograph that, however, shows signs of age; as alive to hear the news, but actually dead; and, finally, as revealing his thoughts and speaking to those holding his photograph, who are nevertheless fully aware that he no longer exists. The same devices of moving freely and unpredictably between past, present and future tenses so as to efface all temporal distinctions, and of handling representational media like portraits, photographs, letters and poems as though they were the actual subjects of representation, so as to resuscitate the subject temporarily – these devices are applied to the grandfather in 'Peters', the father-in-law in 'Spi spokoino, synok', Izol'da in 'Krug', and other figures from the past who play such prominent parts in Tolstaia's fiction.

To grasp the exact time of events, comments or thoughts in Tolstaia's stories is often impossible because temporal distinctions collapse when the past seeps into the present, feeding and infusing it with a prior perspective. With time reconstituted through recollection and absorbed into the narrative present with the aid of animated metonymical objects, the text keeps the dead narratively alive. These metonyms[46] are enlisted in the service of a moral imperative in Tolstaia's universe: to discover and preserve the significance of an individual life through memory. According to Tolstaia, a life may be evaluated only posthumously. Because a retrospective vantage-point is a prerequisite for the appreciation of a given individual's contribution to the total sum of human existence, anyone concerned with values must necessarily keep looking back, engaging in the complex ideational process of recognition, identification and appraisal.[47] Hence the salient role in Tolstaia's fiction of the 'creative and constructive' processes that we call memory (Cassirer, 74), and the proliferation of dreams (both waking and sleeping) in which the past surfaces to confront and invade the present. The process explodes what Paul Ricoeur, following Nietzsche, calls monumental time,[48] whose claims Tolstaia recognises but subordinates to the nuanced complexities of 'soul' time.

The Tolstaian story that most passionately articulates the urge to remember is 'Somnambula v tumane'.[49] There that impulse manifests itself through two highly dissimilar characters: the middle-aged protagonist Denisov, whose subjective point of view dominates throughout, and his fiancée Lora's father, Vasilii Vasil'evich, whose nocturnal antics identify him literally with the story's title. Both try to make sense of the world and its order – Denisov spatially by altering the disposition of oceans and continents on the map in his room, the retired old zoologist taxonomically, by summarising in the simplest terms possible (that is, for children) the defining features of various animals and the seasons. Both are troubled by memory. The older man, during his sleepwalking rampages through the apartment, incessantly repeats, 'I knew, but I forgot' (22). While Tolstaia keeps pregnantly imprecise the object of his forgetfulness, clearly his memory has lost hold of something from the past. By contrast, Denisov's lapse of memory is fully and painfully clarified, within the larger framework of his obsession with immortality.

From the very opening, Denisov's personal anxiety supplies the key to the story's universal concern that human destiny may be reduced to an impermanence synonymous with non-being: 'to die and be forgotten, to be erased from human memory, to be dispersed in the air without a trace' (9). In the course of the narrative Denisov's thirst to be perpetually acknowledged after death as a significant individual instance in the continuum of humanity ('[he] dreams...of fame, of remembrance of immortality...' [10]) develops into an awareness that the dead in general deserve some affirmation of their existence from the living. That realisation is triggered in a revelatory dream in which three figures appear before Denisov, presumably during the time of the Leningrad blockade, demanding that he give them some of the bread he has just bought. His selfish reluctance to do so, within the dream, leads him when he awakens to lacerating self-justification that retraces his steps to a period 35 years earlier (in which, so to speak, the dream comes true). During those grim years, his aunt Rita, whom he recognises as one of his three dream phantoms, perished in the blockade. Characteristically for Tolstaia's fiction, Rita, then a young woman on the verge of marrying, left behind a concrete object as a *memento mori* – a powder compact that the boy Denisov exchanged for a penknife, causing his mother to beat him and burst into tears. The remaining two-thirds of the story is a pilgrimage of penance, tracing Denisov's frantic efforts to salve his conscience and compensate for having forgotten and thus, in a sense, betrayed his aunt. His consciencestricken enterprise assumes the form of a ludicrous substitution.

Appointing himself the 'messenger of the dead', he resolves to immortalise an unremarkable schoolmate of Lora's called Makov, who froze in the mountains during an expedition. No one, including Makov's family, harbours any enthusiasm for Denisov's cause, which degenerates into a Marx Brothers farce as he agitates to obtain a wardrobe for Makov's sister, ostensibly as a gesture of respect for the dear departed.

Denisov's efforts, like all his pangs of impotent sympathy for human sufferers, come to naught. For he, along with the rest of Tolstaia's Strindbergian cast living under the metaphor of the story's title, represents modern humanity: roaming in a fog of metaphysical uncertainty, groping for clues that will shed light on the meaning and goal of life. These spiritually dispossessed include Denisov, the seeker who queries, 'What will remain of us?' (17); and desperately insists that a life should leave behind traces that will have meaning for others; Rita, the narrative's representative of the dead who, accordingly to Denisov's subjective surmise, yearns to have her existence actively incorporated into the general fund of human experience, 'otherwise why [would she] invade our dreams, stretch out her hand, and ask for alms – for bread, or perhaps simply to be remembered?' (17); the enigmatic naval captain who occupies the apartment above him and plays out his fantasies by floating paper-boats in the tub that overflows into Denisov's apartment, before the 'men in white' take him away; Lora, who 'also drags along at random, hands outstretched, rummaging around ledges and clefts, stumbling in the fog; she twitches and huddles in her sleep, she reaches out to will-o'-the-wisps, with her fingers tries to catch reflections of candles, grabs at circles in the water, and throws herself at shadows of smoke ...'(14–15); and Lora's widowed father, who stumbles about in his daughter's apartment, seeking to retrieve what he has forgotten. At the story's ambiguous, open-ended conclusion, he breaks free of his customary pattern to run out into the dark unknown of the night:

> The sleepwalker runs along his roadless path, eyes closed, hands outstretched, with a quiet smile, as if he sees what those with good vision can't see, as if he knows what they've forgotten, is catching during the night what is lost in the daytime. He runs along the dewy grass, along the patches of moonlight and black shadows ...
> Surely he'll reach the light?[26]

The moral imperative of memory as a safeguard of continuity and preservation of culture accounts for the regular excursions into the past found in Tolstaia's works. These internal retrogressive journeys across diverse strata or categories of time represent attempts to recuperate not only past experiences, but also the epistemological stance that enabled them. For in Tolstaia, as in Bergson, memories interlace with perceptions and, conversely, become actual by being embodied in some perception. That convergence accounts for the 'subjectivity' of perceptual images (objects perceived). Thus objects potentially afford their perceivers the opportunity to recover, however imperfectly, former viewpoints, that is, times past, and to integrate them into the present. That insight is inscribed in Tolstaia's own texts, for the dense intertextuality of her prose and its temporal diffusions stylistically convey the enrichment vouchsafed by keeping alive those cultural practices to which a vigilant memory and a receptive imagination offer access.

Notes

1. 'Time Is An Understanding', *Soviet Literature*, 1990, no. 1 (502), p. 143. Further citations from Trifonov refer to this source and hereafter will be identified by page numbers in parentheses in the body of the text.
2. Paul Ricoeur, *Time and Narrative* (Chicago and London, 1983–1985, 3 vols). For Ricoeur, monumental time, 'of which chronological time is but the audible expression', results from 'all the complicities between clock time and figures of authority', of official tabulation (vol. 2, pp. 106 and 112). In his massive study, he takes considerable pains to distinguish between Bergson's spatialised time and his concept of monumental time (vol. 2. p. 190, fn. 23).
3. Henri Bergson made the subjective notion of duration *(durée)* central to his philosophy. He postulated physical time as something spatialised and intellectualised (measurable only through its 'strange and incomprehensible contamination by space', to cite Ricoeur [vol. 3, p.12]), whereas intuition (inner experience) teaches us that 'pure time' or real duration, in the form of directly experienced change, is the 'real' phenomenon of time. Henri Bergson, *Essai sur les donnés immédiates de la conscience* (1889) and *Matière et mémoire* (1896).
4. In his late period, Mikhail Bakhtin equated 'great time' with entire lifetimes, with 'the sense that past events, as they become congealed in institutions, languages of heteroglossia, and genres, pose specific problems and offer specific resources for each present moment that follows'. Saul Morson and Caryl Emerson, *Mikhail Bakhtin: Creation of a Prosaics* (Stanford, 1990), p. 414. To grasp the inner connectedness of past, present and future means to understand 'the fullness of time', with which Bakhtin credits Goethe. See M. M. Bakhtin, 'The *Bildungsroman*

and its Significance in the History of Realism (Toward a Typology of the Novel)', *Speech Genres and Other Late Essays*, ed. Caryl Emerson and Michael Holquist (Austin, Texas, 1986) pp. 10–59.

5. See Ricoeur's discussion of Husserl versus Kant, Vol. 3, pp. 46–47.
6. Ricoeur appropriately stresses the importance for a theory of narrative that both approaches to the problem of time remain open, 'by way of the mind as well as by way of the world. The aporia of temporality, to which the narrative operation replies in a variety of ways, lies precisely in the difficulty in holding on to both ends of this chain, the time of the soul and that of the world' (Ricoeur, Vol. 3, p. 14). Tolstaia's concept of time and its narrative articulation acknowledge both ends, but valorise the 'soul'. Her orientation at first glance seems to ally her, unsurprisingly, with Augustine and his refutation of the cosmological thesis, until a close reading of her texts reveals the extent to which Tolstaia realises that world-time cannot be simply peeled away from soul-time, but interacts with it.

    Unlike Ricoeur, Kermode contrasts 'soul' time with 'simple chronicity' or 'humanly uninteresting successiveness'. Frank Kermode, *The Sense of An Ending* (London/Oxford/New York, 1966/1968), p. 46.
7. Tat'iana Tolstaia. *'Na zolotom kryl'tse sideli'* (On the Golden Porch) (Moscow, 1987), p. 40. Unless otherwise indicated, all citations from Tolstaia's prose refer to this edition and will be identified hereafter by page references in the body of the text. All translations from the Russian are mine.
8. Folkloric elements appear in most Tolstaian stories which recreate childhood: ' "Na zolotom kryl'tse sideli..." ', 'Svidanie s ptitsei' (Rendezvous with a Bird), 'Vyshel mesiats iz tumana' (The Moon Emerged from the Mist) and 'Samaia liubimaia' (The Most Beloved). 'Samaia liubimaia', for instance, shifts into a fairytale mode when it introduces the childhood motif: 'A long, long time ago, on the nether side of dreams, childhood existed [stood/*stoialo*] on earth...'. Tat'iana Tolstaia, 'Samaia liubimaia', *Avrora,* 1986, no. 10, p. 93. All citations from the story refer to this edition and hereafter will be identified by page numbers in parentheses within the body of the text.
9. On the garden topos in autobiography, see Martha Ronk Lifson, 'The Myth of the Fall: A Description of Autobiography', *Genre* XII (Spring 1979), pp. 45–67. (My gratitude to Carol Ueland for acquainting me with this article). On the portrayal of childhood in Russian literature, see Andrew Baruch Wachtel, *The Battle for Childhood* (Stanford, 1990).
10. Edwin Muir, *An Autobiography* (London, 1954), p. 18.
11. Vladimir Nabokov, *Speak, Memory* (New York, 1947/1968), pp. 17, 14.
12. That inability to discriminate between generations is perhaps best illustrated by the classic child's avowed intention of marrying her/his parent, interpolated in 'Svidanie s ptitsei', where Petia decides to marry the 'seven-thousand-year-old' Tamila instead of his mother, as he originally planned: 'Earlier he'd planned to marry his mother, but now that he'd already promised Tamila...' (116). An index of Peter's infantilism is his regressive fantasy of retreat into marriage with his

grandmother: 'nado bylo emu v svoe vremia zhenit'sia na sobstvennoi babushke i tikho tlet' v teploi komnate pod tikan'e chasov' (179). (On the Freudian implications of this, see Helena Goscilo, 'Tolstaian Love As Surface Text', *SEEJ*, vol. 34, no. 1 (1990), pp. 40–52). Nabokov notes: 'the inner knowledge that I was I and that my parents were my parents seems to have been established only later, when it was associated with my discovering their age in relation to mine' (p. 14).
13. For a more thorough analysis of the lapsarian myth in Tolstaia's early stories, see Helena Goscilo, 'Paradise, Purgatory, and Post-Mortems in the World of Tat'jana Tolstaja', *Indiana Slavic Studies*, 1990, No. 5, pp. 97–113.
14. Lifson, p. 50.
15. For Aristotle's treatise on time, see *Physics*, Books III and IV.
16. Augustine's ruminations on temporality are contained in his *Confessions*, especially Book XI. As Ricoeur notes, for Augustine, 'the before-and-after – that is, the relation of succession – is foreign to the notions of present, past and future, and hence to the dialectic of intention and distension that is grafted to these notions' (Ricoeur, Vol. 3, p. 19). Augustine's predilection for the inward and Aristotle's for the scientifically verifiable (largely external) justify Ricoeur's respective labels for their theories of 'time of the soul' and 'time of physics'.
17. Ricoeur, Vol. 3, pp. 16 and 18. Tolstaia's adult 'now' occurs at the moment a child acquires knowledge of mortality (and sexuality). The break is definitive in one sense, for, as Dostoevskii rightly argued, (self-)consciousness, once attained, cannot be voluntarily jettisoned. Yet lapping against the watershed of this 'now' (as opposed to the child's perpetual 'now', to which Aristotle's formula is irrelevant) are memories of irrevocable bliss for which adults yearn and which therefore inform post-'now' experience. So the break in Tolstaia's world is final insofar as childhood resists recapturing, yet paradoxically illusory because the impulse to regain that state persists throughout adulthood.
18. Lewis Carroll, *Alice's Adventures in Wonderland. Through the Looking Glass* (Harmondsworth/Baltimore/Victoria, 1948/1968), p. 254.
19. Kermode, p. 53.
20. See Gérard Genette, *Narrative Discourse* (Ithaca, New York, 1980/1987), pp. 35–40.
21. See, for instance, François Villon's 'Où sont les neiges d'antan?' and Lenskii's lament, overpopularised by the tenor's aria from Chaikovskii's opera, 'Kuda, kuda, kuda vy udalilis'?' (Where, o where, o where have you vanished?).
22. The distinction, codified by Genette, is between *narrated* or *story* and *narrative*. What Tolstaia capitalises on is not only the discrepancy between story time *(erzählte Zeit)* and narrative time *(Erzählzeit)*, but the implications of spatial proximity on the printed page, in *narrating* (Genette, pp. 33–34). This dualism resulting from retrospection is nicely encapsulated in Freud's notion of *Nachträglichkeit*.
23. On this, see, respectively, Ricoeur, passim, and Hayden White, *Metahistory: The Historical Imagination in Nineteenth-Century Europe* (Baltimore, 1973), and *The Tropic of Discourse* (Baltimore, 1978).

24. Emphasis added. Compare these passages with Nabokov's 'walls of time separating me and my bruised fists from the free world of timelessness' and his 'prison of time' (p. 14) with Tolstaia's 'rigid rules of space and time' *(tugie zakony prostranstva i vremeni)* (in 'Sonia', p. 136).
25. On 'multitemporality' or heterochrony *(raznovremennost')* see Bakhtin, 'The *Bildungsroman*...', especially pp. 26, 32–42, and Morson and Emerson, pp. 368, 424, 426.
26. Genette, pp. 113–14.
27. Genette, p. 147.
28. The very issue of Zhenechka's death, however, is less clear-cut than one might suppose, for in a passage that seems to register the 'now' of writing, Tolstaia's narrator muses: 'Perhaps she's somewhere even now, somewhere here, but we simply can't see her' (p. 93).
29. Through that strategy she forces the reader to share the narrator's obsession with the past and her *a posteriori* reassessment of Zhenechka's role in her life.
30. Genette, p. 93.
31. The first line of Fedor Tiutchev's lyric to autumnal passions, commemorating in poetic form his middle-aged love for the young I. Denisieva.
32. But not the items it would be most natural to omit. See David Lodge, *The Modes of Modern Writing* (Ithaca, New York, 1980, pp. 75–6). See Roman Jakobson, 'The Metaphoric and Metonymic Poles', *Fundamentals of Language* (The Hague/Paris, 1975), pp. 90–96.
33. Jakobson, p. 96.
34. E. B. Greenwood, 'Critical Forum', *Essays in Criticism* (July 1962), pp. 341–2.
35. Lodge, p. 93.
36. Whatever their antithetical traits, the two axes obviously share the characteristic of selection.
37. Mikhail Bakhtin, *The Dialogic Imagination*(Austin, Texas, 1981), pp. 155–7.
38. Tolstaia's depiction of Simeonov's 'imagined' world carries so much aesthetic seductiveness and emotional conviction that the hermeneutically-inclined critic is practically forced to read it not as an individual's fantasy, but as a penetration into a transcendent realm accessible only to the elect – an 'extratemporal otherworldly ideal', in Bakhtin's words *(The Dialogic Imagination*, p. 158). Those two options recall E. T. A Hoffman, of course, and above all such works as 'Der Sandmann'. A tropological solution to ontological and metaphysical issues such as Tolstaia's has come under criticism, most notably by Paul de Man. See Paul de Man, 'Impasse de la critique formaliste', *Blindness and Insight*, ed. Wlad Godzich (Minneapolis, 1983).
39. The terms 'tenor' and 'vehicle' coined by I. A. Richards to designate the two components of a metaphor (or simile) tacitly assume that maintaining distance between the two elements under comparison is crucial. A 'holds firm' [tenor], as one 'travels' [vehicle] to B. Tolstaia's frequent tendency is to stay with the vehicle instead of the tenor so as to make unexpected transitions whose abruptness is disguised by the sheer lyrical power of the richly embroidered vehicle.

40. Heidegger in *Sein und Zeit* (1927) usefully observes that things or entities ('stuff' – *Zeug*) for 'use' *(Gebrauch)* that are at hand or 'ready-to-hand' *(zuhanden)* articulate their identity in the process of unreflecting usage and unobtrusively tend to comprise that part of our environment which we take for granted. When the 'unusability' of equipment is discovered, it becomes 'conspicuous' *(auffällig)* and present-at-hand *(vorhanden)* as well as potentially un-ready-to-hand *(unzuhanden)*. See Martin Heidegger, *Being and Time*, trans. John Macquarrie and Edward Robinson (New York, 1962), pp. 95–107.
41. Passages such as these expose the facile nature of many generalisations made by two well-known émigré commentators, Genis and Vail'; here, specifically, their palpably inaccurate claim that 'In Tolstaia, things in general are happier than people – unlike people, they don't change.' See Petr Vail' i Aleksandr Genis, 'Popytka k begstvu: II: Gorodok v Tabakerke – Proza Tat'iany Tolstoi', *Sintaksis,* 1988, no. 24, p. 129.
42. On Solzhenitsyn and Shalamov in this connection, see Matt F. Oja, 'Shalamov, Solzhenitsyn, and the Mission of Memory', *Survey*, Vol. 29, no. 2 (Summer, 1985), p. 62.
43. Raisa Shishkova, 'Nich'i babushki na zolotom kryl'tse', *Kontinent,* 1988, no. 56, p. 399. Genis and Vail' conceive of time's passage as Tolstaia's greatest enemy, but fancifully ascribe what they call her enmity toward the relentless flow of time to her refusal to grow up: 'In brief, the author is a person who refuses to grow up. That's precisely why her main enemy is the unstoppable movement of time.' Vail' and Genis, p. 126.
44. In this context, see Walter Benjamin's conviction that 'To articulate the past historically does not mean to recognize it "the way it really was" (Ranke). It means to seize hold of a memory as it flashes up at a moment of danger.' 'The past can be seized only as an image which flashes up at the instant when it can be recognized and is never seen again.' Walter Benjamin, 'Theses on the Philosophy of History', *Illuminations* (New York, 1969), p. 255. See also Christa Wolf, 'Reading and Writing' and *The Quest for Christa T.*
45. Cited in Ernst Cassirer, *An Essay on Man. An Introduction to a Philosophy of Human Culture* (Garden City, New York, 1944), p. 72. See also Ricoeur's comments regarding the constructions of history (as reconstructions answering to the need for a *Gegenüber*) on the 'relation of indebtedness which assigns to the people of the present the task of repaying their due to people of the past – to the dead'. Ricoeur, Vol. III, p. 157.
46. Operating, as Jakobson noted, on the principle of contiguity (Jakobson, pp. 90–96). The essay in question is entitled 'The Metaphoric and Metonymic Poles', and is part of a larger study, 'Two Aspects of Language and Two Types of Aphasic Disturbances'.
47. Cassirer, p. 72. The appraisal that for Tolstaia is crucial Cassirer explicitly rejects, confining the process to recognition and identification.
48. Ricoeur, Vol. 2, p. 106.
49. Tat'iana Tolstaia, 'Somnambula v tumane', *Novyi mir,* 1988, no. 7, pp. 8–26. All citations from the story refer to this edition and hereafter will be identified by page numbers in parentheses in the body of the text.

4 Myth in the Works of Chingiz Aitmatov
Nina Kolesnikoff

In the late 1970s and early 1980s Soviet critics argued extensively about the role of folklore and mythology in contemporary Soviet literature, particularly in the national literatures of Central Asia, the Caucasus and the Far East.[1] Addressing the question of correlation between myth and Socialist Realism, some critics questioned the appropriateness of blending the archaic and highly conventional forms of mythology with the realistic method of depiction based on verisimilitude and probability. Lev Anninskii in his polemical article 'Zhazhdu belletrizma' (I Crave Fiction) criticised mythological literature for creating some kind of 'superreality' or 'superphilology', by imposing allegorical meaning on simple realistic details, for the stylistic 'oversaturation' of mythological prose with allegories and symbols and for its pretentious ornamental style.[2]

The majority of Soviet critics, however, spoke in favour of mythological prose, arguing that myths enrich contemporary writing by revealing the links between the past and the present, and by accentuating philosophical and moral issues. V. Kubilius distinguished three types of correlation between literature and folklore: 1) simple folk stylisation, 2) the psychological interpretation of folk motifs, and 3) the use of myth as a modelling system.[3] He argued that the third type is the most rewarding artistically, since it brings into the narrative a second level of meaning and a deeper perspective, revealing the genesis of contemporary life and the continuity of human existence.

In similar fashion, I. Panchenko defended the new synthesis of mythological material with a realistic depiction of events as a method that discloses eternal human values. He also distinguished three types of mythological literature, without, however, placing them in a clear hierarchy: 1) mythological prose in which myth or parable exists as the main plot model, 2) folk-like epic prose in which the plot, conflicts, characters and the narrative rhythm are closely connected to a national tradition, 3) realistic prose with embedded elements of myths, legends or fairytales.[4]

It is significant that neither of the above-mentioned critics offered a clear definition of folklore and mythology. Rather they seemed to follow the established practice in Soviet scholarship of distinguishing mythology as a reflection of the most archaic culture, capturing the primitive, animistic concept of the world, and folklore as the product of newer historical developments.[5] Eleazar Meletinskii argued in his excellent study *Poetika mifa* (The Poetics of Myth) that mythology and folklore constitute two distinctive stages whose relation is one of dependence, even though each has a specificity of its own. He demonstrated some fundamental differences between myth and folktale, which could be summarised by the following oppositions: sacred/profane, strictly truthful/not strictly truthful, universal or collective fatum/personal or familial fate, prehistoric era/indefinite time, substantial etiology/ornamental etiology. He also outlined the distinction between myths and epics: the former are concerned with the mythological cosmic struggle, the latter with an ethnic struggle between tribes, states or faiths; the transformation of cosmic language into an ethnic language with geographical and historical names; the replacement of mythological time with a quasi-historical time.[6]

Although Meletinskii's theory is valid for structuralist and ethnographic studies of folklore, for the purpose of this study it is not as vital to maintain a rigid differentiation between myths, legends and folktales. First of all, as indicated by Meletinskii himself, there is a marked genetic interpendence among them, with folktales originating from myths, and archaic epics sharing the characteristics of myths about forefathers and cultural heroes. Secondly, there are no true structural distinctions between these forms in the same archaic culture. Thirdly, there is an underlying similarity in the function they perform in modern literature, for they reveal a new dimension of meaning by illuminating the distinct and localised through the more general and abstract.

Proceeding from these considerations, the working definition of myth in this study is intentionally very broad to include legends, epics and folktales. Myth is understood as an anonymously composed, fictitious tale, embodying some popular ideas concerning natural or historical phenomena, usually including an element of the supernatural.

This definition of myth is very close to that of John White who in his *Mythology in the Modern Novel* offered a solid foundation for the structural investigation of myth in modern fiction, and illustrated it with examples from James Joyce, Thomas Mann, Hans Erik Nossack and other twentieth-century Western European writers. White suggested the following classification of mythological fiction: 1) complete renarration of a classical myth, 2) juxtaposition of sections, with some narrating a myth and others addressing the contemporary world, 3) a pattern of references to mythology running through the work, 4) a mythological motif appearing in the narrative, but without running consistently through the whole narrative.[7]

In applying White's typology to the mythological works of Chingiz Aitmatov, one notices a distinct progression from a few dispersed motifs in his early stories *(Materinskoe pole, Rannie zhuravli)*, to a juxtaposition of sections, some narrating a myth and others concerned with the contemporary world *(Belyi parokhod, Burannyi polustanok, Plakha)*, to a total mythological structure *(Pegii pes begushchii kraem moria)*. In all these works Aitmatov's reliance on mythology appears in overt forms. Occasionally, the importance of myth is signalled by the title itself, as in the case of the original titles of *Posle skazki* (After the Fairytale) and *I dol'she veka dlitsia den'* (The Day Lasts More than a Hundred Years).[8]

In *Rannie zhuravli* (Early Cranes) a mythological motif is alluded to by two literary quotations, one from a Buddhist poem from *Theragatha*, describing the eternal rituals of ploughing and sowing, and the other from the Book of Job, referring to Job's first calamity. In *Materinskoe pole* (Mother Earth) the mythological parallel is introduced in the framework, depicting the heroine of the story confiding to Mother Earth, and seeking her advice.

But the most overt use of myth takes the form of an embedded story, introduced directly into the narrative and juxtaposed with the contemporary story. In *Belyi parokhod* (The White Steamship), depicting the life of three families in a distant San-Tash cordon in the 1960s, there appears the myth of Horned Deer-Mother, who saved two Kirghiz children and led them from the Yenisei river to the Issyk-kul area. According to the myth, Horned Deer-Mother became the protector of the Bugu clan, until people started to hunt for deer horns and forced the animals to flee. In *Burannyi polustanok* (The Buranny Halt), the contemporary plot, encompassing a series of events from the 1930s to the 1970s, includes an embedded story of mankurts, Kazakh youths tortured by their Chinese captors and transformed into robot-like slaves, deprived of memory and family ties. In *Plakha* (The Place of the Skull), set in the contemporary Soviet Union of the 1980s, appears an embedded story of Jesus, contemplating the future of the world on the eve of His crucifixion and debating with Pilate the philosophical questions of human nature and the eternal struggle between good and evil.

In some of Aitmatov's mythological works, the narrative incorporates more than one myth, with the second myth either extending the parallel suggested by the first one, or adding a new dimension to the story. In *Pegii pes begushchii kraem moria* (Spotted Dog Running along the Seashore), in addition to the myth of the creation of earth by the Duck Loovr, there appears the myth of the Great Seal Woman, the totemic forebear of the Nivkh tribe. Both myths underline the eternal struggle between water and land, and the fragile position of man placed between them. In *Plakha*, on the other hand, the Christian myth of Jesus is supplemented with the pagan Indo-European myth of the wolf as the totemic ancestor of man. Whereas the Biblical myth appears in the novel as a typical embedded story, the wolf-myth is only alluded to with such devices as the anthropomorphising of Akbara, who is endowed with the ability to reason as well as to dream. Akbara also carries totemic significance as the representative of all wolves, as well as people. Thus in the novel there are veiled allusions to the similarity between Akbara and Boston, whose name means 'Grey Hide', as well as to the invisible bond between them. Moreover, the narrative signals the significant transformation of her name from Akdaly (White Back) to Akbary, and finally to Akbara (The Great).[9]

As is evident from the above summary, the ethnographic range of the myths used by Aitmatov is very broad: from general Indo-European mythology *(Materinskoe pole, Plakha)*, to some specific myths of Central Asia *(Belyi parokhod, Burannyi polustanok)*, as well as the mythology of the Far East *(Pegii pes)*. In his most recent work, *Plakha*, the mythological material comes from the Christian tradition, more specifically from the Bible. Without going into a detailed discussion of the origin of myths and their fidelity to the originals, it is sufficient to note that for the most part Aitmatov is faithful in his rendering of the existing myths (the myth of Horned Deer-Mother, or the myth of the Duck Loovr).[10] Occasionally, however, he changes the myth in accordance with the overall intention of his work. Thus, in *Plakha* he considerably alters the Biblical story of Jesus, by adding some episodes not recorded in the Gospels (the story of the crocodile), by elaborating on details only briefly mentioned in the Bible (the confrontation between Jesus and Pilate), and generally by changing the focus from the religious aspect to the philosophical and ethical.[11]

In some of his works, Aitmatov creates his own myths, while pretending to follow the existing tradition. The best example of this is the story of Naiman-Ana in *Burannyi polustanok,* which is not based directly on any concrete source, but constructed from elements of the epic tradition of Central Asia. As correctly observed by Katerina Clark,

Aitmatov reverses the epic model, by making the heroine fail in her effort to free her enslaved son, and by portraying the son killing his mother instead of avenging himself on his enemies.[12]

With the exception of *Plakha*, which juxtaposes Biblical myth with contemporary reality in the Soviet Union, all the above-mentioned works have a historical motivation for the myth: they set the modern story in a geographical location once inhabited by the appropriate myth-producing society. The setting of *Belyi parokhod* is that of a distant cordon in the San-Tash canyon near Issyk-kul Lake where, according to the myth, Horned Deer-Mother brought the Kirghiz ancestors from the Yenisei River. The contemporary action of *Burannyi polustanok* takes place at a small railroad stop in Kazakhstan, near the Sarozek cosmodrome, which incorporates the old Ana-Baiit cemetery, associated with the legend of Naiman Ana and her mankurt son. And the events of *Pegii pes* occur in Spotted Dog Bay on the Okhotsk Sea, the area inhabited by the Nivkh clan, who consider themselves descendants of the mythological Seal-Woman.

In addition, in all Aitmatov's mythological works there is psychological motivation for the myth, provided by the connection between the myths and the heroes, who are either very old or very young. As indicated by the Soviet scholars Epshtein and Iukina, the very old and the very young closely follow mythological thinking by identifying their inner world with the outside reality.[13] For children, the world cannot be removed from the realm of fantasy; for the elderly the world is transformed into the realm of memory, and in both these states there is no separation between the subjective world and objective reality. It is therefore not surprising that in almost all Aitmatov's mythological works myth is associated with young children or the elderly. In *Belyi parokhod* the myth of Horned Deer-Mother lives in the memory of Grandfather Momun, who faithfully adheres to the old Bugu tradition. Momun tells the myth to his grandson who believes in it literally: when three marals come to the cordon, the boy believes that Horned Deer-Mother has returned to Her people. Similarly, in *Pegii pes* Nivkh myths are linked with the young boy Kirisk and the old man Organn. While the boy recalls the myth of the Duck Loovr and tries to understand the eternal struggle between sea and land, the old man dreams about the Seal-Woman while contemplating his life and his approaching death. In *Plakha* the myth of Jesus is linked to Avdii Kalistratov, a young idealist who tries to change the world around him with the Christian doctrine of love and forgiveness. Although not a child, Avdii possesses childlike idealism and innocence and approaches the world with childish naivety and openness.

In all Aitmatov's works the embedded myth is also motivated realistically, appearing in the narrative in the form of a dream, a vision or a narrated tale. In *Belyi parokhod* the myth of Horned Deer-Mother is introduced into the plot as a tale narrated by the boy to his new school satchel. In *Burannyi polustanok* the myth of Naiman-Ana is linked to the old man Kazangap who tells it to the local teacher Kutybaev and the geologist Elizarov. But in the narrative it appears as a recollection of Burannyi Yedigei, the protagonist of the novel, during the long journey to the cemetery to bury his friend Kazangap. In similar fashion, the myth of the Great Seal-Woman is introduced into *Pegii pes* as the daydreaming of the old man Organn, who in the quiet hours at sea reflects on his life and his cherished dream of the Seal-Woman. The myth of the Duck Loovr, on the other hand, is remembered by the young boy Kirisk during his sleepless night on the eve of his first seal hunt. Finally, in *Plakha* the embedded story of Jesus appears as a vision experienced by Avdii, who has been thrown from the train and is lying semi-conscious by the railroad tracks.

Myth appears in the form of an embedded story, and is also well integrated with the contemporary story through an extended system of references. In *Belyi parokhod* there are numerous references in the form of proverbial sayings, prayers and traditional sacrifices to Horned Deer-Mother as the totemic forebear and the protector of the Bugu clan. The motif of a cradle, mentioned in the myth as the gift of Horned Deer-Mother to new-born Bugu children, reappears several times in the hallucinations of the feverish boy, who implores Horned Deer-Mother to bring a cradle to his childless Aunt Bekai to avert the anger of her husband. Finally, the motif of horns, mentioned in the myth in connection with the shameful practice of hunting marals and placing their horns on the graves of respected Bugu elders, becomes an essential part of the contemporary plot. The frightful scene of Orozkul's chopping off the maral's horns symbolises the cruelty and sacrilege of killing the totem.

No less elaborate a system of references distinguishes *Burannyi polustanok*, in which the legend of Naiman-Ana is incorporated into the contemporary plot with the help of historical references (the cemetery is called Ana-Baiit, that is, the Mother's Resting Place, while the Malakumdychap precipice is identified as the place where she wept) as well as genealogical links between the protagonist's camel Karanar and the legendary camel Akmaya who carried Naiman-Ana to her son.

Finally, the ending of the novel captures another element of the legend, that of the bird Donenbai, who according to the legend originated from Naiman-Ana's white scarf. In the final scene of the novel Burannyi Yedigei, frightened by the sight of the launched rockets, imagines the white bird flying over and calling: 'Whose son are you? What is your name? Remember your name! Your father is Donenbai, Donenbai, Donenbai, Donenbai, Donenbai, Donenbai.'

In *Plakha* references to the Biblical story appear throughout the entire Avdii subplot, with Avdii portrayed as a true follower of Christ both in his convictions and in his fate.[14] Like Jesus, Avdii tries to change the evil around him with Christian concepts of love and repentance, and like his Teacher he has to pay with his life for his convictions. The scene of Avdii's mock trial by the 'junta' is structurally modelled on the Biblical version of Christ's interrogation by Pilate. Like Pilate, the leader of the 'junta', Ober-Kandalov, proclaims the power of authority and the state, and tries to force Avdii to renounce his views. When this fails, he sentences Avdii to death by crucifixion. Earlier in the novel, the narrative reiterates the Biblical debate on the nature of man in the confrontation between Avdii and Grishan, the leader of the drugrunners. Whereas Ober-Kandalov is presented as a spiritual brother of Pilate, Grishan appears as the Antichrist, the embodiment of pure evil and temptation. Like Satan, Grishan challenges Avdii to a test to prove to him the futility of opposing evil with the Christian philosophy of love and forgiveness.

With the exception of *Pegii pes*, in which the action takes place some time at the turn of the twentieth century, the plots of Aitmatov's other mythological works unfold in contemporary times, that is, the last decades of this century. As a rule, the contemporary plot is presented in a realistic manner, with the depiction of concrete characters and events, clearly localised through spatial and temporal co-ordinates, and with great attention to sociological and psychological details. However, the socio-psychological representation absorbs some elements of the mythological model, including the sharp polarisation of characters into good and evil, the depiction of extreme situations, including deaths, betrayals and disasters and the clear-cut moral postulates, demanding a choice in the light of ethical absolutes.[15] In the realm of artistic devices the contemporary plot relies on a system of binary oppositions, numerical symbolism and a solemn intonation, with repeated phrases and leitmotifs.

In *Belyi parokhod* the mythological influence is evident in the clear-cut view of good and evil, and in the univocal resolution of the conflict at the end of the novella. In the final test, Momun succumbs to the threats of Orozkul and shoots the maral. As correctly observed by I. Panchenko, Momun's killing of the maral is equal to the killing of the totem and is therefore a form of self-destruction.[16] To the boy, it is an act of total betrayal, and the only way he can cope with it is by escaping and plunging into the river. In his rejection of the corrupt world of adults, the boy proves his absolute innocence and idealism. At the same time he demonstrates his total belief in his tale of changing into a fish and swimming into Issyk-kul Lake.

The boy's tale, as well as the contemporary narrative utilise several binary oppositions, so characteristic for mythological structures. First, the opposition land/water. The boy, an earthly being, dreams about changing into a fish and living in water. As opposed to the cruel earth, water will offer him solace and comfort. The boy's dream recaptures the reverence of the Bugu clan for the mother-river Yenisei and for the blue water of Issyk-kul Lake. At the same time, the boy's tale is closely connected with his desire to be reunited with his father who is a sailor on the white ship on Issyk-kul Lake.[17]

The second binary opposition evident in the contemporary plot is that of family and tribe versus others. The family and the tribe are associated in the novella with Momun, the boy, Kulubek and the Buguan people in general. Momun is totally identified with the tribe; he faithfully carries on the Buguan traditions and passes them to his grandson. The boy who is Buguan only on his maternal side, is part of the family, on the one hand, and an 'outsider' on the other. Abandoned by his parents, he is raised in the Buguan tradition by his grandfather, but regarded as an 'outsider' by his step-grandmother and his uncle. Resentful of this label, the boy correctly assumes that it is not he who is actually an outsider, but rather the step-grandmother, Orozkul and the Seidakhmat family.

The opposition of family/others is reinforced in the novella by another binary opposition, that of nature versus culture. All the characters who continue the old tribal tradition are close to nature and respect its laws. Grandfather Momun cares deeply for the forest and the animals that live in it; the boy is totally immersed in the natural world, making friends with rocks, grass and flowers. The 'outsiders', who include Orozkul, Koketai and Seidakhmat, show no respect for nature and destroy it for personal gain. At the same time, they feel ill-at-ease with nature, and dream about moving to big cities.

As demonstrated by the Soviet critic Stepan Ilev, an important role is played in the novella by numerical symbolism, particularly the number 7.[18] According to the myth, Horned Deer-Mother blessed the first Bugu family and promised them many children: seven sons and seven daughters. In the contemporary story, the boy is a seven-year-old, he is one of seven people living in the cordon. Grandfather Momun believes that one of the seven people may turn out to be a prophet, and quotes the saying 'an orphan has seven fates'. During the stormy night seven drivers seek refuge at the cordon; one of them, Kulubek, befriends the boy. The novella is composed of seven chapters, divided evenly by the myth introduced in Chapter 4.

The mythological influence is even stronger in *Pegii pes*, wherein the mythological model becomes the basic structural principle, determining the entire artistic organisation of the material. The novella closely follows the mythological pattern of a rite of initiation, based on the triple formula separation – initiation – return. The narrative openly signals the idea of an initiation, by describing the event as 'a hunting baptism', and 'an inaugural hunting trip', whose purpose is to acquaint Kirisk, a boy of 11 or 12, with the sea.

In depicting the first part of the event – separation – the narrative focuses on the local tradition related to initiation, which includes the taboo on naming the event and its participants, the ways to deceive the evil spirits, and the festivities that follow the successful return. Significantly, all these references appear in the narrative as the reflections of the young protagonist on the eve of the hunt. Following the mythological pattern, the narrative relies on several binary oppositions rendering simple spatial and sensory oppositions, such as land/sea, close/distant, large/small, as well as the oppositions reflecting the tribal social structure: male/female, old/young, home/far away from home.

The largest part of the narrative is devoted to the second stage of initiation – the testing of the physical abilities of the boy. The testing includes three parts: the preliminary test – the seal hunt; the main test – the struggle against the natural elements; and the additional test – endurance and the will to survive.[19] Of the three tests, Kirisk fails the first one (he misses the seal), but is successful in the second and the third. Although he is not directly involved in the struggle against the raging sea, Kirisk displays a remarkable ability to cope with danger and to overcome fear. He proves equally strong in the third test: left alone in the kayak, he manages to endure agonising thirst and hunger, and to retain the will to survive.

In depicting the testing, the narrative deploys mythological oppositions which reflect cosmic spatial and temporal relations, such as sky/sea, day/night, darkness/light. The skilful use of these oppositions introduces into the narrative the sense of a cosmic struggle between chaos and cosmos, man and nature. The idea of the cosmic struggle is strengthened by the metaphorical depiction of the fog as a mythological monster, devouring the entire world and plunging everything into pitch-darkness.

Miraculously, people emerge alive from this uneven struggle, only to be subjugated to an even harder test – the ultimate test of human values, of making the choice between life and death in order to preserve the life of the young boy. In transmitting the thoughts of the protagonists, the narrative relies on fundamental oppositions: life/death, happiness/unhappiness, fear/courage.

In the third rite of passage Kirisk is left alone in the kayak, struggling against thirst, hunger and the feeling of loneliness. The narrative depicts his physical and emotional state with the help of sensory oppositions, such as cold/warm, thirst/water, and fundamental oppositions: solitude/companionship, desire to die/will to live. As befits a mythological hero, Kirisk passes the test of endurance, but before he returns to Piebald Dog Bay he undergoes a symbolic death, a necessary part of an initiation rite. Significantly, when he returns to life, he 'resurrects' in his mind the three men who sacrificed their lives for him: he thinks of the old man Organn as the Friendly Breeze, his father as the Guiding Star, and his uncle as the Waves that Bring Luck on the Sea.

Along with the mythological system of binary oppositions, *Pegii pes* displays a reliance on numerical symbolism, involving the number three. On his initiation hunt, Kirisk is accompanied by three adults. They are heading toward three islets, hoping to get three seals and to return home on the third day. Confronted with the storm and the fog, they undergo three tests that last three days and three nights. The three men sacrifice their lives to save the boy, who in turn will carry their memory with him to the end of his days.

Having examined the typology and the dominant characteristics of Aitmatov's mythological prose, it is important to address the question of the function of myths and the overall artistic quality of these works. The answer to the first question is relatively simple. Myth is used by Aitmatov to imply a comparison between something particular and something universal, and to suggest an analogy or contrast between myth and the contemporary world in which the main events occur. The mythological comparison, as a rule, reveals a deeper level of meaning, by directing the reader's attention to the universal questions of the human condition, the purpose of life, and also the ethical question of man's relations with others, as well as with nature.

As to the question of the artistic quality of Aitmatov's mythological works, it is generally very high. Myth, as a rule, is well integrated into the overall structure, with mythological motifs being well motivated and functioning as central features of the action. Occasionally, however, there is an over-explicit use of mythology, with too-frequent and overt references to myths employed. This tendency is most apparent in *Plakha*, in which the Biblical parallel is superimposed on virtually all characters and events of the Avdii subplot. Such an explicit use of mythology adds a touch of fatalism to the plot of the novel, with events closely following a preordained course and leading to an expected ending.

Apart from the over-explicit use of myth in *Plakha*, Aitmatov's mythological prose is artistically very successful. It manages to present the reader with important contemporary themes, and at the same time to make him feel that the chosen mythological analogy has enriched his understanding of contemporary material. Owing largely to the presence of myth, Aitmatov's prose transcends the particular and localised and acquires universal significance.

Notes

1. See the discussion on the pages of *Literaturnaia gazeta*, 1 March – 7 June 1978; V. Kubilius, 'Formirovanie natsional'noi literatury: podrazhatelnost' ili khudozhestvennaia transformatsiia', *Voprosy literatury*, 1976, no. 8, pp. 23–52; M. Epshtein, E. Iukina, 'Mir i chelovek: K voprosu o khudozhestvennykh vozmozhnostiakh sovremennoi literatury', *Novyi mir*, 1981, no. 4, pp. 236–47.
2. L. Anninskii, 'Zhazhdu belletrizma', *Literaturnaia gazeta*, 1 March 1978, p. 5.
3. Kubilius, p. 52.
4. I. G. Panchenko, 'O fol'klorno-mifologicheskikh traditsiiakh v sovremennoi mnogonatsional'noi sovetskoi proze', *Vzaimodeistvie i vzaimoobogashchenie: Russkaia literatura i literatury narodov SSR* (Leningrad, 1988), pp. 185–207.
5. See A. F. Losev, *Dialektika mifa* (Moscow, 1930); E. M. Meletinskii, S. I. Nekliudov (eds), *Tipologicheskiie issledovaniia po fol'kloru* (Moscow, 1975); E. M. Meletinskii, *Poetika mifa* (Moscow, 1976).
6. Meletinskii, *Poetika mifa*, pp. 262–76.
7. John J. White, *Mythology in the Modern Novel: A Study of Prefigurative Techniques* (Princeton, 1971), pp. 52–4.

8. Cf. the successful English translation of *Materinskoe pole* as *Mother Earth*, and of *Plakha* as *The Place of the Skull*, based on the literal meaning of the Hebrew word Golgotha.
9. See the excellent analysis of the totemic function of Akbara in N. Ivanova, 'Ispytanie pravdoi', *Znamia*, 1987, no. 1, pp. 217–20; and A. Kosorukov, '*Plakha:* Novyi mif ili novaia real'nost?', *Nash sovremennik*, 1988, no. 8, pp. 141–52.
10. Cf. the Soviet studies on Aitmatov's use of folklore and mythology: P. M. Mirza-Akhmedova, *National'naia epicheskaia traditsiia v tvorchestve Chingiza Aitmatova* (Tashkent, 1980); S. Z. Agranovich, 'Fol'klornye istochniki povesti Chingiza Aitmatova "Posle skazki" ', *Problemy istorii kritiki i poetiki realizma* (Kishinev, 1981), pp. 143–59; A. Ibragimova, 'Kraski vsekh iskusstv: Fol'klor narodov SSR v tvorchestve Aitmatova', *Prostor,* 1989, no. 4, pp. 149–52.
11. Many Soviet critics expressed serious reservations about Aitmatov's treatment of the Biblical story; cf. S. Averintsev, 'Paradoksy romana ili paradoksy vospriiatiia', *Literaturnaia gazeta*, 15 October 1986, p. 4; L. Anninskii, 'Skachka kentavra', *Druzhba narodov,* 1986, no. 12, pp. 249–52; A. Nuikin, 'Novoe bogoiskatel'stvo i starye dogmy', *Novyi mir*, 1987, no. 3, pp. 245–55.
12. K. Clark, 'The Mutability of the Canon: Socialist Realism in Chingiz Aitmatov's "I dol'she veka dlitsia den' " ', *Slavic Review,* 43, 4 (1984), 573–87.
13. Epshtein, Iukina, p. 238.
14. In addition to the Christian prefiguration, Avdii appears as a condensation of several other prototypes, most notably Don Quixote and Prince Myshkin; see S. Piskunova, B. Piskunov, 'Vyiti iz kruga', *Literaturnoe obozrenie*, 1987, no. 2, pp. 54–8.
15. See S. Paton, 'Chingiz Aitmatov's First Novel: A New Departure?', *Slavonic and East European Review*, 62, 4 (1984), p. 499–500.
16. I. Panchenko, p. 190.
17. See S. P. Ilev, 'Parabolicheskie povesti Chingiza Aitmatova', *Zagadnienia Rodzajow Literackich*, 20, 2 (1977), 61–90.
18. Ibid., pp. 68–9.
19. Cf. Meletinskii's observations on the structural similarities between initiation rite and magical fairy tale: *Poetika mifa*, p. 277.

5 The Naturalistic Tendency in Contemporary Soviet Fiction: Thematics, Poetics, Functions
Konstantin Kustanovich

Usually literature is referred to as naturalistic when it allegedly strives to show life as it is, including its most repulsive and cruel aspects. Often these aspects become dominant elements of the naturalistic narrative. Like the Russian writers of the 1840s and 1850s belonging to the Natural School, the French writers of the second half of the nineteenth century, for example, Zola and the Goncourt brothers, or such American authors as Stephen Crane (primarily his *Maggie: A Girl of the Streets*), Jack London and James Farrell, the contemporary Soviet writers under consideration here describe such social ills as alcoholism, use of drugs, prostitution, child abuse and the abuse of old people, indiscriminate sexual relations and sex involving children, families falling apart, deterioration of all traditional social institutions, extreme selfishness, crime, senseless cruelty, homelessness, starvation, terrible conditions in hospitals and schools, and other horrors – in a word, the authors present a detailed picture of utterly immoral social relations.

Such special attention to the details of life goes along with very little attention to plot – a violation of a major tenet of Aristotelian poetics which considers plot the most important part of the narrative and proposes that it should have a proper construction: a beginning, a middle and an end.[1] Contrary to this view, Zola, for example, believes that in the naturalistic novel

> plot matters little to the novelist who bothers himself with neither development, mystery, nor dénouement...Instead of imagining an adventure, of complicating it, of arranging stage effects, which scene by scene will lead to a final conclusion, you simply take the life study of a person or a group of persons, whose actions you faithfully

depict...Sometimes, even, it is not an entire life, with a commencement and an ending, of which you tell; it is only a scrap of an existence, a few years in the life of a man or a woman, a single page in a human history, which has attracted the novelist in the same way that the special study of a mineral can attract a chemist.[2]

This characterisation is also relevant to contemporary Soviet naturalistic fiction. In my discussion I am going to concentrate primarily on the works of three writers: Sergei Kaledin, Liudmila Petrushevskaia and Evgenii Popov, whose works fully represent the common features as well as the differences characteristic of contemporary naturalistic literature. Occasionally, however, I will turn to other contemporary authors.

Although Kaledin's works *The Humble Cemetery*[3] and *Stroibat* (The Construction Batallion) have at least some movement and development in the fates of the main characters, the author intentionally plays down the climaxes of these stories by giving them very little space in the text. The events preceding the climaxes serve not only as elements of the plot leading the reader to the dénouement but have their own independent value as parts of a general picture of life.

Popov's stories also contain very few, if any, significant events. One should bear in mind, of course, that the concept of an event is not an absolute one. Yuri Lotman writes that 'the same everyday reality may in different texts either acquire or not acquire the nature of an event'.[4] In other words, an action can be an event in the context of one culture and just an episode in the context of a different culture. Thus, in Bunin's story 'Natali' (Natalie), when a girl, scared by a thunderstorm, runs to the room of a young man with whom she is in love and sees him making love to her friend, her whole life is ruined. In Popov's world such a situation is not an event. In his story 'Svobodnaia liubov' ', (Free Love) two women who accidentally meet in their lover's apartment become friends in a matter of minutes and do not harbour ill feelings towards each other. If one accepts Lotman's definition of an event as a crossing of the border between two artistic spaces in the text,[5] then it is clear that in Popov's world there is no barrier between faithful and unfaithful sexual relations. In his world faithfulness and unfaithfulness do not exist as the elements of a binary opposition; in other words, the notion of faithfulness does not exist here at all.

Petrushevskaia's prose approaches closer perhaps than any other the notion of plotless fiction. Very rarely does she write a story that follows the traditional structural scheme of beginning, development with climax, and end. Generally speaking, her plays follow the same pattern of uneventfulness as her short stories. Something, of course, happens in the course of a play's action, but there is no development in the characters' lives. The play ends usually exactly where it began. In *Syraia noga* (Underdone Leg of Lamb) guests empty several bottles of vodka, the wife gets yet another beating from her husband, but the leg of lamb never appears on the table – the symbol, perhaps, of complete passivity and the inability to achieve anything. Again, actions terrible from the point of view of conventional morality are not events in this world.

The uneventfulness of naturalistic prose excludes, understandably, the figure of the hero. As in naturalistic literature of the past, in contemporary naturalists we do not find active members of society who are engaged in a struggle against social ills. It is here that these writers part company not only with socialist realist literature but also with other contemporary authors who tend to portray dark sides of Soviet life, such as, for example, Astafyev in his *Pechal'nyi detektiv* (A Sad Detective Story), Rasputin in *Pozhar* (The Fire) or Aitmatov in *The Place of the Skull*. Unlike Astafyev's Soshnin and Aitmatov's Avdii, the rare moral persons we find in works by neo-naturalists are not fighters. The only action they are capable of is self-sacrifice. They are also capable of love, but the love that they offer to people is rejected, abused or not understood.

Thus, in emphasising the seamier aspects of life, uneventfulness and lack of a hero, one finds a clear similarity between contemporary Soviet naturalistic writers and those of the past. There are, however, quite significant differences between them. In his book on Russian literature of the nineteenth century, Aleksandr Tseitlin notes that characteristic of the village novella are 'numerous sketches of everyday life, lyrical landscape, careful imitation of specific dialectical features in peasant speech, and a humanist tendency permeating the whole narrative'.[6] Although details of everyday life and imitation of dialect are also typical for neo-naturalistic prose, one does not find much of a humanistic tendency in it.

The humanistic tendency of nineteenth-century naturalistic prose is manifested first of all in the author's compassion for the poor and oppressed. And the nineteenth-century writers see in literature a tool for people's betterment. Zola emphasises the social function of literature: 'We are looking for the causes of social evil; we study the anatomy of classes and individuals to explain the derangements which are produced in society and in man. This often necessitates our working on tainted subjects, our descending into the midst of human follies and miseries.'[7]

Vissarion Belinsky asserts that literature of the Natural School promotes general attention to the plight of the poor.[8] Unlike their forebears, contemporary Soviet naturalists are not interested in didacticism. They do not ascribe educational and moral functions to literature; they seem to have lost the belief in art as an ideological weapon and simply want to show life without teaching anybody how to live. This anti-didactic tendency is common not only in today's naturalistic fiction but in much of contemporary Soviet literature in general. One of the characters, an artist, from a short story by another Popov, Valerii, says: 'I am a superrealist: I draw what I see. That's it. And no conclusions like "This must be stopped and this we should begin".'[9]

The difference between the naturalistic traditions of the past and present is also apparent in the character of social conflicts depicted. In the older literature the oppressors may be one's fellow peasants, as in Grigorovich's novella 'Derevnia' (The Village), yet when naturalistic literature of the past shows the suffering of the poor it is clear that this suffering occurs due to the socio-political situation. The rich are cruel because cruelty is necessary for guarding and increasing their wealth. The poor are cruel because they are afraid of losing what miserable sustenance they still have. But in contemporary prose one does not observe sharp social stratification. In *The Humble Cemetery* among the cemetery employees there are representatives of both the lumpen-proletariat and intelligentsia, including a student and a Ph.D. Popov portrays in his stories a broad spectrum of people from various Soviet social groups. The heterogeneous character of the society depicted, the mixture of different classes within the same limited social space is due, in part, to the lack of strict social partitions in real life. The intelligentsia, blue-collar workers, scientists, labourers and Party functionaries of the lower echelons live in the same neighbourhoods, their children go to the same schools, their wives stand in the same lines. We find in contemporary naturalistic literature not so much social evil as cruelty and abuse generated by selfishness, Now, cruelty is a matter of *byt* (everyday life), unrelated to the social position of either the victim or victimiser. In one of Liudmila Razumovskaia's plays, *Sad bez zemli* (A Garden without Land), a character remembers that her father abandoned her, her one-year-old sister and her three-year-old brother three months after their mother's death: 'When I was ten I became for you both father and mother. I washed your underwear, cooked food for you and took you to nursery school. I was only ten, and I myself still wanted to play with dolls.'[10] The father did not abandon his children out of poverty, but simply left for another woman. A character from Petrushevskaia's play *Tri devushki v golubom* (Three Girls in Blue) leaves her sick little son with her mother, without telling her where she is going, and flies to the Black Sea with her lover. Her mother locks the boy alone in the apartment and checks herself into the hospital. In *Syraia noga* a mother does not feed her little daughter, because she spends all the money she can get on alcohol. When in Dostoevsky's *Crime and Punishment* the Marmeladov family starves because of Marmeladov's drinking, Marmeladov himself senses the tragedy of the situation and is constantly tortured by guilt. In contemporary works conscience and guilt appear only as feigned in order to wring out some additional sympathy from one's neighbour.

If there is a social cause for cruelty it is not made obvious by the authors, perhaps from the same motive of avoiding didacticism. However, one of the motifs common in contemporary naturalistic prose may help in determining the source of everyday rudeness, cruelty and abuse. Although many of the characters seem to belong to the intelligentsia, they lack many characteristic features of this social group. Valentina from Razumovskaia's *Pod odnoi kryshei* (Under the Same Roof) says during one of their customary family squabbles: 'We are the intelligentsia but behave like uneducated boors.' Her mother responds: 'Where do you see the intelligensia here? Your mother is a simple nurse, a hospital maid. Your father did not study in an academy either; he earned his stars in the war.'[11] Soshnin's mother-in-law in Astafyev's *Pechal'nyi detektiv* also claims that she belongs to the intelligentsia, amusing Soshnin by this statement.[12] Svetlana in *Tri devushki v golubom* is more realistic about her social status when she says that she 'hates the cultured' – '*blagorodnykh*'. In pre-revolutionary Russia people of plebeian origins used this word – now an archaism in this usage – to refer to the educated class. Petrushevskaia thus shows that the old social division still holds in the characters' actions, and she uses their illiteracy as a semiotic device. She emphasises the grammatical mistakes her characters make when they speak. She either points out their substandard pronunciation in the stage directions[13] or incorporates in the text the characters' feeling of being unsure about what they say. And these characters include teachers, engineers, doctors; some of them hold a Ph.D. degree.

Thus, the abuse and cruelty one finds in contemporary naturalistic literature are committed by the *kham*, a person with some formal education who lacks the spirituality and morality characteristic of the old Russian intelligentsia. The *kham* is usually very aggressive and rude, especially toward people who he feels are more humane and spiritual than himself. As Petrushevskaia's Svetlana says, 'I prefer to yell first and think second.'[14] The authors seem to suggest that not just illiterate country bumpkins, like Shukshin's Gleb Kapustin in the short story 'Srezal' (Flunked), may develop a militant sense of superiority after picking up one or two ideas. The urban masses, which have replaced the destroyed old intelligentsia, also lack such moral aspects as compassion, love, concern for others and care for children and the elderly. The irony is that the people now responsible for social ills – the victimisers – are descendants of the poor – the victims – described in nineteenth-century naturalistic literature.

Let us turn now to some aspects of poetics that distinguish contemporary naturalistic writers one from the other. Let us also try to distinguish between the functions different techniques perform in different authors. Any good work of art reveals some kind of conflict or tension. A large body of literature is built around the conflict between characters: good guys fighting bad guys. Love stories and novels use the tension between the sexes, or between the lovers and society, or between the lovers and their families. There can also be a conflict of ideas as the main source of tension in a literary work. Tension may also exist between the work's text and the outside world, a previous literary tradition, for example. Kaledin, Petrushevkaia and Evgenii Popov, although they often deal with similar subject matter, differ in many areas of their artistic techniques – styles, plot structures and characters – as well as in the way they create tension in their texts and in the functions of this tension. For my discussion I would like to introduce the concept of an ideological space, that is, a set of ideas, beliefs, principles, values, judgements and prejudices characteristic of a person or a group of people. The three such spaces that I use here are the characters' ideological space, the author's ideological space and the reader's ideological space.

In mainstream Soviet literature of the period, roughly from the 1930s through the 1960s, we do not find tension between these spaces. Usually the protagonist's ideological space, which predominates in the work, coincides with the author's and, presumably, with the reader's. (A reader who does not share the author's/protagonist's ideology cannot find the comfort of an opposing point of view in such texts). The main conflict develops within the characters' space, between the hero and the villain. Kaledin's *The Humble Cemetery* and *Stroibat* at first strike us as a novelty – even in the gloomy *Pechal'nyi detektiv*, *Pozhar* and *The Place of the Skull* we do not see so much seaminess per unit of text. Yet, as in the Russian literary tradition in general, we find the familiar struggle between good and evil inside the characters' space, although it is much more difficult to detect here. In *The Humble Cemetery* the protagonist, a man nicknamed Vorobei (sparrow) is a gravedigger – a job which requires great skill not so much in handling a shovel as in wheeling and dealing and cheating the customers and the administration. Although he is a reformed alcoholic, Vorobei's abstinence is forced by a skull trauma he received in a fight with his brother over a woman. Together, Vorobei and his brother in their youth had made a habit of beating up their own father. In the course of still another fight, with three teenage hoodlums, Vorobei presumably kills one with his bare hands and then steals his watch. He also regularly beats his wife, who became an alcoholic trying to keep up with him when he himself was a heavy drinker.

Thus in the context of customary notions of human decency Vorobei seems a monster. Yet in the world in which Kaledin places his protagonist, Vorobei is a positive hero of the kind we know from Soviet literary tradition, though with some new values added. He cares for the old and defends the weak, twice saving, for example, the old war-veteran Kutia from being fired, the second time sacrificing his own job and, perhaps, life. Though not a believer, he respects religion and does special favours for the priest at the cemetery church. Before going to the district attorney he stops by the church to get the priest's blessing. He cheats customers, but the peculiar code of honour among cemetery-workers is sacred for him. The description of the teenage Vorobei's relations with a warden at the institution for juvenile delinquents could have come from Makarenko's *Pedagogical Poem*. Kaledin constructs the material of the novella in such a way that all Vorobei's vices are easily explainable and justifiable. His father abused his mother and then, when she died, he and his new wife abused Vorobei and his brother. This was the reason the brothers beat their father when they grew up. The three hoodlums, one of whom Vorobei killed, tried to rob him. Taking the watch is a logical action in the context of Vorobei's life since the watch would have been wasted anyway if he left it on the body.

Kaledin creates in this novella a world wherein the level of morality is much lower but the relations between good and evil are the same as in earlier Soviet literature. Like the protagonists in Aitmatov's, Rasputin's and Astafyev's works, Kaledin's Vorobei is on the side of good. And as in their works, he eventually loses his fight, but as long as there is a clear distinction between good and evil in society there is hope.

We do not find such a distinction in the characters' ideological space in Popov's stories. People vomit, urinate, defecate, wipe their behinds and pass gas, and these actions, unusual for Russian traditional literature, do not stand out in a series of other, ordinary, actions. Describing a picture of urinating boys, the narrator in the story 'Vechnaia vesna' (Spring Eternal) passionately asserts that, 'This is beautiful, I'm telling you honestly, this is beautiful because this is life, and everything which is life is very beautiful'.[15] It is important for Popov to destroy the traditional notion that these aspects of our existence are embarrassing and shameful. The same narrator describes a feeling of shame that his friend experiences after accidentally passing gas on his wedding night. Several year later this friend, receiving the narrator in his apartment, paces the room and, in the presence of his wife, passes gas now and then in the course of conversation. The indignant narrator first thinks of him as a fat animal, but then admits that he has no right to this attitude. The friend takes care of his son, helps at home, and is full of creative plans. The narrator concludes his monologue assuring the reader that it is possible to tie together such little things in life as bringing up a son or passing gas with Botticelli's masterpiece *Primavera*.[16]

Thus in the ideological space of Popov's characters there is no tension between high and low, moral and immoral, good and evil – these categories do not exist there. Even when an embarrassing episode involving a natural body function appears decisive in the protagonist's fate, the description clearly has a parodic character, and we understand that the author is not serious and the real source of the protagonist's troubles lies elsewhere. The story 'Palisadnichek' (The Fence) has a very solemn beginning that prepares the reader for a tragic love story: 'Oh, love! Love ruins young people. I myself got ruined because of love. Well, but this is not a story about me...'.[17] The plot, however, unfolds around urination, which undercuts the lofty beginning. In the story a teenager relieves himself in the bushes not knowing that a girl he is in love with and his sister are involuntary witnesses: 'The stream rustled. The beauties patiently waited for a long time but then jumped out the bushes with loud, even obscene, curses.'[18] After this, the narrator says, the boy's life is ruined. In the army he ends up in a penal battalion but later, 'by the fortieth anniversary of the Great October Socialist Revolution',[19] he is amnestied. He then changes jobs 81 times, loses his hair, and grows a beard down to his chest. In a very compact space Popov mixes together ideal love and the vulgarity of the object of this love, urinating in the bushes and the Great October Revolution. He further downgrades the notion of love by having the narrator of this story describe how he himself suffered from love:

> I fell in love with a tall, dark-haired bitch and she ordered me about as if I were a beast of burden. But she gave me her love only after getting pretty drunk on vodka. For this purpose I got used to drinking vodka with her. Then the bitch dumped me, and as for drinking vodka, I still do.[20]

The concepts of good and evil exist here only on the quantitative level, not on the qualitative one. Drinking is morally neither good nor bad, nor is casual sex. The more vodka one can get the better; if there is no vodka one tries to borrow or steal medicine containing alcohol. There is nothing shameful about it. Sex is just another means of social contact, one which also provides physical pleasure. Nothing more. Often sex is only physical pleasure without any social meaning. In Popov's story 'Sir'ia, Boris, Lavinia' (Sirya, Boris and Lavinia), when a woman tells her lover that she loves him, he literally does not understand what she means. The woman, Sirya, is out of place here. Boris's other mistress, Lavinia, seems much more relevant to the reality depicted in the story. This is how Popov describes their first encounter:

> Lavinia did not make any special impression on him. He was not even sure that he liked her...When they were left alone Boris fiercely threw himself on Lavinia. The girl giggled and hurriedly helped him. Soon it became light and she went home.[21]

While the characters in Popov's stories usually lack the criteria that would help them to distinguish between good and evil, between the moral and immoral, there is one voice there which stands apart from the characters' voices and provides an alternative point of view. This is the laughing and mocking voice of the author. The author does not interpose his didactic judgements; his voice is present implicitly in the parodic character and ironic tone of the narration, much as in the works of Gogol and Zoshchenko. And like these authors, Popov laughs not so much at his characters as at life in general. The author's laughter allows some sort of escape from the terrible reality we encounter in his prose.

Another purpose of parody in Popov is to destroy all kinds of stereotypes, those imbued in us by literature or by official propaganda or even by traditional morality. The author conducts a continual polemic with these stereotypes as if trying to tell us that life does not fit their Procrustean bed. What seems insignificant according to a stereotype may be very important in someone's life and vice versa. An old man living a happy, peaceful, harmonious life needs to have his old pot mended. But there is no one in the city who could solder the pot; it is easier to buy a new one. The old man does not want a new one, so the harmony is ruined.²² A worker loses three fingers in a shop accident. After he has recovered he comes back to the shop for his fingers, but finds only two out of three. He quits his job and starts his own little business making and selling candy at a farmers' market. He becomes rich, finds a new wife, buys many good things including a large-screen TV. The only thing which spoils his happiness is the missing finger.²³ Another worker has a loving wife, a beautiful apartment on the thirteenth floor with a great view of a forest, a good salary and no problems but one: the view of the level, green body of the forest is spoiled by one tall tree sticking up. The worker cannot tolerate this violation of harmony, so he destroys the tree. But absolute harmony cannot exist, and the worker in a fit of unbearable anguish falls (or jumps) from his balcony together with his wife.²⁴

To reiterate, the main tension in Popov's stories is between the author and the cultural stereotypes he parodically recreates in his texts, that is, between the author's and the characters' ideological spaces. One of the main stereotypes of the Russian literary past is the assumption that an ideal society – an absolute harmony – may exist. One need only get rid of the people or the social order that stand in its way. Popov destroys this stereotype as he destroys others. The text's main goal in his stories is to show that literature should not stick to the old, well-beaten paths but use everything for its subject matter, even the lowest and most insignificant stuff of life.

Thus if in Kaledin we still find an authorial judgemental attitude toward life, Popov tries to break old, rigid notions and to show that real life will always have an unexpected turn, even in simple situations. A dialogue in 'Zelenyi massiv' (The Green Tract) between Uncle Serezha and the narrator is a good illustration of the author's scepticism:

'I have a question again, Uncle Serezha'.
'What is it?'
'How did it all happen to you?'
'What do you mean all?'
'Well, your life. How did you end up here?'
'First of all, I ended up exactly where I am supposed to be, and then I already asked you not to ask me unnecessary questions because that is not the main thing.'
'And what is the main thing?'
'I don't know. Leave me alone. I've lived a long life and I don't know. Leave me alone.'
'Shall I run to the store again?'²⁵

Uncle Serezha emphatically refuses any didactic role. It is impossible to know what is most important in life – the knowledge that was readily claimed by literary heroes of the past. In Popov's world people prefer to leave the ultimate questions alone and run to the store to fetch another bottle of vodka.

Like Popov's, Petrushevskaia's world has no heroes. But Popov brightens the gloomy life he depicts in his stories with his laughter. Although he does not laugh at people or the way they live, but at stereotypes, there is still tension between the authorial ideological space and the characters' ideological space. In Petrushevskaia's stories there is no tension either inside the characters' space or between the author's and the characters' spaces. There is no opposition here between good and evil as in Kaledin's novellas, nor do we see the irony, play and laughter which betray the author in Popov's works. Her stories are told in a matter-of-fact manner with an almost monotonous intonation. We rarely find here the traditional beginning or dénouement, which usually serve as important devices to introduce and conclude the author's message. The story 'Serezha' (Serezha), for example, opens in a typically Petrushevskaian way: 'I cannot understand one thing – why he left Nadia. He knew that this would finish her, and she really did die a year after his death.'[26] By not introducing the characters but simply telling about an episode from their lives, as if we have just returned from a long trip and are listening to what happened during our absence, the narrator includes us, the readers, in the circle of her intimate friends. And the narrator in Petrushevskaia's stories is usually either the protagonist or someone from the protagonist's surroundings who is well-informed about the protagonist's life. Thus the author's role as an intermediary between the characters and the reader is completely eliminated in Petrushevkaia; hence the authorial point of view is absent too.

The main tension then is realised between the ideological spaces of the characters and the readers. It is based first of all on the difference between the characters' moral makeup and the readers' views on morality. Tatiana Tolstaia makes the following generalisation about Petrushevskaia's female characters: 'a real female tyrant, a passionate and gloomy tyrant with a miserable and inhuman soul; she is unloved and unable to love'.[27] Describing the Moscow of the 1930s Mikhail Bulgakov found that Muscovites are 'people like any others...They're thoughtless, of course, but then they sometimes feel compassion too...They're ordinary people...except that the housing problem has soured them.'[28] Since then, the housing problem and many other problems 'have soured' Muscovites to such a degree that, looking at Petrushevskaia's characters, one cannot say about them, 'people like any others'. Compassion *(miloserdie)* is perhaps one of the main aspects of humaneness, and that is precisely what one does not find in great quantity in Petrushevskaia's characters.

Another source of tension generated by Petruschevskaia's texts is the difference between the characters' acceptance of their reality, however terrible it is, and the horror the reader experiences reading about their lives. The reader's attitude is based on his or her notion of what life should be – a notion cultivated mostly by the literature and other cultural media of the past. In the story 'Skripka' (A Violin),[29] a pregnant patient in a hospital invents her entire life story – a husband, friends, the conservatoire where she allegedly studies the violin – just because her real life would not correspond to common notions about an educated person's life. In real life she has no husband, no friends and perhaps no income and no place to go. She has to fake fainting on the street in order to be picked up by an ambulance and brought to a hospital where she can get free food. Very soon her room-mates in the hospital ward guess the true situation and begin passing her the food packages they receive from relatives, and the doctor keeps her in the hospital as long as he can, knowing that she probably has no home. Yet neither the narrator nor the other characters (the narrator seems to be one of the patients in the ward) nor even the protagonist herself makes a big deal of this tragic situation. The fellow patients just routinely put their food on her bedside table and she just as routinely accepts their donations and eats everything she gets.

When Petrushevskaia's characters betray some recognition of tragedy in their lives, such recognition occurs on the unconscious level. In 'Bogema' (Bohemia) the protagonist is one of Petrushevskaia's misfits:

> She had neither money nor shelter. She had been some kind of correspondence student for eight years at the Library Institute, ate three days a week, and just wandered from house to house in the company of bums like herself without having an affair with any of them.[30]

She becomes pregnant without knowing about it and, after developing abdominal pains, goes to the country to her mother's. There, going out to the garden to urinate, she has a miscarriage. The story ends in the same prosaic tone that dominates the entire narration:

> Later, Klavdiia told many people that she was going to give birth to a boy – in so many months, then so many months ago; she counted

these months like a real mother...In time [she] stopped talking about it, and only her mother, spending a lot of money, for some reason moved the outhouse to a new place, and in the old one, which she had filled in, she planted a mountain ash and a birch tree.[31]

We see that Klavdiia and her mother cannot get over the loss of the child for months. However, they deal with it not consciously but by mythologising the tragedy – Klavdiia by creating an image of a living boy, the mother by removing a profane object – the outhouse – from the sacred burial place. the word *'zachem-to'* – 'for some reason' ('for some reason moved the outhouse to a new place') – emphasises the unconscious character of the mother's action.

At the same time the prepared reader has enough information in this and other stories to recognise the dimensions of the tragedies and horrors described there. This knowledge on the reader's part as contrasted with the characters' all-accepting naivety creates the main tension in Petrushevskaia's stories.

The three writers discussed here count to a significant degree on a certain readership and its stereotypical notions of life. These notions may be reduced to the idea that although such negative aspects of the human experience as, for instance, cruelty, injustice, physical suffering and immorality are encountered in life, they are nonetheless exceptions and can be dealt with in one way or another. Contrary to this idea, each of the writers discussed here depicts a reality in which such aspects are dominant and irremediable. Yet the functions of these naturalistic presentations of life are different. Kaledin simply lowers the general level of morality in relation to the level that Soviet readers have encountered in earlier literature, while preserving the customary oppositions between good and evil. Popov chooses seamy aspects of life as the subject matter for his stories to make the point that anything may serve as literary material and to ridicule old stereotypes. Petrushevskaia creates a horrible world the main horror of which is that its inhabitants perceive it as normal.

Notes

1. Aristotle, *Poetics*, 1450. a5–20, b25–30.
2. Emile Zola, 'Naturalism on the Stage', in *The Experimental Novel*, translated by Belle M. Sherman (New York, 1964), pp. 123–4.

3. I use English titles for works which have been translated into English and Russian titles with their English translations in brackets for works which, to the best of my knowledge, have not been translated. All translations from Russian are mine unless otherwise indicated.
4. Jurij Lotman, *The Structure of the Artistic Text*, translated by Ronald Vroon (Ann Arbor, 1977), p. 232.
5. Op. cit., 238.
6. A. G. Tseitlin, *Russkaia literatura pervoi poloviny XIX veka* (Moscow, 1940), p. 400.
7. Zola, 'To the Young People of France', in *The Experimental Novel*, pp. 102–3.
8. V. G. Belinskii, 'Vzgliad na russkuiu literaturu 1847 goda', in *Sochineniia v odnom tome* (Moscow, 1950), p. 740.
9. Valerii Popov, 'Giganty', *Oktiabr'*, 1987, no. 11, p. 160.
10. Liudmila Razumovskaia, 'Sad bez zemli', in *Sad bez zemli* (Leningrad, 1989), p. 99.
11. Liudmila Razumovskaia, 'Pod odnoi kryshei', in *Sad bez zemli*, p. 22.
12. Viktor Astafyev, 'Pechal'nyi detektiv', in *Padenie lista* (Moscow, 1988), p. 62.
13. See, for example, Liudmila Petrushevskaia, 'Tri devushki v golubom', in *Tri devushki v golubom* (Moscow, 1989), pp. 148–9.
14. Op. cit., 190.
15. Evgenii Popov, 'Vechnaia vesna', in *Veselie Rusi* (Ann Arbor, 1981), p. 141.
16. The Botticelli painting after which Popov names this story is *Primavera*, although the detailed description of the woman's figure better fits the figure of Venus in another Botticelli painting, *The Birth of Venus*.
17. Evgenii Popov, 'Palisadnichek', in *Veselie Rusi*, p. 14.
18. Op. cit., 16.
19. Ibid.
20. Ibid.
21. Evgenii Popov, 'Sir'ia, Boris, Laviniia', in *Veselie Rusi*, p. 146.
22. Evgenii Popov, 'Kotelok pokhodnyi prokhudilsia', in *Zhdu liubvi ne verolomnoi* (Moscow, 1988).
23. Evgenii Popov, 'Dva sushenye pal'tsa iz piati byvshikh', in *Veselie Rusi*, p. 66.
24. Evgenii Popov, 'Zelenyi massiv', in *Veselie Rusi*, p. 43.
25. Op. cit., 46.
26. Liudmila Petrushevskaia, 'Serezha', in *Bessmertnaia liubov'* (Moscow, 1988), p. 158.
27. Tat'iana Tolstaia, 'V strane pobezhdennykh muzhchin', *Moskovskie novosti*, 17 September 1989.
28. Mikhail Bulgakov, *The Master and Margarita*, translated by Michael Glenny (New York and Scarborough, Ontario, 1985), p. 127.
29. Liudmila Petrushevskaia, 'Skripka', in *Bessmertnaia liubov'*, p. 63.
30. Liudmila Petrushevskaia, 'Bogema', in *Bessmertnaia liubov'*, p. 100.
31. Op. cit., 101.

6 Reassessing the Past: Images of Stalin and Stalinism in Contemporary Russian Literature
Rosalind Marsh

Since Gorbachev came to power in 1985 there has been a widespread and unprecedented revaluation of Soviet history and a heated debate about the future development of Soviet society, far surpassing the earlier reassessment which took place under Khrushchev. Literature has played a very important part in this process, opening up new subjects for historical enquiry and challenging historians to produce a deeper analysis of their country's past.

As the development of Soviet historical thought by journalists and historians in the years 1985–8 has already been ably documented by other scholars,[1] this essay will concentrate on works of fiction published in the USSR since Gorbachev's accession which raise questions about Stalin and Stalinism which had either not previously been brought to public attention or not been discussed so frankly before. A consideration of the newly published literature will include a discussion of the way in which works of historical fiction have been presented to the Soviet public, and the controversies they have engendered in the Soviet press. These encompass both debates about the historical accuracy of the facts or interpretations presented in works of fiction, and the political discussions they have provoked among different sections of Soviet society. In Gorbachev's USSR, history has been used as a political weapon in conflicts between neo-Stalinists, Russian nationalists and radical democrats. Since the reassessment of Stalin and Stalinism in Soviet literature is a huge subject which merits much fuller treatment, this essay will be restricted to a discussion of certain general issues raised by the recent literature.

GLASNOST' IN HISTORY

One interesting question is whether *glasnost'* in history – both in literature and in publicistic writing – was planned by the Party leadership, or was an uncontrolled process stemming from below. While the process of *glasnost'* itself appears to have begun with the grass-roots revolt at the fifth congress of the Union of Film-Makers in May 1986,[2] it is unlikely that the reappraisal of Stalin could have occurred without the approval, even encouragement, of the highest Party leadership[3] (although Ligachev and Chebrikov expressed their disapproval of this policy).[4] However, the process of reassessing Stalinism did not happen immediately after Gorbachev's accession. In 1985–6 he made some cautious and contradictory statements warning against obsession with the past; for example, he said at an informal meeting with the Union of Soviet Writers in the Kremlin on 19 July 1986: 'If we were to get too involved with the past, we would lose all our energy. It would be like hitting the people over the head. We have to go forward. We *will* sort out the past. Everything will be put in its place...It must be understood that for us everything lies in the future.'[5]

Nevertheless, by February 1987, perhaps because the aftermath of the Chernobyl disaster of April 1986 had opened Gorbachev's eyes to the magnitude of the problems facing the country, or because he had defeated many of his political opponents at the January 1987 Plenum, Gorbachev publicly reversed his previous position and spoke frankly of the need to explore the 'blank spots' in Soviet history.[6] Gorbachev had clearly come to believe that a reexamination of Stalinism was vital to his policy of *perestroika* and that literature on this subject could help to change people's attitudes. He was correct in the sense that Stalin's totalitarian system, many aspects of which had survived throughout the 'era of stagnation' under Brezhnev, was the major reason for the low morale of the population, poor productivity in the economy, bureaucracy and corruption in society, and the poverty of intellectual and cultural life. Gorbachev had come to understand that in order to repudiate the legacy of the past, it is first necessary to understand it. He hoped that opening up the past would be a means to an end – that it would help the USSR to build a better future.

In practice, however, the reassessment of the past turned out to be an end in itself; by 1987 liberal writers and editors were escaping from official control and raising certain subjects for moral, rather than political reasons. The respected scholar Academician Likhachev, in a telephone message read to a meeting of the Writers' Union in May

1987, stated: 'The past does not die. It is necessary to publish in journals of mass circulation works which were not published in the past. The most important thing in literature is repentance.'[7] Many writers felt that it was an indisputably good thing to tell the truth about past mistakes and crimes, not to conceal them under euphemisms; and they sought through analysing and attacking the Stalinist system to ensure that the past would never be repeated.

THE VALUE OF HISTORICAL FICTION

The second question arising from the recently published literature on historical themes is: does it matter? After all, many of the writers are long dead (and conservative critics have criticised the posthumous publications as 'literary necrophilia');[8] much of the information contained in fiction is not new for a Western audience and has also been discussed in the Soviet press; and some of the works have quite correctly been criticised on historical or artistic grounds.

Nevertheless, in spite of all these qualifications, the role of literature in the process of reassessing the Russian past is very important, for various reasons.

In the first place, literature has played a vital part in opening up new historical questions for discussion. Indeed, fiction *initiated* the whole process: whereas historians and economists only began to treat the subject of Stalin and Stalinism after Party policy changed in the Gorbachev era, novelists and poets had been concerned with this subject since the Khrushchev 'Thaw' and even earlier.[9] During the 'era of stagnation' under Brezhnev they continued to refer obliquely to this theme in print, or to write franker works which either appeared only in the West or were not published at all. It is only since the easing of editorial and official censorship in the Gorbachev era that the full extent of writers' commitment to this subject has become evident, since works of historical fiction have been published which, in some cases, were written more than twenty years earlier (for example, Anatolii Rybakov's *Deti Arbata*[10] (Children of the Arbat) and the plays of Mikhail Shatrov).[11] Although literature and historiography have long been intimately linked within Soviet society, this relationship has been transformed under *glasnost'*, as fiction published in journals of mass circulation became the first medium to introduce new topics relating to Stalin and Stalinism to a wide public in the USSR, playing a particularly valuable role in influencing people too young to remember the limited revelations of the Khrushchev 'Thaw'.

In some cases, novels or literary memoirs have provided factual information new even to a Western audience: for example, Anatolii Zhigulin's memoir *Chernye kamni* (Black Stones) depicts the formation in 1948 of an anti-Stalinist conspiratorial organisation among students in Voronezh, which lasted for about a year until its members were arrested.[12] Konstantin Simonov's memoir *Glazami cheloveka moego pokoleniia* (Through the Eyes of a Man of My Generation) describes Stalin's personal intervention in literary matters, and the harsh attack on Mikoyan and Molotov at the Central Committee Plenum of 16 October 1952.[13] Vladimir Dudintsev's *Belye odezhdy* (White Robes) reproduces a questionnaire issued to secret policemen and informers in order to investigate scientists hostile to Lysenko.[14]

A second reason why literature is important is that it is a powerful means of illustrating the human cost of historical events, the impact of policies on individuals. Striking examples of this are the accounts of 'dekulakisation' in Boris Mozhaev's *Muzhiki i baby* (Peasant Men and Women) and Sergei Antonov's *Ovragi* (Ravines);[15] the depiction of the famine of 1932–3 in Vasilii Grossman's *Vse techet* (Forever Flowing) and Vladimir Tendriakov's *Khleb dlia sobaki* (Bread for the Dog);[16] the cycle of violence and injustice unleashed by the deportation of the Chechens in Anatolii Pristavkin's *Nochevala tuchka zolotaia* (A Golden Cloud Spent the Night);[17] the portrayal of tortures, both physical and mental, used by Stalin's interrogators in Lev Razgon's memoir *Nepridumannoe* (This Has Not Been Invented) and Rybakov's *1935-yi i drugie gody* (1935 and Other Years).[18] Such descriptions have a greater impact on the imagination than dry statistics published in the press or a history textbook.

Writers have been more adventurous than historians in the topics they have raised for discussion, and hence have issued a challenge to historians to tackle formerly taboo subjects and produce their own, more accurate interpretations of Soviet history. Initially, however, Soviet historians displayed a certain reticence about the need to reassess the Stalinist past. In 1987 the senior historian Yurii Poliakov, corresponding member of the Academy of Sciences and head of a department in the Institute of History of the USSR, admitted: 'The writers have long since overtaken the historians in posing sharp questions.'[19] Poliakov complained: 'It's fair enough for writers to present a certain picture of that time, but an historian needs documentation – and our archives, frankly, have been in quite a mess.'[20] Although some radical historians, such as Yuri Afanasyev, who was appointed Rector of the State Historical Archive Institute at the end of 1986, argued that a total reassessment of Stalin's role was essential, since Soviet textbooks distorted history and passed over sensitive issues in silence,[21] it has only been since 1987-8 that serious historical and biographical works on Stalin and Stalinism have begun to be published in the USSR: Dmitrii Volkogonov's biography of Stalin, *Triumph and Tragedy*, Roy Medvedev's *On Stalin and Stalinism*,[22] articles in the revitalised journal *Voprosy istorii*, and translations of works by foreign historians, such as Stephen Cohen's biography of Bukharin and Robert Conquest's *The Great Terror*.[23]

THE BREAKING OF TABOOS

It is instructive to trace how and why some of the major works on historical themes have been published in recent years, in order to demonstrate how taboos have gradually been broken in the Gorbachev era. In 1986 literature on the theme of Stalin and Stalinism began to be published as a contribution to Gorbachev's drive for 'reconstruction' and greater economic efficiency. The first literary work to treat this theme – Aleksandr Bek's novel *Novoe naznachenie* (The New Appointment), posthumously published in October and November 1986, was introduced by Grigorii Baklanov, the editor of the journal *Znamia*, as a work which would aid Gorbachev's policy of *perestroika*.[24] Bek's novel, published in the West in 1971, frankly portrays the minister Onisimov, based on Stalin's Minister of Ferrous Metallurgy Tevosian, who is slavishly loyal to Stalin, and finds it difficult to adapt to the changed climate of the post-Stalin era. Bek's treatment of the theme of 'Stalin's heirs' did not venture far beyond what had been permitted under Khrushchev, but the well-known economist and reformer Gavriil Popov used the evidence of the novel to draw far-reaching conclusions about what he called the 'Administrative system' of the Soviet economy.[25]

A work which had greater popular impact was a film, Tengiz Abuladze's *Pokaianie* (Repentance), put on general release in December 1986, which approached the subject of dictatorship, guilt and responsibility in an oblique, surrealistic way. The sociologist Lev Ionin provided an interesting analysis of the film, arguing that society was at fault for permitting the crimes of the dictator Varlam to be shrouded in silence after his death; repentance of this sin was necessary in order to rouse society out of its hypocrisy, immorality and lack of faith.[26]

At the beginning of 1987 some major works by dead writers, which had long circulated in *samizdat* among the Soviet intelligentsia, were posthumously published, simply to set the historical record straight. One was Anna Akhmatova's moving poem *Rekviem* (Requiem),[27] about which one critic commented ironically: 'Ecstasies on account of *Rekviem* would now appear belated.'[28] Another was Aleksandr Tvardovskii's poem *Po pravu pamiati* (By the Right of Memory),[29] which rethinks the experience of collectivisation, and attempts to expiate the guilt which the author felt in relation to his father's deportation as a 'kulak'.

After this the floodgates opened, and from 1987 onwards many new subjects were aired in literature almost simultaneously, in works not previously known either in the USSR or the West. The effect of Lysenkoism on science was treated in Dudintsev's *Belye odezhdy*, Vladimir Amlinskii's *I opravdan budet kazhdyi chas* (And Every Hour Will Be Justified) and Daniil Granin's fictionalised documentary *Zubr* (The Buffalo)[30] (which also dealt with the imprisonment on charges of treachery of Russians who had lived abroad). Stalin's deportation of whole peoples in 1944–5 was highlighted in Pristavkin's *Nochevala tuchka zolotaia* and Iosif Gerasimov's *Stuk v dver'* (A Knock at the Door).[31] The cost of 'dekulakisation' and collectivisation was exposed in novels by Mozhaev, Antonov and Vasilii Belov.[32] The general atmosphere of fear and mistrust prevalent during Stalin's Terror was conveyed in Yurii Trifonov's *Ischeznovenie* (Disappearance) and Boris Yampolskii's *Moskovskaia ulitsa* (Moscow Street); the excessive tempos of the First Five Year Plan were illustrated in *Vas'ka*, Antonov's story about the construction of the Moscow metro.[33] Shatrov's play *Brestskii mir* (The Peace of Brest-Litovsk) explored Stalin's relationship with Lenin. But perhaps the greatest literary sensation of 1987 was the publication of Rybakov's novel *Deti Arbata,* suppressed for many years, which provides a detailed reconstruction of Stalin's psychology and what Rybakov has called his 'philosophy of power', and an elaborate account of the preparation of a purge trial in the period leading up to the assassination of Kirov in 1934, in which, it is hinted, Stalin was implicated.

In 1987 a new orthodoxy seemed to be emerging: Soviet history was yet again being presented by writers and journalists in a biased way, although the bias was less extreme and more acceptable to the West than formerly. Most works of fiction either stated or implied that Stalin and a few of his closest associates had been personally responsible for the tragedy of the 1930s; no institutional causes were identified. There were no works of fiction published in 1987 which explicitly stated that the oppositionists of the 1920s, whether Trotsky or Bukharin, might have had a valid case (although Bukharin is sympathetically portrayed by Shatrov, and Mozhaev's *Muzhiki i baby* implicitly propounds a Bukharinist view of economic development). Lenin was still placed on a pedestal, and there was no hint that he might have bequeathed ideas and institutions to Stalin which had enabled him to carry out the purges. In the works of Rybakov and Shatrov, Lenin is seen as a wise leader, not as Stalin's mentor. In particular, his democratic tendencies are over-accentuated and his New Economic Policy over-praised as the most suitable model for the future development of the economy; there is no discussion of the tightening of political control during the 1920s, or of whether Lenin intended the NEP merely as a temporary measure.

By the end of 1988, following Bukharin's legal rehabilitation in January 1988, his alternative view of Soviet economic development was increasingly being accepted as viable, both in literary works like Shatrov's *Dal'she, dal'she, dal'she!* (Onward, Onward, Onward!) and many works of non-fiction.[34] In 1988 it also became possible to publish works like the memoirs of Zhigulin and Razgon, which graphically expose atrocities committed by Stalin's security services and the terrible conditions in the prison camps. Perhaps the most remarkable literary event of 1988 was the posthumous publication of Vasilii Grossman's powerful novel *Zhizn' i sud'ba* (Life and Fate),[35] which draws a direct parallel between Nazism and Stalinism, and implies that the Second World War was a conflict between the two totalitarian systems of Germany and the USSR on the one hand, and the spirit of human freedom on the other. Rybakov's second, less successful novel *1935-yi i drugie gody*,[36] which depicts Stalin's preparation of the trial of Zinoviev and Kamenev, treats certain themes which *Deti Arbata* was criticised for omitting:[37] collectivisation and the famine, the purges in the army and secret police, and the activities of Stalin's henchmen Kaganovich, Ezhov and Beria.

1989 was the year when it became possible to publish works overtly critical of Lenin. Grossman's *Vse techet* links Stalin with Lenin, who is presented as a supporter of dictatorship. Grossman regards Russia as having always been enslaved, and cherishing its 'non-freedom'. 1989 was also marked by the long-awaited publication of Solzhenitsyn's *Arkhipelag Gulag* (The Gulag Archipelago) in a version abridged by the author.[38] Sergei Zalygin, the editor of *Novyi mir*, prefaced its publication with the comment that even though 'we certainly do not agree with everything said by the author,...intelligent and honest opponents are more necessary to our society than friends who have been cheaply acquired, and even sincere, but dull-witted friends'.[39] Remarkable though the publication of *Gulag* would have seemed even a year or two earlier, it is not surprising that it finally appeared in 1989, as by this time the press had already treated some of Solzhenitsyn's more controversial themes: prison camps in the 1920s; secret police tortures; Lenin's introduction of the Red Terror; and certain positive aspects of tsarist Russia.

1990 witnessed the publication of the first three parts of Solzhenitsyn's epic, *Krasnoe koleso*, (The Red Wheel),[40] which paint a very hostile picture of Lenin and praise Stolypin as the one tsarist statesman whose policies might have prevented revolution. Simultaneously, *Novyi mir* published the revised, 98-chapter version of Solzhenitsyn's novel *V kruge pervom* (The First Circle),[41] first published in Paris in 1978, which contains a satirical portrait of Stalin, attacks Marxism-Leninism and speaks favourably of the Constituent Assembly, dissolved by Lenin in 1918. Both *The First Circle* and *The Red Wheel* implicitly pose the question: was the Revolution necessary at all? It seemed at the beginning of 1990 that no historical subjects were now taboo, but the third (March) number of *Novyi mir* took a long time to appear; the official reason was shortage of paper, but such was the suspicion of the authorities still prevalent in the USSR that Soviet intellectuals in June 1990 were claiming that 'it is because they are publishing Solzhenitsyn'. Whatever the truth of the matter, it is nevertheless fair to say that in 1990 there seem to be no issues relating to Stalinism which are officially banned, now that the sensitive subjects of the Molotov-Ribbentrop Pact and Soviet responsibility for the massacre of Polish officers at Katyn have been broached in the press. A genuine pluralism has emerged in contemporary Russian historical fiction; since 1988 Soviet writers have discussed such contentious issues as Lenin, the NEP, collectivisation and Stalin's purges from different points of view.

THE PROBLEM OF HISTORICAL ACCURACY

Many works of literature have been criticised for their alleged historical inaccuracy. It is certainly true that there is still little knowledge of Western historiography among either Soviet writers or historians, and many writers have had only limited access to historical information. But how important is historical accuracy in literature?[42] On the one hand, writers of historical fiction possess a certain leeway to invent, and in the West readers have long been accustomed to allowing writers full licence to make of historical characters and events what they will; an obvious example is Schiller's *Maria Stuart*, which depicts a dramatic meeting between Elizabeth I and Mary, Queen of Scots, who in reality never met. In the twentieth century, however, with the increasing concern for accuracy which has come to permeate historical scholarship, certain works of historical fiction have aroused controversy because of what Joseph W. Turner has called 'the tension inherent in the genre'.[43] A certain degree of historical accuracy does appear to be a conventional expectation of most contemporary readers of 'documented historical novels'[44] – that is, novels in which actual people from the past appear – even though it need not necessarily be a fundamental requirement of the genre, or play any significant role in the critical assessment of a work of literature. Nevertheless, many Western readers, concerned less with factual accuracy than with a writer's ability to convey the spirit of a historical period, might consider, for example, that Rybakov has skilfully exploited his freedom as a novelist when he posits an imaginary last meeting between Kirov and Ordzhonikidze in Moscow in November 1934 shortly before Kirov's assassination.[45]

However, the writing of historical fiction in the USSR raises certain special problems. Perhaps historical accuracy is more important in a Soviet literary context than in other cultures (although in view of the dearth of historical works and archival material, its absence is more understandable). Because of the shortage of accurate works by historians, writers of fiction in the USSR in the era of *glasnost'* have a great responsibility, as their work may be the first medium to raise new and important topics before a mass audience. In view of the potential their works possess for exerting great psychological and political influence in the USSR, it is incumbent upon writers to get their facts straight as far as possible, or to make it clear to their readers which parts of their work are fictional and which are based on fact. Some writers of historical fiction, notably Solzhenitsyn and Rybakov, are clearly aware of their responsibility and claim that they are striving for historical accuracy.[46] However, most contemporary works of fiction depicting Stalin – for example, those of Bek, Rybakov, Shatrov and Solzhenitsyn – to some extent fall into the danger of 'psycho-history' – the limited view that history is merely a result of the ideas and actions of individuals, with no reference to political systems or wider economic, ideological and international factors. This is partly an inevitable result of the demands of the novelistic or dramatic genre, which focuses on the thoughts and actions of individual characters. Rybakov, despite his desire for historical accuracy, was to some degree guilty of concentrating on Stalin's personality in his novel *Deti Arbata,* but the second volume of his trilogy also depicts other aspects of the *system* which Stalin created (in particular, it provides insights into the workings of the secret police).

Certain fictional works contain controversial conclusions which have been rightly challenged by historians and economists. Mozhaev's *Muzhiki i baby* implies that members of the Leftist deviation in the 1920s – particularly Trotsky, Zinoviev and Kamenev – were responsible for the policy of collectivisation, and that local officials, especially a Jew and a Tartar, behaved with excessive zeal until Stalin's moderate article 'Dizzy with Success' (1930) put an end to their ruthless activities. Mozhaev demonstrates little knowledge of Western scholarly disputes about the cause of the grain crisis of 1927–8 and the viability, or otherwise, of NEP. The eminent economic historian Academician Danilov has challenged Mozhaev's somewhat disingenuous interpretation of collectivisation,[47] with its nationalistic, partially anti-Semitic overtones (Mozhaev's views are, however, by no means as extreme as those of Belov in *Kanuny).* Rybakov's *1935-yi i drugie gody* suggests that ten million peasants were dekulakised, and estimates the total number of deaths during collectivisation and the famine as thirteen million. These are still extremely controversial issues in the West; such high figures have repeatedly been challenged by Stephen Wheatcroft and others, and have recently been called into question by information from Soviet archives which supports a much lower excess mortality figure of three to four million or, at most, four to five million during the years 1929–34.[48]

Although the debate is by no means over, Rybakov may be guilty of contributing to the popularisation of a new myth in the USSR at a time when the high estimates of Solzhenitsyn, Conquest and Medvedev have been questioned by Western scholars.

HISTORICAL FICTION AND POLITICAL DEBATE

Historical fiction and the critical responses it has engendered have played an important role in political and historical debate in the Gorbachev era. This subject cannot be examined in detail here, but two prominent examples are *Deti Arbata,* which initiated a heated debate about Stalinism and the origins of the Terror, and Shatrov's *Dal'she, dal'she, dal'she!,* which sparked off a discussion about the relationship between Lenin and Stalin. Works on historical themes have also been used in contemporary debates to support certain political viewpoints, either in defence of *perestroika* or of nationalism.[49] Many denouncers of Stalinism are Jewish (for example, the writers Rybakov and Shatrov, and Korotych and Baklanov, the editors of the liberal journals *Ogonek* and *Znamia*, respectively), so they are regarded as suspect by members of the Russian nationalist movement, particularly by the extremists in Pamiat. Although most critical responses to Rybakov's *Deti Arbata* and Shatrov's play have been positive, some neo-Stalinists threatened to denounce Rybakov to the KGB;[50] and Shatrov's *Dal'she, dal'she, dal'she!* was attacked as 'irresponsible' by Viktor Afanasyev, the editor of *Pravda*.[51]

ANTI-UTOPIAN LITERATURE

Some great literary works of the past newly published in the Gorbachev era which are not directly, or are only implicitly concerned with Stalinism, have also played a huge, though incalculable part in undermining the whole utopian concept of 'remaking history' which inspired both Lenin and Stalin. 1988 saw the publication after many years of Pasternak's *Doktor Zhivago* (Doctor Zhivago),[52] which concentrates on the experiences of an individual who remains true to himself in a time of historical cataclysm. It contains the statement that 'the remaking of the world' is a triviality in comparison with the individual's experience of nature, love or art (it is worth noting that Pasternak actually uses the word *perestroika!*). Other anti-utopian works like Zamiatin's *My* (We) and Platonov's *Kotlovan* (The Foundation Pit),[53] as well as the newly-published works of émigré writers such as Nabokov and Brodsky, also emphasise the importance of the individual's experience and undermine the great social experiment attempted in the USSR since 1917. Such works venture beyond realistic novels and essays on historical subjects in their defence of the free human spirit and their advocacy of a spiritual dimension beyond both history and ideology.

CONCLUSIONS

Our consideration of contemporary historical fiction raises three important issues: the nature of the relationship between history and fiction in the Gorbachev era; the future of the historical novel in the

USSR; and the political effects of the reassessment of history.

The close link between literature and historiography in the contemporary USSR[54] has had both beneficial and detrimental effects on both literature and the understanding of history. On the one hand, it has considerably widened the subject matter of literature and has introduced a mass readership to crucial questions about Stalinism and the origin of the Terror; on the other hand, it frequently produces a distorted picture of Soviet history, and not all the historical works produced have been of high artistic quality. Somewhat paradoxically, artistic quality and historical accuracy may sometimes come into conflict; for example, Rybakov's *Deti Arbata,* much criticised on artistic grounds, does at least tell a compelling story, and is artistically superior to its sequel, which is arguably more historically accurate. Yet distortion of historical truth, perhaps inevitable in works of fiction, does not matter very much as long as the issues raised by writers are investigated in greater detail by historians (and Soviet historians, initially silent, have since 1988 at last begun to rise to the challenge). Literary investigations of Stalin and Stalinism, whatever their degree of historical accuracy, are in the last resort only fictional, and are no substitute for historical or biographical studies of Stalin. Literature has created new myths and clashing interpretations which can only be resolved by historical scholarship.

How important will literary works on historical subjects be in the future? I would argue that it is no longer enough to raise controversial issues; it is important to write well. Literature is likely to have greater impact if it is of high artistic quality (hence the republication of major works by dead writers and Russian émigrés). Much historical writing in the USSR in recent years – both factual and fictional – has been sensational; perhaps the time has come for a deeper and more sober assessment of the past. Will the works of Soviet historians obviate the need for more historical fiction? One critic has argued that Shatrov's plays have been made to bear too great a historical burden,[55] and another has claimed that by 1989 Soviet society had begun to grow out of Rybakov's novels.[56] Historical fiction may become less important as a genre, but the tradition of treating historical issues in fiction is so deep among Russian writers and so familiar to Russian readers (far more so than in the West) that it is unlikely to disappear altogether, despite the anti-ideological stance of many younger writers.

Since in the USSR the main purpose of recalling the past is to shed light on the present and to attempt to avoid further mistakes in the future, a revaluation of Soviet history will probably continue to be an important theme in literature published in the USSR. However, in the immediate future the Stalin era is likely to become less important as a subject of literature than the fall of tsarism, the Russian revolution and the character and activities of Lenin. Interesting new discussions about the fall of the monarchy and the February and October Revolutions may well be engendered by the publication of Solzhenitsyn's *V kruge pervom* and *Krasnoe koleso*. The critic Alla Latynina has already produced a sensitive, measured response to Solzhenitsyn's work, which recognises his total rejection of the regime established by the Bolshevik Revolution, but is careful to differentiate his ideas from the crude opinions of some extreme Russian nationalists in the USSR, since she expects his views to exert a great influence on contemporary Soviet society.[57]

THE POLITICAL RESULTS OF *GLASNOST'* IN HISTORY

On the one hand, literature and journalistic writing on historical themes have led to many constructive political and economic discussions about the present and future development of the USSR. Writers still possess a privileged position in the USSR as the 'conscience of the nation', so works by Rybakov and Shatrov praising Lenin's NEP have fostered a favourable attitude towards a mixed economic system; while novels by Mozhaev, Antonov and others attacking the dispossession of efficient farmers during collectivisation have promoted the concepts of private and cooperative farming. Moreover, all the recently published works attacking Stalin and Stalinism implicitly warn against the dangers of a return to dictatorship, corruption, terror and an immovable bureaucracy, features characteristic of Brezhnev's 'era of stagnation' as well as of the Stalin era itself.

On the other hand, confronting the past has had some destructive effects on the contemporary USSR (at least, destructive from the point of view of the Soviet leadership). The processes which Gorbachev unleashed – *glasnost'* and the reexamination of Soviet history – have led to much of the current unrest in the USSR. Examining the legacy of the past meant confronting the full horror of what had happened under Stalin, which has involved a deeper investigation of the role of the Party in the Stalin period, a reconsideration of the origins of Stalinism and the role of Lenin, and even a discussion of whether the Bolshevik Revolution should ever have happened at all. If the Party originally hoped to limit the process of historical exploration, after 1987 the flood of works on historical themes and the plurality of voices became so powerful that the Party could no longer control them all, unless it chose to resort to repressive measures. So this process of historical reassessment, initially 'encouraged by the Party, has now far surpassed the Party's original intentions, and has unleashed forces which undermine the legitimacy of the regime and threaten to sweep it away, as has already occurred in Eastern Europe. The reexamination of Stalin and Stalinism has led the Baltic states to reassess the Nazi-Soviet Pact and to express a desire to secede from the USSR; Moldavia wishes to rejoin Romania; and Russian nationalists want to return to the values of the past. Many Soviet people, especially young people, horrified by the revelations of past crimes, now adopt a nihilistic attitude to the Soviet regime, and wish to dismantle what they now perceive as the whole disastrous social experiment initiated in 1917. It is unlikely that Gorbachev predicted all the consequences of his actions – in the cultural field as in many others – and perhaps he now regrets them, but now that the floodgates have been opened, it will be difficult to control the tide of freedom. The amnesty for all the victims of Stalinism announced in August 1990 may reflect Gorbachev's desire to limit the destructive effects of confronting the past and to lay the subject of Stalinism to rest once and for all. It remains to be seen whether writers and editors feel that this welcome decision has also exhausted the need for any further literary works on the subject.

Notes

1. R. W. Davies, *Soviet History in the Gorbachev Revolution* (London, 1989); W. Laqueur, *The Long Road to Freedom: Russia and Glasnost* (London, Sydney and Wellington, 1989), pp. 48–77; A. Nove, *Glasnost in Action: Cultural Renaissance in Russia* (Boston and London, 1989), pp. 15–102; S. Wheatcroft, 'Unleashing the energy of history', *Australian Slavonic and East European Studies*, Vol. 1, no. 1 (1987), pp. 85–132; idem, 'Steadying the Energy of History', ibid., Vol. 1, no. 1 (1987), pp. 57–114.
2. I. Christie, 'The Cinema', in J. Graffy and G. Hosking (eds), *Culture and the Media in the USSR Today* (London, 1989), pp. 44–5.
3. M. Dejevsky, 'Glasnost and the Soviet Press', in ibid., p. 38; Davies, pp. 129–30; G. Hosking, 'At Last an Exorcism', *The Times Literary Supplement*, 9–15 October 1987, pp. 1111–12.

4. E. Ligachev, *Pravda*, 24 March 1987, p. 2; 17 September 1987, p. 2; *Sovietskaia kul'tura*, 7 July 1987, p. 2; V. Chebrikov, *Pravda*, 11 September 1987, p. 3.
5. 'Mr Gorbachev Meets the Writers', transl. R. Sobel, *Detente*, no. 8 (Winter 1987), pp. 11–12.
6. M. S. Gorbachev, 'Ubezhdennost' – opora perestroiki, Vstrecha v TsK KPSS', *Pravda*, 14 February 1987, p. 1.
7. *Literaturnaia gazeta*, 6 May 1987, p. 10.
8. Ibid., p. 7.
9. R. Marsh, *Images of Dictatorship: Portraits of Stalin in Literature* (London and New York, 1989).
10. A. Rybakov, *Deti Arbata*, *Druzhba narodov*, 1987, nos 4–6.
11. M. Shatrov, *Diktatura sovesti*, *Teatr*, 1986, no. 6; *Brestskii mir*, *Novyi mir*, 1987, no. 4; *Dal'she...dal'she...dal'she!*, *Znamia*, 1988, no. 1.
12. A. Zhigulin, *Chernye kamni*, *Znamia*, 1988, nos 7–8.
13. K. Simonov, *Glazami cheloveka moego pokoleniia*, *Znamia*, 1988, nos. 3–5.
14. V. Dudintsev, *Belye odezhdy*, *Neva*, 1987, no. 3, pp. 46–7; the novel is serialised in nos 1–4.
15. B. Mozhaev, *Muzhiki i baby*, *Don*, 1987, nos 1–3; S. Antonov, *Ovragi*, *Druzhba narodov*, 1988, nos 1–2.
16. V. Grossman, *Vse techet*, *Oktiabr'*, 1989, no. 6; V. Tendriakov, *Khleb dlia sobaki*, *Novyi mir*, 1988, no. 3.
17. A. Pristavkin, *Nochevala tuchka zolotaia*, *Znamia*, 1987, nos 3–4.
18. L. Razgon, *Nepridumannoe*, *Iunost'*, 1988, no. 5; A. Rybakov, *Tridtsat' pyatyi i drugie gody*, *Druzhba narodov*, 1988, nos 9–10.
19. *Literaturnaia gazeta*, 29 July 1987, p. 1.
20. *Observer*, 8 November 1987, p. 11.
21. Iu. Afanasyev, 'Unleash the Energy of History', *Soviet Weekly*, 21 February 1987, p. 10.
22. D. Volkogonov, *Triumf i tragediia*, *Oktiabr'*, 1988, 10–12; R. Medvedev, *O Staline i stalinizme*, *Znamia*, 1989, nos 1–4.
23. S. Cohen, *Bukharin: politicheskaia biografiia* (Moscow, 1989); R. Konkvest, *Bol'shoi terror*, *Neva*, 1989, nos 9–12; 1990, nos 1–8, etc.
24. G. Baklanov, *Znamia*, 1986, no. 10, pp. 3–4; Bek's *Novoe naznachenie* was published in *Znamia*, 1986, nos 10–11.
25. G. Popov, 'S tochki zreniia ekonomista (o romane Aleksandra Beka "Novoe naznachenie" ', *Nauka i zhizn'*, 1987, no. 4, pp. 54–65.
26. L. Ionin, '...i vozzovet proshedshee (razmyshleniia sotsiologa o novom fil'me T. Abuladze', *Sotsiologicheskie issledovaniia*, 1987, no. 3, pp. 62–72.
27. A. Akhmatova, *Rekviem*, *Oktiabr'*, 1987, no. 3, pp. 103–5.
28. A. Urban, 'I upalo kamennoe slovo', *Literaturnaia gazeta*, 22 April 1987, p. 4.
29. A. Tvardovskii, *Po pravu pamiati*, *Znamia*, 1987, no. 2; *Novyi mir*, 1987, no. 3.
30. V. Amlinskii, *I opravdan budet kazhdyi chas*, *Iunost'*, 1986, nos 10–11; D. Granin, *Zubr*, *Novyi mir*, 1987, nos 1–2.
31. V. Gerasimov, *Stuk v dver'*, *Oktiabr'*, 1987, no. 2.

32. V. Belov, *Kanuny,* Part 3, *Novyi mir,* 1987, no. 8.
33. Iu. Trifonov, *Ischeznovenie, Druzhba narodov,* 1987, no.1; B. Iampol'-skii, *Moskovskaia ulitsa, Znamia,* 1988, nos 2–3. S Antonov, 'Vas'ka', *Iunost',* 1987, nos 3–4.
34. See Davies, pp. 36–8; Nove, passim.
35. V. Grossman, *Zhizn' i sud'ba, Oktiabr',* 1988, nos 1–4.
36. A. Rybakov, *Tridtsat' pyatyi i drugie gody, Druzhba narodov,* 1988, nos 9–10.
37. See, for example, N. Kuznetsova, 'Pokaianie ili preklonenie?', *Russkaya mysl',* 30 October 1987, pp. 12–14; discussed in Marsh, pp. 95–6.
38. A. Solzhenitsyn, *Arkhipelag Gulag; glavy iz romana, Novyi mir,* 1989, nos 8–11.
39. S. Zalygin, *Novyi mir,* 1989, no. 8, p. 7.
40. The first three parts of Solzhenitsyn's *Krasnoe koleso – Avgust chetyrnadsatogo, Oktiabr' shestnadtsatogo,* and *Mart semnadtsatogo –* were published in 1990 by *Neva, Zvezda* and *Nash sovremennik; Aprel' semnadtsatogo* has been announced for publication by *Novy mir* in 1991.
41. A. Solzhenitsyn, *V kruge pervom, Novyi mir,* 1990, nos 1–4, etc.
42. For a more detailed discussion, see Marsh, pp. 1–10, 142–3, 207–10 and passim.
43. J. W. Turner, 'The Kinds of Historical Fiction: An Essay in Definition and Methodology', *Genre* (Oklahoma), Vol. xii (Fall 1979), p. 342.
44. Ibid., p. 337.
45. For criticism of this episode, see A. Latsis, 'S tochki zreniia sovremennika: zametki o romane *Deti Arbata',* *Izvestiia,* 17 August 1987; J. Barber, 'Children of the Arbat', *Detente,* 1988, no. 11, pp. 9–11.
46. A. Rybakov, *Literaturnaia gazeta,* 19 August 1987, p. 6; A. Solzhenitsyn, 'On the Fragments by Boris Souvarine', in J. Dunlop, R. Haugh and M. Nicholson (eds), *Solzhenitsyn in Exile: Critical Essays and Documentary Materials* (Stanford, 1985), p. 338. On the historical accuracy of Solzhenitsyn's portrait of Stalin in *V kruge pervom,* see Marsh, pp. 135–73.
47. V. Danilov, 'Tret'ia volna', *Voprosy istorii,* 1988, no. 3, pp. 21–4. For a different view, see D. Gillespie, 'History, politics and the Russian peasant: Boris Mozhaev and the collectivisation of agriculture', *Slavonic and East European Review,* Vol. 67, no. 2 (April 1989), p. 203, fn. 29.
48. See, for example, S. Wheatcroft, 'More light on the scale of repression and excess mortality in the Soviet Union in the 1930s', *Soviet Studies,* 42, no. 2 (April 1990), pp. 355–67 (p. 367); A. Nove, 'How many victims in the 1930s?', ibid., p. 370; for a review of the Western literature by a Soviet scholar, see V. Danilov, *Voprosy istorii,* 1988, no. 3, pp. 116–21.
49. On Rybakov's *Deti Arbata,* see *Current Digest of the Soviet Press,* Vol. XXXIX, no. 33 (1987), pp. 1–6, 19–20; no. 40, pp. 11–13; on Shatrov's *Dal'she...dal'she...dal'she!* see ibid., Vol. XL, no. 7 (1988), pp. 11–16; for a Russian nationalist, anti-Semitic attack on Rybakov and Shatrov, see V. Kozhinov, 'Pravda i istina', *Nash sovremennik,* 1988, no. 4, pp. 160–75.
50. See the letters from K. Sidorova, L. Strizhalova, *Literaturnaia gazeta,* 19 August 1987, p. 4.

51. Cited in D. Spring, 'Stalin exits stage left', *The Times Higher Education Supplement*, 12 February 1988, p. 14.
52. B. Pasternak, *Doktor Zhivago, Novyi mir*, 1988, nos 1–4.
53. A. Platonov, *Kotlovan, Novyi mir*, 1987, no. 6. A. Siniavsky's *Sud idet* and *Liubimov*, which also treat this subject, have also recently been published in the USSR: see *Tsena metafory ili Prestuplenie i nakazanie Siniavskogo i Danielia*, compiled by E. Velikanov, ed. L. Eremina (Moscow, 1989), pp. 279–424.
54. See the 'round-table' discussions on the relationship between history and fiction, *Voprosy istorii*, 1988, no. 3, pp. 3–57; *Voprosy istorii*, 1988, no. 6, pp. 3–114.
55. J. Shapiro, 'Shatrov and his critics: on the debate about *Dal'she...dal'she...dal'she!*', unpublished paper presented to Soviet Industrialization Project Seminar, CREES, Birmingham, May 1988, p. 9.
56. A. Latynina, *Literaturnaia gazeta*, 14 December 1988, p. 4.
57. A. Latynina, 'Solzhenitsyn i my', *Novyi mir*, 1990, no. 1, pp. 241–58.

7 Village Prose: Chauvinism, Nationalism, or Nostalgia?
Kathleen Parthé

> 'See what **your** nihilists are doing!
> They're setting Petersburg on fire!'
> (An acquaintance of Turgenev[1])

> And what we said of it became
> A part of what it is...
> (Wallace Stevens)

One of the thorniest critical debates about the legacy of Russian village prose at the end of the 1980s had to do with the relationship between rural literature and the rise of extreme Russian nationalist groups, especially Pamyat. Such actions as the public expression by several erstwhile *derevenshchiki* of affinity with some of Pamyat's ideas, the way some of these same writers wielded power in the RSFSR Writers' Union, and the signing – along with many urban writers – of collective letters of a generally xenophobic and specifically anti-Semitic character have led to a linking both in the USSR and the West of village prose with chauvinism. Among the contemporary rereadings of post-revolutionary works and movements is the rereading of *derevenskaia proza* as a 'seedbed' for chauvinism. To a certain extent, this view has replaced previous assessments of the same literature as being primarily nationalistic or just nostalgic. My chapter will attempt to untangle this complex situation first by defining this literary movement, and then by distinguishing the legacy of canonical village prose from the activities of people who at one time wrote this type of literature, and from literary critics and ideologues who have adapted metaphors from village prose for their own uses.

Russian village prose began in the 1950s and lasted as a coherent literary movement until the late 1970s. The commonly accepted date for the move towards a new type of rural literature is 1952, when the first instalment of Valentin Ovechkin's 'District Routine' appeared; the conventional date for the beginning of the movement's break-up is 1976 when Valentin Rasputin's *Proshchanie s Materoi* (Farewell to Matyora) was published.[2]

Village prose has most often been defined as a literature that began with articles critical of the way collective farms were being managed and which developed into an insider's view of rural life not just as it was changing in the postwar period but as it used to be before the war, before collectivisation, even before the Revolution. Theme-based definitions of village prose (that it is a literature about: the postwar village, the environment, the rural/urban split, a search for roots and national values) are not in themselves wrong, but they simply do not capture enough of the important qualities of this material, and give little indication of the crucial ways in which it was a force for aesthetic as well as ideological renewal in Russian literature. A number of critics have suggested that a more comprehensive approach to the new rural literature would involve the drawing up of a 'system of coordinates' comprising a 'code of reading' or a semiotic.[3]

Village prose can be contrasted at almost every point with socialist-realist kolkhoz literature, and indeed, contrast (between old/new, endings/beginnings, old age/youth, submitting to nature/ruling nature, preservation/destruction, local/national, spiritual/material, continuity/revolution, past/present, and hand/machine) is used in both these types of rural literature as a structural principle. In moving along a spectrum from kolkhoz literature to village prose, the positive and negative poles of these contrasting elements are reversed.[4]

The parameters of canonical *derevenskaia proza* are: the centrality of the village, nature, the peasant home and its simple inventory, all that is implied by *rodnoe* (that which is felt to be native and dear), an orientation in time that focuses on the past, memory, nostalgia and childhood, and an interest in and reverence for authentic language. In a given work, of course, there can be a great deal of overlapping – between properties of village prose and war prose, for example, or even between village and urban prose.

Canonical village prose flourished for more than two decades, but by the 1980s it no longer functioned as a viable literary movement; Rasputin's *Farewell to Matyora* seemed to both the author and the majority of Soviet critics to 'logically complete the village theme'.[5] The apocalyptic finale of the work – with fire, flood, and the outside world disappearing in an impenetrable fog, was the strongest possible image for expressing the sense that the traditional village had reached the end of its history. *Farewell to Matyora* may have been the most important work on rural themes in the second half of the 1970s, but it was hardly the only one; Astafyev *(Tsar'-ryba* [Kingfish], Belov (the first parts of *Kanuny* [The Eve] and *Lad* [Harmony]), Abramov *(Dom* [The House]), Mozhaev (the first parts of *Muzhiki i baby* [Peasant Men and Women], and Lichutin ('Babushki i diadushki' [Grandmothers and Uncles] and *Poslednii koldun* [The Last Wizard]) all published major works between the years 1976 and 1980. There was a lively and protracted discussion of village prose primarily in *Literaturnaia gazeta* in 1979 and 1980 as there had been in 1967–8.

The elegiacal period of village prose, centred on memories of a rural childhood, drew to a close. *Derevenskaia proza* went through that period of decline and transformation to which all literary movements are subject. Critics had noticed that village prose was in danger of repeating itself endlessly and sounding as clichéd and predictable as collective-farm literature. One problem was that the popularity of village prose – and the relative ease with which it was published – attracted a large number of epigones as well as very gifted writers. The conventions of village prose began to be the subject of parodies as well as outright criticism.

The years 1980–85 were relatively quiet ones for the village writers, partly due to accidents of fate: for example, the vicious attack on Rasputin in March 1980 and his long recovery period, and the deaths of Kazakov (1982), Abramov (1983) and Tendriakov (1984).[6] Censorship and editorial timidity had hindered the natural evolution of the movement towards franker accounts of wartime in the countryside and the process of collectivisation.

Village prose as a movement was waning: a number of older and young writers – Boris Ekimov and Vladimir Krupin, for example – continued to write on familiar themes, but their work simply did not have the same impact it would have had in the previous two decades. Village prose had experienced the natural fate of all literary movements; also, as a memory-driven 'witness' literature, it could not survive the ageing of the last generation of writers who had known firsthand something of the traditional Russian village.

The works that emerged in the period after 1985 show that village prose as a whole had fragmented, with writers moving in several directions. Along with those writers who continued to write lyrical stories and reminiscences, there were four major developments:

(1) Some writers carried village prose themes into urban settings; new settlements, provincial cities and Moscow became more important than the village itself. The emphasis in such works as Rasputin's

'Pozhar' (The Fire) Astafyev's 'Pechal'nyi detektiv' (A Sad Detective Story), Belov's *Vse vperedi* (Everything Lies Ahead) and Lichutin's *Liubostai* (The Demon) is on the consequences not just of one uprooted person or village, but on the uprooting of the Russian peasantry, who for so long had made up the largest single group in the population. These works are not simply pro-village, they are also anti-city. In fact this new line of works by erstwhile *derevenshchiki* has been called *anti-gorodskaia literatura* (anti-urban literature). In canonical village prose the city was far away, it was exciting and even forbidding for villagers but it was not irredeemably evil and foreign, as it became in the 1980s. The numerous colourful and wise old peasants of village prose have been reduced to a few isolated 'righteous ones' *(pravedniki)* who seem like cranks to their urban neighbours. The 'radiant past' has been replaced by a sense of emptiness in the present and anxiety about the future.

(2) Several rural writers were engaged in finishing long-term projects in the 1980s. Mozhaev and Belov published further volumes of the historical novels they had begun in the 1970s: respectively, *Peasant Men and Women* and *The Eve*. Both writers used more archival material and relied less on personal anecdotes as they concentrated on the events of 1929–30 in the countryside. In the November 1989 issue of *Nash sovremennik* Belov indicated an interest in pursuing the story of collectivisation; under the title 'Nezazhivaiushchaia rana' (The Wound That is Not Healing) he introduced a selection of the letters he received from readers telling him what they or their families experienced during these years of upheaval. This is, of course, reminiscent of the gulag archive that Solzhenitsyn began to amass after the publication of *One Day in the Life of Ivan Denisovich;* we might, then, see long gulag-type volumes on this subject from Belov in the future. Viktor Astafyev published further instalments of his massive rural memoir *Poslednii poklon* (The Final Bow) along with a group of new stories, some of which – especially 'Lovlia peskarei v Gruzii' (Fishing for Gudgeon in Georgia) – aroused a great deal of controversy because of its unflattering remarks about Georgians, among others.

(3) The literature that evolved from village prose, what I call 'post-village prose', was noticeably less lyrical and more publicistic than its predecessor.[7] Rural writers began to speak directly to the public and devote a greater proportion of their time to publicistic and openly political activities. Some of the essays they wrote were primarily ethnographic in character (Rasputin about Siberia, Belov and Lichutin about northern Russia), but they have also spoken as conservative

ideologues, anxious and angry about what they perceive to be the threat to their nation. Readers of such periodicals as *Nash sovremennik* and *Literaturnaia Rossiia* are regularly treated to their ideas and theories.

(4) A final development in the 1980s involving *derevenskaia proza* is the publication of works that were written in the 1960s, but kept in the drawer until recently. These works include Soloukhin's 'Pokhorony Stepanidy Ivanovny' (Stepanida Ivanovna's Funeral) and 'Smekh za levym plechom' (Laughter Behind My Left Shoulder), Tendriakov's trio of rural stories 'Para gnedykh' (A Pair of Bays), 'Khleb dlia sobaki' (Bread for a Dog) and 'Parania' (Paranya), and Abramov's 'Poezdka v proshloe' (A Journey into the Past).[8] These works are wonderfully written, rich accounts of rural life, greatly increasing our estimation of these writers' talents, and, by extension, of the possibilities of village prose; they also give the lie to the widely held assumption that censorship had little effect on village prose during the period of 'stagnation' and that writers were free to publish everything they were capable of writing.

During the years when village prose was a flourishing literary movement, it stimulated a vast body of literary criticism. 'A whole pleiad of critics...entered the literary process with articles about "village prose" and its creators.'[9] While some commentators were interested in a criticism based on aesthetic criteria, for the most part these articles were 'emotional, subjective, or exclusively publicistic in character'.[10] As the *derevenshchiki* evoked the past in elegiac, at times idyllic tones, basing their stories to a large extent on childhood memories supplemented by stories told them by older villagers, they had also raised such issues as the need to use the peasant's labour more efficiently and to compensate it more justly, the importance of preserving examples of traditional rural architecture and other physical aspects of the old village, respect for the rural contribution to the war effort, the need to strengthen spiritual aspects of Russian life weakened by atheism, materialism and urbanisation, the need to find one's roots and the rapidly fading 'memory' of the past, and the importance of protecting the environment from the ravages of progress.

Critics picked up on these extra-literary issues using them for their evaluation of village prose as anything from patriarchal and anti-Soviet to deeply patriotic and necessary for the health of the nation. A whole 'ideological infrastructure' grew up around the new rural literature, 'with critics and journalists supplying the rationale for this new Russophile culture'.[11]

In the late 1970s, just before the rise of Pamyat, the village prose movement, now twenty years old, was seen as a 'moderate element' in the 'spectrum of Russian ethnocentricity'.[12] But mournful evocations of picturesque – but dying – villages were not entirely neutral; at the very least they had 'radical implications' for the Russian people.[13] In the works of the late 1970s mentioned at the beginning of this chapter, there is no Russian chauvinism, but there is the 'potential espousal of the cause of Old Russia'.[14] In Mozhaev's and Belov's books there is increased attention to the fate of the middle peasant during collectivisation; in these works the 'luminous sadness' *(svetlaia pechal')* of canonical village prose is giving way to a darker anger and resentment, which is expressed, among other ways, in some stereotyping of the urban activists who introduced the new rural policies to the villagers.

In works written during the period from the mid-1950s to the end of the 1970s there is a great deal of nostalgia; that is, the reconstruction of the essence of what is basically a 'personally experienced past'.[15] There is a palpable contrast in village prose to the unlived, artificial past of kolkhoz literature. Sociologist Fred Davis has noted that nostalgia is a 'distinctive aesthetic modality' lacking 'a position in objective time' (73,77). He sees the time-perspective as the characteristic that differentiates nostalgia from other forms of consciousness:

> Unlike the 'vivid present' of everyday life – that intersection of clock time and our inner time sense – nostalgia leaps backward into the past to rediscover and revere it. Here present clock time loses much of its relevance, and because the rediscovered past is clothed in beauty, temporal boundaries are extended in imagination well beyond their actual chronological span (80–1).

The frequent ambiguity about exactly when the action of a given rural work is taking place led Geoffrey Hosking to remark that the *derevenshchiki* preferred to depict the village 'not as it was *at the time of writing*, but as it used to be somewhat earlier'.[16]

Nostalgia in literature – when it is not used superficially – can be a complex emotion, even a spiritual quality. It involves a sense of sadness at loss, but a sadness that is leavened by 'radiance' or 'luminousness', what Russians express with the words *svetlost'* and *svetlyi*. The 'radiant past' *(svetloe proshloe)* and 'radiant/luminous sadness' *(svetlaia pechal')* are central to village prose – as they are to other memory-oriented literature.[17] The 'warm glow from the past'

(Davis, 16) is a universal quality of nostalgia.

The sense of time in village prose is slow, cyclic, mostly focused on the patterns of everyday life *(byt)*, and often directed towards the past. Even when the setting is the present, it is in the past that narrator and characters look for roots, beauty, traditions and values. There is a fear that in losing the rural past, Russians will also lose their distinctive identity and their future. The older characters provide a natural access to the past, as do the authors' personal memories of a rural childhood. Individual memories are blended with the national 'memory' of the rapidly vanishing peasant way of life to create works of great intensity.

There is another side to the nostalgia of village prose, another voice of an 'inner dialogue' between a good past and a bad or problematic present (Davis, 15–16). This inner dialogue can break out into the expression of angry, bitter feelings about what seems to have been carelessly and needlessly lost:

> This is what we might call, perhaps, 'black' nostalgia: far from being sentimental, it is an outburst of despair or protest against the wanton murder of the countryside, village, and even town, a lament for the deliberate destruction of beauty.[18]

Village prose provides many examples of this angrier, darker nostalgia that borders on an urgent sense of apocalypse. The urgency, the sense of 'borrowed time' has to do with the rapid, often poorly-planned process of rural transformation, and the destruction of nature in the age of the NTR (scientific-technical revolution) and the GES (hydroelectric station). Realising that they are the last generation to know the ancient patterns of rural life has led the *derevenshchiki* to take their writing very seriously as a legacy to the Russian people.

Nostalgia is the aspect of village prose that has the most universal appeal. Any country that has moved from a predominantly rural life in which subsistence agriculture was the main activity to a more urban, industrialised way of life – with all the losses that implies – has much in common with the Russia depicted in *derevenskaia literatura*. The South of Faulkner's novels, the England of Ronald Blythe and Flora Thompson, and the France of John Berger – not to mention the developing world – are closer to rural Russia than the map might suggest. And the radiant nature-and family-centred world of childhood, the very essence of Russian village prose, is the most personal and universal land of all.

Nationalism is also a part of village prose; in the works of Soloukhin, Astafyev and a number of other writers there are references to ancient

Rus, to the Slavs, and to the Russian homeland or *rodina* and its people, to whom unique qualities are often assigned.[19] But far more important in village prose is regionalism or localism; *rodina* is most commonly used in the sense of *malaia rodina*, 'native region' (e.g. central Russia, the north, Siberia, the Ryazan area). On an even more intimate level it can refer to the village of one's childhood. For instance, in Vladimir Tendriakov's 1974 essay 'Den' na rodine' (A Day in My Native Village), *rodina* is used to mean only one thing, the particular village, Makarovskaia, where Tendriakov was born. The strictly local sense of 'homeland' is further emphasised when Tendriakov mentions that his mother is from the nearby village of Ignashikha, and thus they do not have the same *rodina*.[20] The *rodina* of village prose is part of a whole constellation of words using the root *rod-*, which link land, language, home, renewal, and a bond between the dead, the living and those not yet born. Vladimir Lichutin stresses the importance of an awareness of *rod* (relatedness in time, place and person), calling it *rodovaia pamiat'* (literally, generational or ancestral memory). While these ideas are overtly discussed in Lichutin's essays, they are implied in the works of Rasputin, Astafyev, Belov, Krupin, Abramov and many other writers of rural literature.

There is a multitude of little 'homelands' in Russian village prose, each a microcosm – a miniature, complete universe. While village prose may have reflected or even fuelled the revival of strong Russian nationalist sentiment, it is most often orientated towards one village or region. Village prose turns away from gigantism – the large, impersonal, multinational state whose citizens move freely from one 'territory' to another, or, as officials, from kolkhoz to kolkhoz. Rural writers and critics have spoken about the crucial difference between 'homeland' and 'territory': 'a person living on a territory has no sense of home, of a small or large native land'.[21] These writers speak of something smaller, more authentically and deeply personal and familiar.

If it is true that nostalgia is one of the core elements of Russian village prose, and that nationalism is more often than not present in the sense of a personal *malaia rodina* than of Russia as a whole, how does one account for the perceived connection between extreme Russian nationalism – chauvinism – and *derevenskaia proza*? If chauvinism is not actually located in canonical village prose, where does the sense of linkage originate?

It was said that the rural literature that developed after Stalin's death which focused on the loss of the old ways had a 'deep resonance', 'radical implications', and represented the 'potential espousal of the cause of Old Russia'. Where was this resonance, implication and potential realised? In other words, how does one get from the lyrical description of the traditional village full of old women, birch trees and decrepit peasant houses to the 'disclosure' of a Jewish-Masonic conspiracy to destroy the Russian people?

One place where the link was being made was in the commentary on village prose of the 1960s and 1970s. The rural writers did raise many issues of social, economic and political importance that stimulated extra-literary debate. But while canonical village prose engages these ideas mostly at the level of metaphor, character, setting and dialogue, critics and demagogues used these metaphors as ideological stepping-stones. In the process, the chronotope of the traditional village became what might be called a 'paraliterary space':

> the space of debate, quotation, partisanship, betrayal, reconciliation...not the space of unity, coherence or resolution that we think of as constituting a work of literature... .[22]

In this politicised – at times highly charged – literary context, village prose has been not so much an object of literary-critical study as 'an occasion for argument about the most important contemporary problems'.[23] For instance, when Belov's essays on folk aesthetics *(Harmony)* appeared, only a few critics actually discussed the content of the book; the rest argued over the implications of its idyllic view of traditional rural life.

At first the new rural literature was read as a liberating force for both literature and society – it did, after all, appear in the wake of such dreadfully written and palpably false socialist-realist works as Babaevsky's *Cavalier of the Golden Star* and Nikolaeva's *Harvest*. It seemed to critics reading works that went 'beyond socialist realism' (to use Hosking's term), that because of these bold new stories and essays the collective farms would be better run, peasants would be appreciated, the past – whether in the form of buildings or customs – would be honoured, and the countryside would be protected from uncontrolled development. Then village literature began to be read – both positively and negatively – as a powerful conservative voice. The sparring pitted such conservative figures as Chalmaev, Viacheslav Gorbachev, Kozhinov, Lobanov and Seleznev against an equally committed opposing force (including Starikova, Zolotusskii, Kariakin, and Bocharov) that was disturbed by what they saw as the idealisation of patriarchal Rus.

There were no critics of the stature of Belinsky, Chernyshevsky, Dobroliubov or Pisarev in the post-1953 years, but there were powerful voices in the very large critical establishment. To understand how the literary-critical process transformed village prose, one must look back to the mid-nineteenth century and see how such works as Goncharov's idyllic novel *Oblomov,* Turgenev's narratives of gentry life, and Ostrovsky's play *The Storm* were used by politicised critics for ideological ends. Village prose has been used in much the same way for reactionary purposes.[24]

Along with conservative, even reactionary commentary on village prose, there were a number of other important factors in the rise of a more extreme form of Russian nationalism in the 1980s: a backlash against anti-Russian outbursts by other ethnic groups in the Soviet Union, residual Russian xenophobia, the resentment felt against those who were not only allowed to emigrate but then were also allowed to visit their former homeland, the worsening of the economy (which historically results in the search for a scapegoat), a broadly based anti-urbanism that saw the cities as wickedly 'cosmopolitan', pro-Russian feeling surrounding the celebration of the millenium of Russian Orthodoxy in 1988, the increased opportunities for self-expression afforded by *glasnost',* compounded by the alarming failures of *perestroika,* and, finally, the legacy of official government anti-Zionist propaganda and of urban right-wing underground movements.

The final factor is the one that is least understood or known by those who see the *derevenshchiki* as the chief architects of chauvinism. The samizdat archives of the 1970s include essays whose content is very similar to Shafarevich's 1989 essay 'Russophobia', to the 'Letter of the 74 Russian writers' and to other similar documents of the *glasnost'* years.[25] In fact, the samizdat essays are so extreme in nature that Shafarevich and Solzhenitsyn are accused of being Russophobic agents of Zionism. There is ample evidence of the development of a conservative and xenophobic ideology outside artistic literature in the years before *glasnost'.*

Despite all the non-literary sources of contemporary Russian chauvinism, it would, of course, be inaccurate to say that erstwhile *derevenshchiki* have no links to this phenomenon. Pamyat arose without their direct help, but some rural writers have joined with urban writers such as Yuri Bondarev, Stanislav Kuniaev and other members of the conservative intelligentsia in expressing affinity for a number of the group's ideas and have defended its right to exist. Of the 74 original signatories to the March 1990 'Letter of Russian Writers', at least five (Proskurin, Lichutin, Likhonosov, Rasputin and Krupin) could be classified as present or former rural writers (though the mediocre

Proskurin could hardly be called a *derevenshchik)*. Belov asked to have his name added a few weeks later. This letter defends Pamyat, attacks those whom it sees as trying to carry out a policy of 'genocide' against Russia, and even goes so far as to accuse Jews of complicity in pogroms and the Holocaust. While the opinions expressed in this document have no link to canonical village prose, and the signatories are primarily urban writers and critics, at least five former *derevenshchiki* felt comfortable enough with these ideas to lend their names and their credibility with the public (which in the case of Rasputin is substantial). For those who would see this as a singular occurrence, there are other occasions on which these and other rural writers such as Belov and Astafyev have expressed similar sentiments (Belov primarily during meetings of the Writers' Union of the RSFSR and Astafyev in his infamous response to Natan Eidelman's letters).[26] Whether or not interviews with these writers and reports of their public remarks have always been recorded with complete accuracy, the body of evidence is simply too large to ignore.[27] Their artistic sense has not been matched by political wisdom or by a generosity of spirit towards those whom they identify as 'alien' *(chuzhoi)*.

Evidence of Russian chauvinism has also been observed in some of the works of what can be called 'post-village prose', for example in Astafyev's 'A Sad Detective Story' and 'Fishing for Gudgeon in Georgia', Belov's *Everything Lies Ahead* and *The Critical Year* ('God velikogo pereloma'; this is the continuation of *The Eve)* and Lichutin's *The Demon*. This ranges from negative epithets and characterisation to the foregrounding of the participation of Jews in the collectivisation of the Russian countryside. Literary critics have heard echos of the Avvakum-Gogol-Dostoevsky-Solzhenitsyn rhetorical line in these post-1985 works. Perhaps the most embarrassing of these works – both artistically and ideologically – is Belov's novel *Everything Lies Ahead*, where a Jewish character breaks up a Russian family, mocks Russian bravery in the war, annoys people with his complaints about anti-Semitism, and plans to emigrate to Arkansas with his Russian wife and stepchildren. Other targets of Belov's 'Avvakum-like' indignation are: Freemasons, lesbians, hypnotists, pure-bred dogs, computers, alcohol, rock music, and the very smell of foreigners (their shampoo, their perspiration).[28] These and other similar remarks in some of the works that evolved from village prose complement what was being stated simultaneously by Pamyat and other groups.

The chauvinistic remarks made by several former writers of village prose both in literary works and elsewhere has gained a great deal of attention both in the USSR and the West. 'Third wave' émigré writers and critics have reacted vigorously to this development, but in their well-founded anxiety they have sometimes focused too narrowly on the *derevenshchiki,* who have been termed collectively 'writer–Nazis' by Vasily Aksenov.[29] The appointment of Valentin Rasputin to Gorbachev's council was viewed with alarm in the West by those who do not understand that the author was reluctant to accept, and that he is actually much more moderate in his beliefs than many other prominent nationalists. Nationalist feeling in Russia is not one kind of emotion or political stance; it ranges from the commendable 'cultural ecology' of Dmitrii Likhachev at one end of the spectrum to something close to neo-Nazism at the other end; 'conservative' is also a problematic term.

Were the members of Pamyat nurtured on village prose? Perhaps, but they also read Pushkin, Dostoevsky, and other Russian and Soviet classics. Besides, xenophobia and anti-Semitism have a very long history in Russia and periodic outbreaks are independent of a particular writer or group of writers or type of literature. Take away Astafyev, Belov, Rasputin and all their writings and the results would be just the same; it is important to realise that they began to express an extreme nationalism not only after village prose ended but several years after Pamyat and other likeminded organisations had begun their activities; rather than inspiring chauvinism they seem to have been inspired *by* it.[30] This does not lessen their guilt; it does put their remarks in the larger context of a broad-based, primarily urban movement, whose real leaders and ideologists are not rural writers. The wave of chauvinism that began to be noticed in the late 1980s is the result of many factors, only one of which is nostalgia for the rural past that eventually turned into anger at those thought to be the architects of change.

In answering the question posed by the title of this paper: 'Village prose: chauvinism, nationalism, or nostalgia?' it is helpful to think of the Aksakovs, the nineteenth-century literary family, with a nostalgic father (Sergei), and two sons, one a nationalist (Konstantin), and the other a chauvinist (Ivan). The works of the father Sergei Aksakov, the benignly conservative memoirist of rural childhood, are closest to canonical village prose (indeed he is acknowledged as one of their predecessors). Village prose was very nostalgic, somewhat nationalistic, but only in the use made of it by ideological critics and in the activities of some of its erstwhile writers can it be linked to Russian chauvinism.

We are accustomed to following the evolution of literary style, themes and genres, but are apt to forget that 'codes of reading' change as well. The village prose that seemed an important and valuable development for literature and society from the 1950s through the 1970s – coming as it did in the wake of some of the worst of the collective-farm novels – may be read differently now, its legacy obscured. However, in any thoughtful rereading of the post-Stalinist years, village prose will continue to play a central role for having greatly contributed to loosening the grip of socialist realism and returning Russian literature to its roots, and for having restored some of the dignity and value of the Russian peasants, their traditions and their folklore, that had been lost in the first half of the Soviet period. Whether such erstwhile *derevenshchiki* as Rasputin and Belov return to the lyrical fiction that made them famous, or whether they continue to exercise their – at times pernicious – influence as public figures, such past achievements as *Farewell to Matyora, Borrowed Time, That's How Things Are* and *Harmony* have permanently enriched Russian literature.

Notes

1. This was said to Turgenev by an acquaintance who met him on Nevsky Prospect shortly after the publication of *Fathers and Sons* in the spring of 1862, when the city was plagued by a rash of fires attributed to revolutionaries; quoted by Avrahm Yarmolinsky in *Turgenev. The man, his art and his age* (New York, 1959), p. 204. The Wallace Stevens quotation is from 'A Postcard from the Volcano'.
2. Those who wish – for positive or negative reasons – to see village prose as a highly nationalistic type of literature, tend to push the starting date forward to 1963 when Aleksandr Solzhenitsyn's 'Matryona's home' came out in *Novyi mir*, and extend the date of the disintegration of the movement far into the 1980s. This alternative dating does not withstand rigorous analysis of the movement from an aesthetic, thematic, or even an ideological point of view. For a more complete characterisation and chronology of Russian village prose, see: Kathleen Parthé, *The Radiant Past: Russian village prose from Ovechkin to Rasputin* (forthcoming, Princeton University Press).
3. Several critics have proposed non-thematic approaches to village prose. See Galina Belaia, 'Pol'za intuitsii. Proza 70-kh godov v zhurnal'nykh stat'iakh 1980 goda. Opyt problemnogo obzora', *Literaturnoe obozrenie*, no. 6, 1981, pp. 9–14; and, by the same author, 'O "vnutrennei" i"vneshnei" teme', in her book *Literatura v zerkale kritiki. Sovremennye problemy* (Moscow, 1986), pp. 158, 170–1. See also: Liliia Vil'chek, 'Derevenskaia proza', in *Sovremennaia russkaia sovetskaia proza*, Part

II, ed. A. G. Bocharov and G. A. Belaia (Moscow, 1987), pp. 52–3; and by the same author, 'Vniz po techeniiu derevenskoi prozy', *Voprosy literatury*, 1985, no. 6, pp. 35, 72. Georg Witte warned against seeing the evolution from kolkhoz to village prose as merely a change of themes: see *Die sowjetische Kolkhos- und Dorfprosa der fünfziger und sechziger Jahre. Zur Evolution einer literarischen Unterreihe* (Munich, 1983), p. 1. It has also been said that writers like Rasputin, Abramov and Belov created not merely a style but a 'mode of thought': Peter Vail' and Aleksandr Genis, *Sovremennaia russkaia proza* (Ann Arbor, 1982), p. 93.

4. Witte, p. 15. Georgii Tsvetov lists the following contrasts: 'city-village, new-old, young people-old people, life-death, progress-stagnation' in *Tema derevni v sovremennoi sovetskoi proze* (Leningrad, 1985), p. 26.
5. Vil'chek, 'Vniz po techeniiu...', 72. Rasputin declared that this work represented a turning-point in his creative life as he 'left' the island for life in the new settlements; Valentin Rasputin, 'Ne mog ne prostit'sia s Materoi', *Literaturnaia gazeta*, 16 March 1977; trans. as 'I had to say goodbye to Matera', in *Soviet Studies in Literature*, Vol. 14, no. 3 (Summer 1978), 43. As one critic said while discussing the work of Vladimir Lichutin, 'Everyone knows that "Village Prose" ended approximately in the middle of the seventies' (Vladimir Voronov, ' "Uberegis" ot iskushenii..." O proizvedeniiakh russkoi poezii i prozy, vydvinutykh na Gosudarstvennuiu premiiu SSSR', *Literaturnaia gazeta*, 6 September 1989, p. 4).
6. Shukshin, Dorosh, Ovechkin and Rubtsov died between 1968 and 1974; Solzhenitsyn had left the USSR and in any case no longer wrote about rural Russia.
7. One critic asked pointedly whether the very writers who had helped to rid Russian literature of politics had done so simply in order to make room for their own ideological agenda. A. Khvatov, 'Znaki podlinnosti. Zametki o sovremennoi literature', *Zvezda*, 1987, no. 3, p. 186, see also F. Gilis, 'My pochemu takie-to?', *Neva*, 1985, no. 5, p. 162; and Aleksei Gorshenin, 'Ukhodiashchee i nastaiushchee', *Sibirskie ogni*, 1967, no. 6, p. 154.
8. The Soloukhin works were published respectively in *Novyi mir*, 1987, no. 9 and in *Moskva*, 1989, no. 1. The Tendriakov stories appeared in *Novyi mir*, 1988, no. 3; and the Abramov story came out in *Novyi mir*, 1989, no. 5.
9. A. Petrik,' "Derevenskaia proza": Itogi i perspektivy izucheniia', *Filologicheskie nauki*, 1981, no. 1, p. 66.
10. Petrik, p. 66.
11. George Gibian, 'Reviving Russian nationalism', *The New Leader,* 19 November 1979, pp. 13–14.
12. Catherine Theimer Nepomnyashchy, 'The search for Russian identity in contemporary Soviet Russian literature', *Ethnic Russia in the USSR. The dilemma of dominance,* ed. Edward Allworth (New York, 1980), pp. 95–6; see also George Gibian's comments on this and other articles, 'Comment – beyond Soviet categories of literary ethnocentrism', in the same volume, pp. 98–101.
13. Philippa Lewis, 'Peasant nostalgia in contemporary Russian literature',

Soviet Studies, Vol. XXVII, no. 4 (Oct. 1976), p. 552.
14. Geoffrey Hosking, *Beyond Socialist Realism. Soviet fiction since 'Ivan Denisovich'* (New York, 1980), p. 82.
15. Fred Davis, *Yearning for Yesterday. A sociology of nostalgia* (New York, 1979), pp. 8–10. Further references are indicated in the text.
16. Geoffrey Hosking, 'The Russian peasant discovered: village prose of the 1960's', *Slavic Review*, Vol. 32, no. 4 (Dec. 1973), p. 724, footnote 26.
17. One of the alternative names suggested for village prose was *nostal'-gicheskaia literatura*, 'the literature of nostalgia'; Petrik, pp. 65–8. Abramov insisted that what the rural writers felt towards older peasants and their way of life was not nostalgia, but gratitude; see F. Abramov, 'O khlebe nasushchnom i khlebe dukhovnom', *Sobranie sochinenii v 3-kh tomakh* (Leningrad, 1982), III, p. 631.
18. Richard Coe, *When the Grass was Taller. Autobiography and the experience of childhood* (New Haven, Connecticut, 1984), p. 64.
19. Brodsky described village prose as 'largely unpalatable [with a] strong tendency toward nationalistic self-appreciation'; see Joseph Brodsky, *Less Than One. Selected essays* (New York, 1986) pp. 294–5.
20. Vladimir Tendriakov, 'Den' na rodine', *Nauka i religiia,* 1964, no. 11, p. 44.
21. Tsvetov, p. 28.
22. Rosalind Krauss, 'Poststructuralism and the paraliterary', *The Originality of the Avant-garde and other Modernist Myths* (Cambridge, Massachusetts, 1985), pp. 292–3; as quoted in Catherine R. Stimpson, 'Woolf's room, our project', in *The Future of Literary Theory*, ed. Ralph Cohen (New York, 1989), p. 131.
23. Petrik, p. 66.
24. In this context, Sidney Monas remarked that what he was criticising was 'the ideological place Solzhenitsyn has found for the *derevenshchiki*'. See: 'Sidney Monas replies [to John Dunlop]', *Slavic Review*, Vol. 40, no. 3 (Fall 1981), 463.
25. The samizdat material is discussed in 'The debate over the national renaissance in Russia', Section VI of *The Political, Social and Religious Thought of Russian 'Samizdat' – an anthology*, ed. Mikhail Meerson-Aksenov and Boris Shragin, trans. Nickolas Lupinin (Belmont, Massachusetts, 1977), pp. 345–448; of special interest are Mikhail Agurskii's discussion of 'The intensification of neo-Nazi dangers in the Soviet Union' (pp. 414–19), and the two appendices that follow (pp. 420–48). David Shipler (Moscow bureau chief of *The New York Times* 1977–9) discusses some of these contributors to samizdat in the 1970s in *Russia. Broken idols, solemn dreams* (New York, 1984), pp. 323–46. Igor' Shafarevich's essay 'Russofobia' appeared in two instalments in the June and November 1989 issues of *Nash sovremennik*. The collective letter 'Pis'ma pisatelei Rossii. V Tsentral'nyi komitet KPSS' was published in the 2 March 1990 issue of *Literaturnaia Rossiia*. Although the original letter was signed by 74 people, several hundred more (among them Belov on 23 March 1990) subsequently wrote to *Literaturnaia Rossiia,* expressing their full support for the document and their desire to be considered as signatories.

26. Transcripts of the RSFSR Writers' Union meetings are printed in *Literaturnaia Rossiia;* the Astaf'ev-Eidel'man exchange of letters was circulated in samizdat and then printed in the émigré journal *Kontinent,* 1987, no. 17, pp. 80–7.
27. See, for instance, Valentin Rasputin's remarks to an interviewer from *The New York Times,* in Bill Keller, 'Russian nationalists. Yearning for an iron hand', *The New York Times Magazine,* 28 January 1990, pp. 48, 50. Rasputin later claimed that his remarks had been distorted and mistranslated; see V. Rasputin, 'O moem interv'iu', *Izvestiia,* 14 July 1990. Even Vladimir Soloukhin, who has generally stayed within the bounds of nationalism, has sparred with the anti-Stalinist group Memorial for dating the purges from 1934 and not from 1929 when collectivisation and dekulakisation began; see 'Pochemu ia ne podpisalsia pod tem pis'mom', *Nash sovremennik,* 1988, no. 12, pp. 186–9. Soloukhin expressed sympathy for the urban victims of the purges, whereas other ideologues (e.g. theatre critic Mark Liubomudrov) have blamed prominent Jewish victims of the purges for having earned their terrible fate by 'destroying' Russia. Village prose writers have been included in the parodies of Russian chauvinism by Tatiana Tolstaia *(Ogonek,* 1990, no. 14), Vladimir Voinovich *(The Tribunal* and *The Fur Hat),* and in the pages of *Knizhnoe obozrenie* and *Ogonek.*
28. Vladimir Lakshin, 'Po pravdu govoria: Romany o kotorykh sporiat', *Izvestiia,* 3 and 4 December 1986. Excerpts from this article were translated in *Current Digest of the Soviet Press,* Vol. XXXVIII, no. 51 (21 January 1987), pp. 7–9, 14.
29. Vasilii Aksenov, 'Ne vpolne sentimental'noe puteshestvie', *Novoe russkoe slovo,* 16 March 1990, pp. 10–11; trans. by Moira Ratchford and Josephine Woll in *The New Republic,* 16 April 1990, p. 215. Aksenov sees these writers, under Belov's leadership, as worse than the leaders of Pamyat. His condemnation of the *derevenshchiki* for being members of the Party is somewhat strange, considering that Aksenov and a number of other urban writers came from solid Party families, who suffered during the purges (though not because they had lost faith in communism).
30. Galina Belaia has said that the *derevenshchiki* and Pamyat may seem to have met on the road, but they arrived there from different directions; remarks made at a panel on 'Contemporary Soviet and American fiction: Soviet perspectives', MLA Annual Convention, 29 December 1989, Washington, DC.

8 Brodsky's Poetic Self-portrait
Valentina Polukhina

> Рассматривать других имеешь право,
> лишь хорошенько рассмотрев себя.
>
> Бродский[1]

The theme of the poetic self-portrait is closely tied in with the problem of identifying the author in the body of his work, and unmasking the literary incarnation of his personality, its psychological and physical traits. Traditionally researchers have seen it as involving the complex problem of how far one can justifiably go in equating the author with the voices emanating from his text, whatever one choses to call them – lyrical hero, poetic persona, fictional ego, narrative mask or general lyrical subject.[2] For many researchers the extent of their affinity with the author remains a matter for speculation for, to date, we have found no reliable criteria for establishing the similarities and dissimilarities between the writing 'I' and 'I' in writing.[3]

The mechanism I propose to use in order to elicit information about the poet's self from his text was suggested to me by a remark made by Jerzy Farino: 'if you can make judgements about the [lyrical] subject from the characteristics of his speech then one can make a judgement about the author by studying the features and the functions of his created subject (by answering the questions how and for what purpose this subject has been constructed)'.[4] With no pretension to present a full, three-dimensional interpretation of the poet's personality, this paper attempts to clarify the principles which lie behind and the means used by Brodsky to paint his self-portrait.

If, instead of seeking for doubles, for biographical coincidence between author and lyrical subjects, we concern ourself rather with describing the means used to represent the subjects he has called into existence, with explaining their functions in Brodsky's poetic world, we will discover that the principal distinguishing traits ascribed to the self by the poet are to be found at the point where the aesthetic, poetic, thematic and conceptual levels intersect. If we exclude any one of these levels we run the risk of ending up with a portrait that, even if it is not somewhat distorted, will be by no means a full portrait, for it is precisely at these levels that the form and extent of the poet's presence in his work can be determined. Because the author's presence in a poem is, as a rule, poetically masked, it is expedient for us to begin our search by determining the distance from which his observations are made, and that amounts to determining the distance the author placed between himself and his work.

In any systematic schema of Brodsky's views on art pride of place has to be given to his conception of distancing. This is what he said in one of his essays: 'The ability to distance is a unique thing in general, but in the case of a poet..., it also indicates the scale on which his consciousness is working. In the case of the poet, distancing is not 'one more boundary', it is going beyond the boundary'.[5] In his poetry that principle of 'going beyond the boundary' is also actualised in his self-portraiture: 'This, in essence, is a self-portrait. / A step to the side, out of one's own body' (U:176);[6] 'Thus, simultaneously, one gazes at oneself from out of nowhere' (C:68). That aspect of his aesthetics has been perceptively commented upon by Anatoly Naiman: 'he doesn't just see himself from a detached point of view, he also sees himself through several different sets of eyes: his own; those of the lover he embraces; those of the bird perched upon a branch; those of the worm wriggling in the latter's beak; those of the tea running down someone's throat; those of the empty space occupied by his body just a moment before. And all of these points of view are given equal weight.'[7]

The multiplicity of points of view inevitably engenders a great number of different self-descriptions. The ability of the poet to take 'a step aside, away from his own body', gives rise not just to the simple transformation of self into object under observation, now 'from the point of view of the crow' (C:100), now 'from the point of view of air' (C:90), but also to a transformation of self into 'fleshless observer' (S:235), when he finds an absolutely new point of view – 'the point of view of time' (N:140), the extreme limit of distancing, not just away from one's own body, but away from the universe itself. From the point of view of time, the 'I' is simply annihilated, turns into dust. The poet begins to use the device of *via negativa*, replacing the lyrical subject, and the contingencies of his existence, with negative pronouns and adverbs: 'absolutely nobody' (C:40); 'From nowhere with love'; 'not yours but no-one else's devoted friend' (C:77); 'A winter evening with wine in nowhere' (C:80); 'Draw on the paper a simple circle. / That will be me: nothing within' (U:148).[8] Is this the reason why the reader gets the false impression that there are no self-portraits to be found in Brodsky's poetry?[9]

Here Brodsky obviously puts into practice ideas which he discussed with Evgenii Rein back in the 1960s. He said that the dimensions of lyrical poetry had to be changed because almost always its range 'depends upon the author's field of view. This is wrong. The range of a poem has to be wider, it could be country-wide, continent-wide, or measure up to some abstract notion or other.'[10] In Brodsky's case, the *idée fixe*, as will be demonstrated, is time.

At the poetic level, 'the Greek principle of masks is again in vogue' (O:171). But the very many-sidedness and ambiguity of the masks which the poet uses demands that we find the general principle which lies behind their semantics. Systematically analysing the various ways in which the lyrical subject manifests itself, a definite trend begins to appear, both in the choice he makes of formal structures for his self-portrait and in the material with which he fills out those structures. Some of Brodsky's masks have already been described by other Brodsky scholars, in particular the associations of Brodsky's lyrical subject with mythological and historical characters, such as 'the contemporary Orpheus' (S:207), 'the unknown Hephaestus' (S:233), Theseus (O:92; C:27), Aeneas (O:99), Odysseus (C:23), 'the new Gogol' (O:171), 'the new Dante' (C:9) or Plato (U:8). Professor Loseff writes: 'the serious and almost pious attitude of the poet towards the other Joseph Brodsky expresses his conception of the poet's mission as a votary of the Muse and performer of God's will, whose fate is unravelled in the form of the Christian mystery or of the tragedy of the Titans (Dante)'.[11]

A master of contrast and paradox, Brodsky tries on not only the tunic of Orpheus or mantle of Dante, but also the 'costume of the clown' (N:77): 'I am one of the deaf, bold, gloomy ambassadors / of a second-rate power' (K:58); 'I am a singer of nonsense, superfluous thoughts and broken lines' (U:112). It is no longer 'a mould with a sorrowful gift' (K:61) but a self-portrait painted 'in an ironic key' (N:47), that is far from flattering and goes beyond the bounds of the poetic tradition:[12] 'I am a stepson of a wild power / with a bruised face' (U:93); 'a tired slave – of that breed / that is seen more and more often' (U:95); 'a renegade, son-of-a-bitch, outlawed' (U:161). The external details of his self-description are banal, disparaging, and anti-romantic:

> I, who hide in my mouth
> ruins comparable with those of the Parthenon,
> a spy, a scout, fifth columnist
> of a rotten civilisation – in everyday life
> a professor of rhetoric
>
> (C:28)

> я, прячущий во рту
> развалины почище Парфенона,
> шпион, лазутчик, пятая колонна
> гнилой цивилизации — в быту
> профессор красноречья ...
>
> (Ч:28)

Such a persistent tendency in the poet's depiction of his lyrical persona demonstrates Brodsky's rejection of the time-worn romantic image of the poet. This is confirmed by Brodsky's critical attitude to the traditional lyrical hero in the poetry of his contemporaries. In his afterword to a collection of Kublanovskii's poems he writes: Kublanovskii's lyrical hero lacks that self-disgust which he needs in order to be really convincing'.[13] To be convincing, neutral and objective – these are Brodsky's aesthetic principles. In the way in which he delineates his self-portrait these principles are actualised, not just through a system of derogation, which deserves deeper study on its own account, but also, as Lev Loseff has noted, through being 'underlined by the objective word-image',[14] the most important of which is 'man'. The homeless, nameless 'man in a cloak' (C:40) who appeared in 'Lagoon' trails in his wake a whole host of lexical doublets: 'a man on the veranda with a towel wrapped around his throat' (C:103); 'a man muses on his life like the night about the lamp' (C:107); 'a man in brown / sitting on the veranda' (U:38); 'a man brings with him a dead-end wherever / on the globe he is' (U78); 'a man in a suit eaten by a moth' (U:80); 'a man who has nothing / and, most important, nobody to confess to' (U:84); 'a man differs from himself only by the degree of despair' (U:173).

Such universalisation of the 'I', achieved not by substituting 'we' but by completely identifying with man in general, takes on the character of an archetype, and bears witness to the fact that Brodsky had found the long-sought means of objectifying his own personality. It should be noted in passing that only such a large personality can portray itself with such impersonality. Many self-portraits are built upon the persistent conjunction of the inconspicuousness and the anonymity of man with concrete, prosaic details, some of which are deliberately earthy: 'a man is just an author of a clenched fist' (N:110); 'a passer-by with a creased face' (U:43); 'it's no matter what four-lettered word one calls oneself / a man is always to be overtaken by his own snoring' (U:134). It is also significant that the vocabulary chosen to describe the situations in which this nameless, common man finds himself is wan and colourless.

It is fully in keeping with the spirit of twentieth-century philosophy and literature that Brodsky's lyrical subject should be decentred, fragmented, contradictory. Between the extreme poles of his self-portraiture, such as 'the new Dante' (C:9) and the nameless man who 'sups from the exile's chalice' (S:97) and who 'survives like a fish on the sand' (C:106), there are to be found a vast number of tropes, periphrases and similes substituting for his lyrical subject, and, at first glance, they are endowed with a plethora of heterogeneous meanings. But if we cut a cross-section through the tropic axis we find a quite obdurate primal situation governing the existence of the lyrical subject in his verse:

> Stifling. Even the shadow on the wall, weak as it is,
> repeats the movement of the hand that wipes the forehead's sweat.
> The smell of the old body is stronger than the body's outline.
> The soberness of a thought loses its defined edges. Brain in
> a soup-bone is melting. And there is nobody
> to set the proper focus of your eyes.
>
> (C:105)

> Духота. Даже тень на стене, уж на что слаба,
> повторяет движенье руки, утирающей пот со лба.
> Запах старого тела острей, чем его очертанья. Трезвость
> мысли снижается. Мозг в суповой кости
> тает. И некому навести
> взгляда на резкость.
>
> (Ч:105)

Here anonymity is achieved through fragmentation of the representation of the lyrical subject; to be precise, through the use of synecdoche: hand, forehead, body, thought, brain, skull ('a soup-bone'), eyes. 23 per cent of all Brodsky's tropes depicting the lyrical subject depend on synecdoche and metonymy. The fact that there are a great number of lexical doublets amongst them hints at a link, a unity, in such a dismembered ego's existence, ensuring its semantic stability: 'the body has repented of its passions' (C:24); 'the body in a cloak' (C:42, 112); 'the body scatters its steps on the walk from its crumpled trousers' (C:46); 'the body, frozen, extends a chair. / Resembles a Centaur' (U:20); 'For a homeless body and idle rake, / there is nothing dearer than the sight of ruins' (U:111). As if in an anatomical theatre, the body is dismembered: muscles, larynx, heart, brain, eyes are dissevered, dissected, discarded. This is the lexical key to self-description: 'the mind, diminished by our parting' (K:82); 'eyes, stung by a horizon, weep' (C:23); 'the heart, grown savage, still beats for two' (C:82).

It is precisely this preference for the part over the whole ('we are just a part / of a great unity', N:132) which brings Brodsky closest to being categorised as an impersonal poet because the lyrical 'I' is almost totally squeezed out of his poetry. The technique of *pars pro toto* as a metonymical means of self-portrayal is cultivated by Brodsky throughout the whole of his work: 38 per cent of all similes which play a part in the delineation of his lyrical subject rest upon a metonymic basis:[15] 'And my pupil being blinded by the Fontanka, / I break myself up into a hundred parts. / I put my five fingers over my face. / And in my brain, as in the forest, / the snow crust is settling' (O:136); 'And my consciousness whirls like a propeller / around its own unbending axis' (O:143); 'two thighs are as cold as ice' (K:110); 'and the face with its eyes / spreads out over the pillow like an egg in a frying pan' (N:144). Once more we have a reduplication of the situations in which the lyrical 'I' finds itself: 'in the darkness my whole body is repeating / your features like a mad mirror' (C:77); 'the body rests on its elbow / like moraine out of an iceberg' (C:80) 'Like a fine mirror, the body stands in the darkness: / on its face, in its mind, nothing but ripples' (C:109).

Brodsky further complicates his very idiosyncratic metonymical depiction of the self by using reification as a special type of transformation of semantics in that trope: 'There it is – what I'm talking about: / about the transformation of the body into a naked / thing!' (C:27). No less explicit a reification of his lyrical subject is actualised in the richly alliterated metonymy such as *oskolok* (a splinter, O:95); *otbrosy* (garbage, O:202); *ogryzok* (a stub, U:95); *oblomok* (a fragment, U:173); *obrubok* (a stump, U:180):

> Caesar's stub, an athlete's,
> what's more, a singer's stub
> in a variation on a self-portrait.
>
> (U:95)

> Огрызок цезаря, атлета,
> певца тем паче
> есть вариант автопортрета.
>
> (У:95)

Such metonymical objects as throat, hand, brain, which stand for poetry in Brodsky's work, are depicted in the process of being frozen, turned to stone or to wood: 'my larynx, once wet and damp, hardens now into firm, moribund matter' (C:27); 'In the distance the hand on / the armrest turns to wood. An oaken gleam / covers the bones' joints. The brain / beats like an ice-cube against the edge of a glass' (C:101); 'with a brain hardening like a nut' (C:102).

Since 'any expression of the face is simply a reflection of what the man has gone through in his life', as Brodsky put it,[16] we should try to find a common semantic focus for the heterogeneous analogies used to paint a picture of the lyrical 'I', as seen, for example, in the poem 'Afterword':

> In profile I, too, now can hardly be set
> apart from some wrinkle, domino, patchwork, fig leaf,
> fractions or whole, causes or their effects –
> from all that can be ignored, coveted, stood in fear of.
>
> (U:186)[17]

> Я теперь тоже в профиль, верно, не отличим
> от какой-нибудь латки, складки, трико паяца,
> долей и величин, следствий или причин –
> от того, чего можно не знать, сильно хотеть, бояться.
>
> (У:186)

The analogy of the 'I' with things ('domino, patchwork, fig leaf'), with dust ('you are the worst scoundrel, dust under the fence' U:92),[18] with dryness ('touch me – and you'll touch dry burdock stems' U:187), together with abstract notions ('fractions or whole, causes or their effects') are linked with the motif or mortality and time. What Brodsky writes of Cavafy is relevant here: 'More often than not, the protagonist of these lyric poems is a solitary, ageing person who despises his own features, which have been disfigured by that very time which has altered so many other things that were central to his existence' (L:61).

An early and profound consciousness of the temporality of man's existence ('that's how time will treat me too', S:194; 'I sense the breath of mortal darkness / with every fibre of my being', C:25) has determined the motif of age, of mortality ('It's death we carry within ourselves', S:78; 'Ageing! The body reeks more and more of mortality', C:25) and it is one of the key motifs of Brodsky's poetry. Such an acute sense of mortality has, in Olga Sedakova's opinion, a 'liberating force':

> mortality when a man does not close his eyes to it makes him free of a whole host of things, politics, etc., etc. That vantage point presents one with broad views of the world ('the view of the planet from the Moon', N:114) and of oneself (the self-deprecatory portraits of Brodsky in his verse are also like a view from the Moon), it frees one

from petty pretensions, from grievances, from attachments. It's this which brings Brodsky's poetry close to the poetry of the Middle Ages, of the Baroque, but most of all towards the poetry of Ecclesiastes... .[19]

What places Brodsky somewhat apart from most other poets, even the greatest, is his indomitable urge to 'take everything to its logical conclusion – and further' (M:22). Like Tullius, the hero of his play *Marbles*, Brodsky tries not to let slip his chance of 'finding out what things are going to be like afterwards' (M:60). By attributing to man, to his spiritual and intellectual activities, the characteristics of things, the poet is, as it were, imitating the action of time itself.[20] The theme of time is, by Brodsky's own admission, the central theme of his work: 'As I see it, I write about one thing only: about time, and about what it does to man.'[21] In his poetry this is expressed most clearly in 'Strophes':

> All that we call personal,
> what we pile up, in our sin,
> time, accounting it superfluous,
> as the tide does a pebble,
> grinds it down, now with a gentle stroke,
> now with a cutting blade –
> so as to end up with a Cycladian
> thing, a face with no feature.
>
> (N:109)

> Все что мы звали личным,
> что копили, греша,
> время, считая лишним,
> как прибой с голыша,
> стачивает — то лаской,
> то посредством резца —
> чтобы кончить цикладской
> вещью без черт лица.
>
> (Н:109)

The 'absolutism of thought' (M:22) which he cultivates prompts one to the thought that a thing too, with time, 'loses its profile' and 'having received a name, straightaway / becomes a part of speech' (O:204). Words are not just 'devouring' things (O:205), but are also man, reducing him to the status of a grammatical category: 'What is left of a man is a part / of speech. / A part of speech in general. A part of speech' (C:95). Following this merciless logic, we should not be surprised at his next step, 'the transition from words / to numbers' (U:20), to the sign in general, to the hieroglyph: '...there stands the Wall. / Against its background man is monstrous, dreadful, like a hieroglyph; / like any other indecipherable script' (U:88).

All these tropes bear witness to the poet's deeply thought-out and dangerous game with time which is luring him into a boundless nothingness. Brodsky explains: ' The transformation of man into a thing, into a hieroglyph, into a number – that is a vector into nothingness.'[22] That entry into the realms of pure abstraction is endorsed by his associating the 'I' image with mathematical terminology: 'I am a circle cleaved' (O:184); 'therefore who else but me, a quadrant, invisible and dumb' (K:79) and by the poetic definition of man:

>   his cheek tear-silver flecked,
>   man is his own end
>   and juts forth into time.
>   (C:109)

>   слезой скулу серебря,
>   человек есть конец самого себя
>   и вдается во Время.
>   (Ч:109)

When observations are made 'from the point of view of time' (N:140), man's accepted view of the universe turns out to be incomplete and even defective, change is needed in the principle of relativity which the poet applies to everything without exception: 'of any great faith, / as a rule, only holy relics remain' (O:173); 'of the face, there remains just the mere profile' (K:103); 'of great things, there remain the words of language' (C:109); 'of great love, only a sign of equality remains' (U:18); and finally, 'taking the greater from the lesser – subtracting Time from man – /what you have left over are words, which stands out more distinctly on a white background / than the body is capable of / while it's alive' (U:79). These formulae betray Brodsky's heightened interest in the most extreme existential situations, such as death and orphanhood in both senses, being abandoned by man and by God. They also underline his ethical position, which is that of a stoic:

>   A stoic who knows the truth
>   is only one third of stoic.
>   The dust settles on the table
>   and it won't be wiped off.
>   (N:115)

> Знавший истину стоик —
> стоик только на треть.
> Пыль ложится на столик,
> и ее не стереть.
>
> (H:115)

In Brodsky's work, 'dust' is a metaphor for time: 'dust is the flesh of / time; its flesh and blood' (K:110). Only a one-hundred-per-cent stoic has the courage not just to accept the world (and his self in the world) as it (he) is, but also to make the attempt to 'merge with Time' (M:14). And the more logical his philosophical reasoning is, the more cheerless is the tragic situation of his self. But the stoic in him adds: 'The bleaker things are, for some reason, the simpler' (N:100).

It is precisely at the thematic and conceptual levels of Brodsky's poetic world that it becomes clear that his lyrical subject is involved in all of the speculative meditations upon the themes of life and death, of time and space, of language and faith. Even if it is not made explicit the lyrical 'I' is an integral part of all constituent members of the metaphorical rectangle that the poet draws up: Spirit – Word – Man – Thing. That rectangle stands as a sign for Brodsky's extended journey, not just into the realm of the Spirit, but also in the opposite direction, 'into that "nowhere" in which the thought can linger, but the pupil can't' (C:43). Brodsky's universal range of thought allows him to give equal weight to all four categories in his rectangle and by that means construct a new system of analogies and oppositions. The traditional type of semantic transformation, by means of personification, is neutralised by an infusion of its opposite, matter, a transformation into a thing rather than Spirit. All four members of the rectangle are involved by Brodsky in this process. It should be noted here that if the first type of transformation of meaning is motivated by the way man sees the world, and his reflection in it, the second type is dictated by a view of the world and man himself as seen from the most extreme limit of detachment, 'from the point of view of time'. That two-way transformation is, however, more complex than that, since change can be brought about by involving any one of the four categories: any one of them can be made spirit, made man, made thing, or transformed into a sign by means of language.

The word, with the aid of which Brodsky has reorganised the classical triangle (Spirit – Man – Thing) into a rectangle, is drawn into all types of transformation of the real world into the poetic world, and is no less ambiguous than man. Being divine by nature, the word, standing metonymically for language in general, resists the destructive force of time and is capable of defending the poet who is the faithful servant of language:

> It's true, the thicker the deposit
> of black on the page,
> the more indifferent the species is
> to the past, to the emptiness
> in the future.
>
> (N:111)

> Право, чем гуще россыпь
> черного на листе,
> тем безразличней особь
> к прошлому, к пустоте
> в будущем.
>
> (H:111)

This 'species' is one that writes, a man of letters, a modern *scriptor*, and 'the deposit / of black on the page' is simply 'the moulded copy of the sorrowful gift' (K:61). Hence, all the comparisons of the self with the word and its black letters. The poet is just 'a mumbling heap of words' (C:33), 'an instrument of language',[23] who is capable of being 'transformed into the rustle of pen on paper, into the rings, / the noose, the wedges of letters and, because it is slippery, / into commas and full stops' (C:112). 'The all-seeing eye of words' (K:81) possesses prophetic power: 'Of my own – and of any – future – / I've learned from the letter, from its black colour' (U:113). Brodsky's so called 'linguistic' metaphors and similes bear witness to the complete dissolution of the self into the word: 'How did you live in those years?' – 'Like the letter "g" in "ogo".' (C:47). Bearing in mind that the letter 'g' in the Russian interjection 'ogo' is pronounced like the sound [η], which is not represented by a separate letter in the Russian language, the comparison of the disgraced poet with a non-existent letter reflects Brodsky's official status in official Soviet literature, until, that is, his gaining the Nobel Prize. No less striking is the comparison of the self with the last letter of the Russian alphabet – я which also means 'I': 'Like the thirty-third letter, / all my life I am advancing backwards' (N:111). That graphic-synaesthetic image of the lyrical 'I' is interpreted by Professor Loseff as a metaphor for Brodsky's position in relation to Russian literature. The Russian letter я resembles a man moving from right to left, while Russian writing moves in the opposite direction.[24] It is yet another self-portrait of Brodsky in a contemporary poetic setting.

Thanks to his own logic, the poet's relations with the word are not reducible to one single meaning. The word, having entered the metaphorical rectangle, is not only infused with spirit, it is also transformed into an object, a thing: 'But if you look from aside, / then you can, in general, make the remark: / the word is also a thing' (O:205). The word in its role as a sign is subject to the action of time, just as all the other members of the rectangle are, and its future seems to be a very sorry one: 'The distant screech / of the police sirens / is the future of words' (U:152). In other poems Brodsky hints at the annihilation of the word by comparing his own speech with 'the clatter of flies' (U:61).

And so each of the members of his metaphorical rectangle are now equated, now compared with one another. This two-way traffic within the square secures its semantic stability and might be considered as the unifying principle of the associations which run through the entire system of Brodsky's tropes and figures of speech. It also excludes any one entrenched reading of any of the possible oppositions, which would contradict the very nature of poetry, the essence of which lies in the engendering of new meanings which are not equivalent in meaning to the component parts of the poetic structure. Thanks to the inclusion of the word in the metaphorical rectangle each of the terms is seen in a fresh light, and can be described in a new way. At a certain level of abstraction all members of the equation can be replaced by a sign.

It seems to me to be a sound proposition that Brodsky's self-portrait is drawn, to a significant extent, in accordance with his concept of time and language, which allows him to identify his lyrical subject with the most heterogeneous objects and abstract phenomena of the world without losing its unity. Brodsky's self-image is projected on to existence in general and reflects the antinomic nature of man's existence. The sharpness of conflict at the conceptual level has a direct bearing upon the degree of disparity to be found in the delineation of the self-portrait. These disparities are neutralised, to a significant extent, by the equation of spirit and matter, part and whole, high and low, essential and trivial. The regularity of that principle guarantees the semantic unity of the decentred and fragmented 'I', for it is upon that same principle that the whole organic unity of the world is built.

Brodsky's self-portrait is the embodiment of his own sharp-eyed, scrupulous attitude towards himself. 'He was so impudent as to strive to know himself. No more and no less than to know himself' – that is how Brodsky's text on Rembrandt starts.[25] The Socratic dialogue with himself, begun in 'Gorbunov and Goncharov' (O:177–218), continues.

It has merely changed its form. In one of his interviews, Brodsky was asked what life meant for him in exile. He replied: 'It helps you to win a notion of yourself unimpeded. It's not pleasant, but it is a more clinical notion of yourself.'[26] That process of getting to know oneself, a search devoid of either passion or fear, cannot fail to have an impact upon the principles which lie behind his poetic self-portrait: 'absolute calm in the face of absolute tragedy', as Aleksei Parshchikov sees it.[27] It is worth noticing that Brodsky sees Rembrandt's self-portrait in the same way:

> to replace anger, sorrow, hope
> and astonishment comes the mask
> of tranquillity...
> Such he saw his own face
> and concluded that a man is capable
> of bearing any blow of fate.
> That sorrow and joy in equal measure
> suit him – like the robes
> of a tsar or the rags of a beggar.
> He tried them all on and found that all
> he tried turned out just right.

> на смену гневу, горечи, надеждам
> и удивленью приходит маска
> спокойствия...

> Таким он увидал свое лицо
> и заключил, что человек способен
> перенести любой удар судьбы.
> Что горе или радость в равной мере
> ему к лицу — как пышные одежды
> царя и как лохмотья нищеты.
> Он все примерил и нашел, что все,
> что он примерил, оказалось впору.[28]

Brodsky's self-portrait could not have assumed the form I have described if the poet were not fascinated by the realms of language, time and spirit.[29] The universality of Brodsky's world-view leaves its imprint upon the semantics of his self-portraiture. It is of a type never before seen in Russian poetry and it reflects new directions, both in Brodsky's own thought and in Russian poetics in general.

Notes

1. Iosif Brodskii, 'Rembrandt. Oforty', *Stikhotvoreniia i poemy*, ed. V. Maramzin (a 'samizdat' production, Leningrad, 1973–77), Vol. 3, p. 233.
2. W. G. Weststeijn in his articles 'The role of the "I" in Chlebnikov's poetry. (On the typology of the lyrical subject)', *Velimir Chlebnikov (1885–1922). Myth and reality*, ed. W. G. Weststeijn (Amsterdam, 1986), pp. 217–242, and 'Liricheskii sub'ekt v poezii avangarda', *Russian literature*, XXIV, II (1988), pp. 235–57, puts forwards a number of convincing arguments against linking lyrical subject and author too closely together but offers no principles for differentiating between them. See also the interesting works of S. T. Zolian, ' "Ia" poeticheskogo teksta: semantika i progmatica (k probleme liricheskogo geroia)', *Tynianovskii sbornik. Tret'i tynianovskie chteniia* (Riga, 1988), pp. 24–8, and K. G. Petrosov, 'Teoreticheskie i istoriko-literaturnye aspekty izucheniia problemy literaturnogo geroia', *Izvestiia Akademii nauk SSSR, seriia literatury i iazyka*, Vol. 48, 1989, No. 1, pp. 3–16.
3. Jerzy Farino touches upon this problem in his article 'Bul'var, sobaki, topolia i babochki (Razbor odnoi glavy "Okhrannoi gramoty" Pasternaka)', *Studia slavica Hung.* 33/1–4, 1987, pp. 277–301.
4. Jerzy Farino, *Vvedenie v literaturovedenie*, Part II (Katowice, 1980), p. 12.
5. Joseph Brodsky, preface to *Modern Russian Poets on Poetry* (Ann Arbor, 1974), p. 8.
6. The following abbreviations are used for Brodsky's works repeatedly cited in this article:
   S – *Stikhotvoreniia i poemy* (New York, 1965), O – *Ostanovka v pustyne* (New York, 1970), K – *Konets prekrasnoi epokhi* (Ann Arbor, 1977), C – *Chast' rechi* (Ann Arbor, 1977), N – *Novye stansy k Avguste* (Ann Arbor, 1983), U – *Uraniia* (Ann Arbor, 1987), M – *Mramor* (Ann Arbor, 1984), L – *Less Than One* (London, 1986)
7. Anatolii Naiman, 'Velichie poeticheskogo zamysla', *Russkaia mysl'*, 25 May 1990, *Spetsial'noe prilozhenie*, p. iii.
8. In Brodsky, the use of negation for a definition of the self is also connected with the theme of exile. Lev Loseff writes: 'There is no doubt that in Brodsky's mythopoesis Nobody is not just a pronoun, it is also a name. Odysseus calls himself "Nobody" to escape punishment by Polyphemus whom he has blinded.' 'Rodina i chuzhbina u Brodskogo', a paper given to the International Conference 'Under Eastern Eyes: the Depiction of Western Life in the Work of Russian Writers of the Third Wave of Emigration', 19–21 September 1989, University of London.
9. One cannot disagree with Professor G. Nivat when he says that Brodsky's poetry 'shuns the pronoun "I" '. See his article 'Kvadrat v kotoryi vpisan krug vechnosti', *Literaturnoe prilozhenie*, no. 7, p. 1, of *Russkaia mysl'*, 11 November 1988. Dealing with the same subject, Professor Loseff *à propos* of the theme 'Motherland and foreign land in Brodsky' says: 'What is characteristic for these works is how rarely the pronoun

"I" appears. Where one would expect to find it one finds impersonal, indefinite constructions such as: "One can live here and forget about the calendar", "When one sleeps here", or "it is impossible to live, without brandishing a fist", etc.' ('Rodina i chuzhbina u Brodskogo'). However, this does not mean that in his poetry 'there is no self-portrait, no relation with the self', as S. A. Lurye contends. That terrifying octopus, the giant squid which appears in 'The New Jules Verne' and which Lurye mentions, is nothing but an ideogram of the author's name: 'Os'minog (sokrashchenno – Osia) karaet zhestokoserdie / i gordyniu, votsarivshiesia na zemle' (U:45) – 'The Octopus (abbreviated – Osia) punishes hard-heartedness / and pride which dominate the earth'. It is also significant that upon meeting the poet Ol'ga Sedakova in Venice in December 1989 the first thing Brodsky said was, 'We've all got a bit of monster in us, haven't we?' (from a private letter to the author). The manuscript of S. A. Lurye's paper, presented to an audience at the Theatre Museum in Leningrad on 6 May 1988, was given to me by Era Korobova.

10. Evgenii Rein, in 'Russian poetry's last outstanding innovator', an interview given to the author for her collection: *Brodsky Through the Eyes of His Contemporaries* (Macmillan, in preparation).
11. A. Loseff, 'Niotkuda s liubov'iu... Zametki o stikhakh Iosifa Brodskogo', *Kontinent*, 1977, no. 14, p. 309.
12. In the footnotes to his commentaries on 'the new realism in poetry' in 'Twenty Sonnets to Mary Queen of Scots' Loseff remarks: 'our author artfully does not don the cynic mask, which would be fully in keeping with poetry, acceptable, familiar, but that of a vulgarian, which is, according to the ruling canons of poetry, intolerable' ('Niotkuda s liubov'iu...'). E. Rein sees here one more 'even more subtle layer' that is 'an attempt to break with the notorious romantic pose which Russian poets have favoured, one which elevated them above the crowd...'. (From the above-cited interview with E. Rein).
13. Iosif Brodskii, 'Posleslovie k knige' Yu. Kublanovskogo *S poslednim solnstem* (Paris, 1983), p. 364.
14. Lev Loseff, 'Rodina i chuzhbina u Brodskogo'. In Rein's opinion, it even smacks of something completely new: not to be outside, not 'to shepherd the people', as Gumilev put it, not a lesson read from the lectern or pulpit, but complete fusion with the crowd' (Rein, interview).
15. For a more detailed account of Brodsky's similes, their structure, semantics and conceptual functions, see my article 'Similarity in disparity' in *Brodsky's Poetics and Aesthetics*, eds L. Loseff and V. Polukhina (London, 1990), pp. 150–75.
16. Iosif Brodskii, 'Rembrandt. Oforty'.
17. Translated by Jamely Gambrell; Joseph Brodsky, *To Urania: Selected Poems 1965–1985* (London, 1988), p. 117.
18. In Krivulin's opinion, Brodsky's metaphor 'dust under the fence' is 'a metaphor of Anna Akhmatova's which he stretches as far as it will go': 'If you only knew from what sort of trash / poetry grows without any shame, / like *the yellow dandelion by the fence,* / like the burdock, or the goosefoot'. Krivulin, interviewed by the author for her collection *Brodsky Through the Eyes of his Contemporaries*.

19. Ol'ga Sedakova, 'A rare independence', an interview for the collection *Brodsky Through the Eyes of His Contemporaries*.
20. Rein considers that Brodsky's 'persistent references to tooth decay, to ageing flesh, to hair loss' is 'a merging of the self with everything that time destroys, with everything that dies with the flesh' (Rein, interview).
21. From an unpublished interview of mine with Brodsky, 10 April 1980. Brodsky persistently singles out that major theme of his in other interviews as well. 'The fact is that what I'm interested in, what I've always been interested in (it's just that earlier I wasn't fully conscious of it myself) is time and the effect it has on man, how it changes him, how it grinds him down, that is, real time in extension. It is, if you like, what happens to a man in the course of his life time, what time does to a man, the way in which it transforms him. On the other hand, it's just a metaphor for what time does, in general, with space, with the world.' (Brodsky, interviewed by John Glad, *Vremia i my*, 1987, no. 97, p. 166.) 'I'm most of all interested in books, and in what happens to man in time. What time does to a man. How it changes his conceptions of values. How time, in the final analysis, makes man like itself.' (Brodsky, interviewed by B. Ezerskaia, *Mastera* (Tenefly, N.Y., 1982), p. 109.
22. From an unpublished interview with the author, 10 March 1980.
23. Joseph Brodsky, 'Perhaps the most precious thing we possess is our language'; Brodsky, interviewed by N. Gorbanevskaia, *Russkaia mysl'*, 3 February 1983, p. 8.
24. From a letter to the author from L. Loseff concerning the article 'Similarity in disparity', 10 August 1988.
25. Iosif Brodskii, 'Rembrandt. Oforty'. From Maramzin's comments we learn that it was really a script intended for a documentary film commissioned by Lennauchfilm. For this reason instead of a title it is given as 'Spoken text. Rembrandt. Etching'. 'The film has been made (the director was Kinarsky), but naturally Brodsky's contribution wasn't used in the final version and he didn't get a kopek.' *Stikhotvoreniya i poemy*, Vol. 3, p. 298.
26. Richard Eder, 'Joseph Brodsky in the US: poet and language in exile', *The New York Times*, 25 March 1980, p. 2.
27. From my interview with Aleksei Parshchikov for the collection *Brodsky Through the Eyes of His Contemporaries*.
28. Iosif Brodskii, 'Rembrandt. Oforty'.
29. For a more detailed account of Brodsky's main themes, see my book *Joseph Brodsky: A Poet for Our Time* (Cambridge, 1989).

Translated from the Russian by Chris Jones and the author.

9 A Matter of (Dis)course: Metafiction in the Works of Daniil Kharms
Graham Roberts

Although Daniil Kharms spent most of his adult life writing independently of any artistic alliance or creed, his name is usually mentioned in connection with the literary group the 'Oberiu' (a distorted acronym of 'Ob'edinenie real'nogo iskusstva', or 'The Association of Real Art').[1] This group, whose official members were Kharms, Igor' Bakhterev, Boria Levin, Konstantin Vaginov, Aleksandr Vvedenskii and Nikolai Zabolotskii, was particularly vociferous in its rejection of literary convention. One of their central claims was that literature in Russia should reflect the significant changes brought about by the October Revolution, principally by reflecting the aesthetic tastes of the growing proletariat. As the group put it in their 'manifesto':

> The momentous revolutionary changes in culture and in life in general, so characteristic of our era, are being held up in the arts by a number of abnormal phenomena. We have not yet fully understood the irrefutable truth that as far as art is concerned the proletariat cannot be satisfied by the ways of the old schools, for their artistic principles go much deeper and undermine the very roots of the old art.
>
> (Kharms, 1974, p. 287)[2]

Hand in hand with this expression of concern for artistic accessibility and social relevance came the vehement attack on the notion that the 'logical' laws governing reality should also apply to art. Describing themselves as 'poety novogo mirooshchushcheniia i novogo iskusstva' ('poets of a new world-view and a new art'), the 'Oberiuty' maintained that their art would supersede conventional literature, which they dismissed wholesale as 'mir, zamusorennyi iazykami mnozhestva gluptsov, zaputannyi v tinu "perezhivanii" i "emotsii" ' ('a world cluttered up by the jabbering of a multitude of fools, and bogged down in the mire of "feelings" and "emotions" ') (Kharms, 1974, pp. 288–9).

The advent of the 1930s, however, saw the dissolution of all 'non-official' literary and artistic groups on the charge that they constituted counter-revolutionary class enemies.[3] Writers such as Kharms had been engaged until that time in a search for new art forms and new modes of writing to translate their equally new world-views; throughout the decade which was to follow they were, with increasing urgency, to ask themselves 'how to write?' in order to answer the much more tangible question 'how to live?'.

One solution which Kharms appears to have tried (although there are those who argue that he was merely giving free and playful expression to his 'childlike' imagination)[4] was to turn to children's literature. Indeed, it is as a children's writer that the Soviet literary establishment – not to mention thousands of Soviet children – have, until recently at least, preferred to remember Kharms. During these trying years, however, Kharms continued to write material not intended for children's journals – not intended, perhaps, for any reader other than himself. In these poems and short prose pieces he never stopped asking questions of a metafictional nature.[5] Not only do such questions reflect Kharms's precarious position in a society profoundly suspicious of the kind of eccentric individuality which motivated him; they also imply a rejection of empiricist models of thought, language and reality, and all discursive practices underpinned by them. These questions concern the writing process, as both a textual and a social enterprise, and they left an indelible mark on the work – verse, prose and drama – which Kharms produced over fifteen long and frequently 'absurd' years. Kharms's metafiction emerges at the intersection of writer, language, reality and reader, and this chapter is an attempt both to examine these points of intersection, and to analyse their ramifications for the theory – and practice – of writing.

A significant element in Kharms's metafictional inquiry is the subversive attitude towards various forms of authority manifest in the production of text and textual meaning. In some works, Kharms mocks the very notion of 'Literature' as 'high' art, worthy of special reverence. As Loshkin prepares to talk about drama in 'O drame' (On Drama), for instance, his interlocutors all take their hats off, in an ironic gesture of exaggerated respect.[6] Much more frequently, however, Kharms turns his parodic gaze not to the concept of 'Literature' in general, but to specific genres. Although a number of his texts take their title from a certain genre or discursive mode, none of them conforms more than remotely to the relevant generic model. One such work is 'P'esa' (A Play), which is not, as might be expected, a play, but actually constitutes a brief monologue by a man whose wife has just left him, and who consoles himself with the thought that he knows the German for 'stomach' (Kharms, 1974, pp. 118–19).[7] Other texts, while they do not have a generically explicit title, are nevertheless modelled on a particular genre or mode of writing. 'Rak' (A Crayfish)[8] is a parody of a fable, for example, while 'Svyaz' ' (The Connection) begins as a letter which is being written primarily, according to its author, in order to preempt its own reply (Kharms, 1988, pp. 500–3).[9]

The generic self-consciousness in 'Skazka' (A Fairy Tale) has a different emphasis, however. For as Vanya tries to write a fairy story, Lenochka rejects every suggestion with the reminder that *takaya skazka uzhe est"* ('there already exists a fairy tale like that one') (Kharms, 1988, p. 275), before proceeding to relate the story in question. Each of Lenochka's narratives, with its proliferation of senseless violence, defeats our generic expectations in a way typical of Kharms. And yet at the same time, there is the suggestion, later to become an obsession in much Western postwar narrative fiction, that originality in art is no longer attainable.

These two ideas – namely the frustration of expectations based on generic models and the denial of the possibility of creative autonomy – are developed most explicitly in *Elizaveta Bam* (Kharms, 1988, pp. 175–205). There are two versions of this play, whose 'absurd' subject-matter concerns the arrest of a woman, Elizaveta Bam, by two men, one of whom she is alleged to have murdered. In the first version, the text is divided into nineteen untitled sections (each of which, rather strangely, is not referred to as a 'scene', but instead as a *'kusok'*, literally 'a piece') of varying length, with each section approximately corresponding to a particular genre. The second, 'scenic' *('stsenicheskii')*, version of the play is sub-divided in the same manner, but with the important distinction that each section is now given a title suggesting the genre to which it 'corresponds'.[10]

At first these sections and their titles conform to more or less recognisable models, as in the first *'kusok'* entitled 'Realisiticheskaia melodrama' (Realistic Melodrama), and the second, headed 'Zhanr realisticheskii, komediinyi' (Realistic Genre, Comic). As the play progresses, however, it becomes increasingly difficult to judge whether or not a particular *'kusok'* conforms to its generic heading. This is either because the two elements which the title contains are not usually associated together (for example, *'kusok'* number seventeen, entitled 'Fiziologicheskii pafos', or 'Physiological Pathos'), or else it is due to the fact that the 'genre' is 'invented' by Kharms, as in 'Kusok chinarskii' (A 'Chinar' Piece), or 'Bytovoi radiks' (Everyday Radiks).[11] And as Jenny Stelleman, in a recent article on Elizaveta Bam[12] has suggested, many of these generic headings are realised in an ironic and unexpected way. Whereas, for example, the title 'Spich' (Speech, '*kusok*' number eleven) may refer to the language of the text (and particularly Ivan Ivanovich's declamation around which the scene is constructed), it may equally well be a pun on the fact that throughout the scene Ivan Ivanovich keeps lighting matches *(spichki)*.

Such generic ambivalence in *Elizaveta Bam,* and the literary self-consciousness which it produces, have two main functions. First, since changes in genre are announced (either on the page or, as Stelleman believes was also the case, on the stage) *before* they take place in the text, they emerge as the cause of the various shifts in context which also occur within the play, rather than their consequence. This suggests that the subject-matter on which the play is constructed, rather than existing independently of, and prior to, the text, is instead largely dependent upon the writer's initial choice of genre. The inauthenticity of realism as 'analysis after the event' is thus exposed. Second, the ironic fulfilment/non-fulfilment of various genre expectations helps not only to undermine the parameters which we, as readers, often place around them, but also to emphasise the extent to which these genres – and the literature they underpin – are essentially contrived. As the title character of 'Rak' puts it, when asked a question by a frog, *'ia ne znaiu, kak tebe na eto otvetit' (...) My zhe - umnye tol'ko v basniakh, kotorye pishet pro nas chelovek'* ('I do not know how to answer your question (...) You see, we are clever only in fables which humans write about us').

As well as problematising various genres – and, indeed, the very concept of 'genre' – Kharms also parodies specific texts within those genres. Indeed, his frequent irreverent allusions to the 'Greats' of Russian – and particularly Petersburg – literary history have resulted in comparisons being made between himself and that textual embodiment of the Russian parodic spirit, Koz'ma Prutkov.[13] One of his earliest works is *Komediia goroda Peterburga* (The Comedy of the City of Petersburg)[14] an 'absurdly' comic piece written in dramatic form and dealing, initially at least, with the arrest of Tsar Nicholas II by the Communists. As Anatolii Vishavskii points out, this 'topsy-turvy' play contains a plethora of parodic references to works by Pushkin, Gogol, Lermontov, Dostoevsky, Bely and Blok, amongst others.[15] In this generically hybrid text (it switches between drama, verse and prose) the Petersburg tradition as a whole is also debunked; the foreboding, phantasmagorical ambience with which it is usually associated is virtually unrecognisable here, as the play resembles an absurd farce, with Nicholas questioned by a *komsomolets* (a member of the

Communist Youth League, or 'Komsomol') as to where it is that tsars usually spit, and Prince Meshcherinskii (a parodic inversion of Dostoevsky's Prince Myshkin) flying in from Switzerland to give his opinion on the proceedings.

Whenever Kharms is parodying particular genres (as in *Elizaveta Bam),* or specific works within a genre (as is the case with *Komediia goroda Peterburga),* the intertextual 'overkill' and the 'surrealist' textual/contextual collage which it engenders means that, as Patricia Waugh puts it, 'not only is Literature as sacred system challenged but also the Artist as inspirational alchemist. Instead, texts/writing is explicitly seen to produce texts/writing' (Waugh, 1984, p. 145).[16] At these moments, the author is no longer at the origin of meaning; instead s/he is seen to be working within a set of cultural 'codes' which can be either adhered to or subverted, but which can never be eliminated.[17] The 'author' with which Kharms presents us in these texts looks forward in some respects to Michel Foucault's definition of this 'figure' as no more than the moment of individualisation in the structuring of discourse.[18] As Margaret Rose points out: 'One of Foucault's theses [...is that] the liberation of art from the mimetic representation of reality has been accompanied by the disappearance of the author as the structurer of representation' (Rose, 1979, p. 124). At the same time, these works themselves resemble to a significant degree that archetypal 'text', as defined by Roland Barthes:

> a text is not a line of words releasing a single 'theological' meaning (the 'message' of the Author-God) but a multi-dimensional space in which a variety of languages, none of them original, blend and clash. The text is a tissue of quotations drawn from the innumerable centres of a culture.[19]

Such a definition is particularly applicable to works like *Elizaveta Bam* and (perhaps even more so) to *Komediia goroda Peterburga.* As Meilakh puts it in his discussion of the former:

> As they are composed of autonomous theatrical moments, albeit underpinned by a scenic plot, these 'theatrical elements' can be regarded ... as containing in condensed form information *about whole layers of culture to which they refer.*
> (Meilakh, 'O "Elizavete Bam" ', p. 175, my emphasis)

If Kharms questions the author's role as the origin of discourse, he also engages in a polemic with the respectful awe with which canonical authors are conventionally regarded. In a verse piece dated January

1935, Kharms complains about the 'slow' and 'predictable' tales of these 'old men':

> Mne starikov medlitel'nyi rasskaz protiven.
> Poka tiaguchee skripit povestvovan'e,
> nachalo frazy v pamyati bledneet,
> i vse, chto budet, napered umu poniatno.

> I hate the slow tale old men tell,
> For while their narrative creaks wearily along,
> the beginning of their sentence is already fading
>   from memory,
> and all that is yet to come has already been
>   grasped by the mind.[20]

Just who these 'old men' might be is not discussed here. Elsewhere, however, Kharms is more specific, complementing his parodic references to the canonical texts of particular authors by 'de-bunking' their canonised image. Pushkin is, of course, traditionally held to be the 'father' of modern Russian literature. Yet he is depicted in 'Anekdoty iz zhizni Pushkina' ('Anecdotes from Pushkin's Life', a text which thereby also parodies a certain mode of biographical writing) as a peasant-fearing half-wit, obsessively hurling stones and ridiculously unable to grow a proper beard. As for his sons, these are presented, not as great authors, but instead as children pathetically incapable of sitting on a chair without falling off it (Kharms, 1988, pp. 392–3). And at a time when the Soviet Communist Party was, or had recently been, exhorting writers to copy Leo Tolstoy, Kharms has the Count appear to one of his characters in a dream in 'Sud'ba zheny professora' (The Fate of the Professor's Wife), in which he holds his chamber-pot out to her, eager to show her its freshly-deposited contents (Kharms, 1988, pp. 328–30).

But if writers can appear ridiculous, they can also be ethically dubious, either because of their moral convictions, or on account of their willingness to compromise their ideals in order to appease a 'higher' authority. The end of the 1920s saw the termination of the NEP experiment, and the dawn of the Stalinist era. The most important consequence of this development, in the world of Soviet literature, was the emergence, and subsequent dominance, of the All-Russian Association of Proletarian Writers (RAPP). The increasingly vehement proscription, by official organs of the Soviet regime, of non-RAPP writers meant that the question of a writer's moral and social responsibility was brought into sharper and sharper focus, often with tragic consequences for those authors who refused to bend to the monologising will of the state. This dilemma is focused upon in 'Mest'' (Vengeance), written in 1930 (the very year in which adverse criticism in the official press had forced the 'Oberiuty' to cease working as a group), where not just one writer, but many (albeit anonymous) writers appear in the text (Kharms, 1988, pp. 92–101). One of the main themes of this work, evoked through the figure of Faust and the dialogue which he conducts with the writers, is that of the artist's conscience. The writers are initially depicted in a very bad light, as they are contrasted with the Apostles. Even Faust himself, that archetypal soul-seller, condemns them. The presence of the pure Apostles serves further to underline their moral entropy and their fear. The writers declare: *'Nebesnaia mudrost' / ot nas daleka. ... My boimsia, my triasemsia'* ('Celestial wisdom / is out of our reach. ... We are afraid, we tremble') (Kharms, 1988, pp. 92–3). When Faust banishes the hapless writers, however, they later return to present the doctor with a new composition, which they describe as *'slov bessmyslennye kuchi'* ('meaningless heaps of words') (Kharms, 1988, p. 100), and this radically changes Faust's opinion of them. The text finishes with a recital of a few of these lines, which Faust appears to like. Yet to the end the writers manifest their moral cowardice, insisting on their desire not to offend and expressing the hope that no one will condemn their work.

The figure of the narrator is, like that of the writer, also deprived of its conventional authority, both textual and moral. Kharms's narrator speaks in anything but the implicitly objective voice characteristic, if not, perhaps, of all 'realist' fiction, then at least of much Russian 'psychological' and 'socialist' realist literature. Kharms frequently leaves the narration of his texts to the kind of unreliable narrator found elsewhere in modernist prose fiction. In 'Zabyl, kak nazyvaetsia' (I Forget What It Was Called) the narrator sets out to tell us the story of the Englishman who could not remember the name of a particular bird. It soon transpires, however, that the narrator too has forgotten, and so, after trying desperately to jog his memory, finally admits defeat and brings his 'narrative' to an abrupt and premature conclusion.[21] In 'Piat' neokonchennykh povestvovanii' ('Five Unfinished Narratives', Kharms, 1988, pp. 498–9), the narrator is unable to prolong any of his narratives for more than a few moments, not because he is forgetful, but rather, so it would seem, because he is simply not sufficiently interested in any of them.

The act of narration also appears in much of Kharms's work as an ideological act, and as such, potentially morally dubious. In making such a claim, Kharms is engaging in a dialectical criticism of the unwritten convention according to which, as Shlomith Rimmon-Kenan puts it, 'the ideology of the narrator-focalizer is usually taken as authoritative, and all other ideologies in the text are evaluated from this "higher" position'.[22] Time and time again, Kharms distances the reader from the narrator's 'problematic value-scheme' (Rimmon-Kenan, 1983, p. 100), as implied by this narrator's attitudes and by his priorities.

At 'best', the Kharmsian narrator appears indifferent to suffering. In 'Vyvalivaiushchiesia starukhi' ('Plummeting Old Women', Kharms, 1988, p. 356), for example, not only does the narrator add nothing to his purely factual account of six tragic fatalities, but he also demonstrates his profound indifference to such suffering by leaving the scene in order to witness the (comparatively banal) presentation of a scarf to an old man. And at the end of his account of a neighbourhood brawl in 'Nachalo khoroshego letnego dnia. (Simfoniia)' (The Start of a Fine Summer's Day. (A Symphony)) all he can find to say is the ironic *'takim obrazom nachalsia khoroshii letnii den' '* ('and thus began a fine summer's day') (Kharms, 1988, p. 394). At worst, however, it is the narrator himself who perpetrates acts of senseless violence and victimisation. Perhaps the most (in)famous example of this in Kharms's *oeuvre* occurs in the profoundly shocking 'Reabilitatsiia' (Rehabilitation).[23] In what must be one of the most gruesome works in the history of Russian literature, Kharms's anti-hero kills one man, kills and then rapes a pregnant woman before decapitating her (still-born) baby, licking up the pools of blood, literally wiping a dog all over the floor, before finally defecating on the corpses. The narrator of this text is just as bloodthirsty in deed as the writer in 'Rytsary' (Knights) is in thought; the latter's sadistic transcription of acts equally bloody is interrupted only when he runs out of ink.[24] At a time when the ruling hierarchy in the Soviet Union was busy extolling the virtues of literary forms underpinned by an apparently objective and morally responsible narrative voice (whether Tolstoy's *Anna Karenina* or Ostrovsky's *How the Steel was Tempered*), Kharms's fiction is particularly subversive.

In texts such as these, the narrator/writer figure has a function similar to that of the *iurodivyi*, or 'holy fool' in medieval Russian literature; in other words, he highlights, albeit exaggeratedly, the profoundly unethical conduct which writing in the Soviet Union of the Stalinist era had come to constitute.[25] The figure of the *iurodivyi* represented a profound moral criticism of his culture, which by his actions or words he revealed to be an 'anti-culture'. As Dmitrii Likhachev and Aleksandr Panchenko put it:

> he criticises his society by revealing the extent to which that society does not conform to the standards set by Christian morality.... By his behaviour the holy fool shows that it is precisely the world of culture which is an unreal world, a world of anti-culture, of hypocrisy and injustice, and one which does not conform to standards of Christian morality.[26]

If the literary canon and the figure(s) of author/narrator are disenfranchised as sources of authority, then the opposite is true of the reader, for the reception process in general is foregrounded by Kharms in a way which underlines the role of the reader in the production both of text and of textual meaning. The most explicit way in which this is achieved by Kharms is the thematisation of such a process by the inscription of a reader-figure in the text. In 'Chetyre illiustratsii togo, kak novaia ideia ogorashivaet cheloveka, k nei ne podgotovlennogo' (Four Illustrations of the Fact That a New Idea Distresses Those Who Are Not Ready For It), the reader's insult serves to question the equation author = authority:

Pisatel': *Ia pisatel'*.
Chitatel': *A po-moemu, ty g...o!*

(*The Writer* : I am a writer.
The Reader: As far as I'm concerned, you're s...t!)
(Kharms, 1988, p. 372)

In *Komediia goroda Peterburga* the reader-figure (this time a '*zritel'* ' or 'spectator') engages in a page-long dialogue with one of the characters, who asks his opinion as to a third character. This is important for its implicit affirmation of the role of the reader not just as judge of character, but, ultimately, as arbiter of textual meaning. Such an affirmation comes first and foremost from the nature of the question posed. Then there is the spectator's reply, '*ishchite, gde khotite*' ('look wherever you want [for the answer]') (Kharms, 1978, p. 94), which, given the plethora of defamiliarisng textual strategies in the play, can be read as a metaphor for interpretive freedom.[27]

As well as being thematised, the reading process is frequently problematised in Kharms's texts. This occurs primarily whenever the reader is obliged, during the act of reading itself, to revise the way in which s/he reads. In 'Fedia Davydovich', for example, Fedia and his wife engage in an apparently trivial, not to say absurd, dispute as to whether he has stolen the butter from the kitchen (he has in fact just popped the whole block into his mouth with a view to selling it). It is only about halfway through the text, however, as Fedia rushes out of the flat to escape his incensed spouse, that the narrator suddenly reveals that his wife cannot chase after him as she is naked (Kharms, 1988, p. 390). As a result of this new information, the reader has consequently to 'repicture' the scene, as it were, to recontextualise, mentally undressing Fedia's wife before the reading process – and the act of communication which it constitutes – can continue successfully.

In texts such as 'Fedia Davydovich' the epistemological and ontological 'gaps' in the diegese[28] can be closed by the reader without too much difficulty. Such closure becomes virtually impossible, however, in a work such as *Elizaveta Bam*, where contextual indeterminacy and instability are pushed to the extreme in a way which runs parallel to, and to a large extent is produced by, the shifts in genre which have already been noted. The reader/spectator is taken from the opening scene, where Petr Nikolaevich and Ivan Ivanovich attempt forcibly to arrest Elizaveta, through a magic show (where the two men become magicians, and Elizaveta and her mother a willing audience), a children's game of 'tag', a pseudo-rustic scene and a quasi-mythical realm before the initial 'plot' is reinstated, and Elizaveta is finally arrested and led away by the two men (one of whom is the person she is alleged to have killed!) (Kharms, 1988, pp. 175–205).

'Fedia Davydovich' is typical of those texts where the reader is made aware of the necessarily linear nature of writing/reading, while *Elizaveta Bam* forces the reader constantly to establish new codes of interpretation, to reformulate concepts such as 'sense' and 'significance'. In these works, and in others like them, there is 'mimesis of process' (where fiction imitates a view of its own linguistic and literary production), rather than, as conventionally, 'mimesis of product' (where fiction imitates an empirical world).[29] As Linda Hutcheon puts it:

> Metafictions...bare the conventions, disrupt the codes that now *have* to be acknowledged. The reader must now accept responsibility for the act of reading, for the act of decoding. ...He must self-consciously establish new codes. ...[The text] no longer seeks to provide just an order and a meaning to be recognized by the reader. It now demands that he be conscious of the work, the actual construction that he too is undertaking, for it is the reader who, in

Ingarden's terms 'concretizes' the work of art and gives it life.

(Hutcheon, 1984, p. 39)

If more than one reference has thus far been made to *Elizaveta Bam*, this is because this play is central to any study of Kharms's metafiction. For it shows that if the writer uses fiction to undermine a host of conventional attitudes towards extradiegetic instances of the literary process (essentially the literary tradition, notions of genre, the 'creativity' and ultimate authority of the writer, and the passivity of the reader), then his metafictional strategies also function on an intradiegetic level. In other words, the world(s) which Kharms depicts, and the characters which people it (them), are subject to textual strategies which are analogous to those which have already been discussed, and thus also raise a series of questions of a metafictional nature.

In much of his work, Kharms questions the notion that not only literary-fictional discourse but discourse of any kind is capable of 'imitating' the 'real' world and its inhabitants. As regards his characters, the fact that almost all of them are given specific names belies the 'anonymity' which they otherwise enjoy, as the narrator rarely allows us even the merest glimpse at their emotions, their thoughts or anything else which might help to define them as human beings. They have all either already lost their individuality, or lose it during the course of the text. In the course of *Elizaveta Bam,* Petr Nikolaevich and Ivan Ivanovich tell the same story from the same point of view, appropriating the same 'I', thereby becoming one and the same person (Kharms, 1988, p. 186). And in 'Zhil-byl chelovek' (There Was Once a Man) a certain Kuznetsov (= Smith!) goes out to buy some wood-glue, only gradually to forget why he left home in the first place and, eventually, who he is. The process of alienation from the self becomes complete, as Kuznetsov tries frantically, and unsuccessfully, to remember who he is:

— *Nu i nu!* — *skazal Kuznetsov, pochesyvaia zatylok.* — *Ia...ia...ia...Kto zhe ia? Nikak ia zabyl, kak menia zovut...Vot tak istoriia! Kak zhe menia zovut? Vasilii Petukhov? Net. Nikolai Sapogov? Net. Pantelei Rysakov? Net. Nu kto zhe ia?*

('Well, well, well', said Kuznetsov, scratching his head. 'I...I...I... Just who am I? I just can't remember my name...How strange! Just what is my name? Vasilii Petukhov? No. Nikolai Sapogov? No. Pantelei Rysakov? No. So who am I then?').[30]

These 'characters' emerge as little more than the 'motivation', in the Formalist sense, for these tales of nonsense and senselessness, thus drawing attention to what Boris Tomashevsky claimed to be their primary function in a text:

> The protagonist is by no means an essential part of the story. The story, as a system of motifs, may dispense entirely with him and his characteristics. The protagonist, rather, is the result of the formation of the story material in a plot. On the one hand, he is a means of stringing motifs together; and on the other, he embodies the motivation which connects the motifs.[31]

In what is by now one of the best-known of all Kharms's works, 'Golubaia Tetrad' No. 10' (Blue Notebook No. 10), it is not the concept of individuality which is questioned, but rather the very existence of the character upon which the text is apparently based. The narrator begins by introducing the reader to a *'ryzhii chelovek'*, or ginger-haired man. In the very first sentence, however, we are told that this man had neither eyes nor ears. And it soon transpires that he had nothing at all – including no ginger hair! The text is thus shown to be constructed around the (apparent) existence of the (actually) non-existent, and, logically, is aborted with an embarrassed apology from the narrator: *'Nichego u nego ne bylo! Tak chto ne poniatno, o kom idet rech'. Uzh luchshe my o nem ne budem bol'she govorit'* ' ('He didn't have anything at all! So it's not at all clear who we are talking about. We'd better not say anything more about him') (Kharms, 1988, p. 353).

Kharms deconstructs the world(s) these characters inhabit just as much as he does the characters themselves. A question-mark is placed against the unity and 'three-dimensionality' of the Kharmsian world, due to the fact that these texts characteristically do not conform to conventional plot models. At times, for example, the plot unexpectedly and irrevocably changes direction. Such is the case in 'Kassirsha' (The Check-Out Girl), where the initial details concerning the mushroom which Masha picks soon appear superfluous, as the story is transformed into an account of her job as a check-out girl in a grocer's shop (even this, it soon transpires, is not central to the 'plot', which ultimately concerns the store manager's attempts to fool his customers into believing that the now dead Masha is in fact alive behind her cash-register!) (Kharms, 1974, pp. 79–82). In other texts, elements of the plot are erased, as in 'Molodoi chelovek, udivivshii storozha' ('A Young Man Who Surprised a Guard', Kharms, 1988, pp. 370–1). The text presents a brief conversation which takes place between a 'guard' and a young man who asks him the way to heaven. What is significant here is that this question and its posing are presented in the text in isolation, without either that which, logically, at least, precedes it or that which comes after it. An in 'Vstrecha' (A Meeting), there is simply no 'plot' at all:

> *Vot odnazhdy odin chelovek poshel na sluzbu, da po doroge vstretil drugogo cheloveka, kotoryi, kupiv pol'skii baton, napravlialsia k sebe vosvoiasi. Vot, sobstvenno, i vse.*
>
> (One day a man went off to work, and on the way he met another man who, having bought some Polish bread, was on his way home.
> That's about all.)
>
> (Kharms, 1988, p. 378)

If the creation of minimalist, episodic and fragmentary worlds in texts such as these is one way in which Kharms problematises conventional notions of diegetic parameters, another is the transcendence of such boundaries, which the writer achieves by blurring the distinction between the intradiegetic and extradiegetic levels of the text. At times, figures who are conventionally inhabitants of the latter of these two worlds cross over into the former. In *Komediia goroda Peterburga*, as has already been mentioned, not only does the spectator appear in the text; so, apparently, does the author, in the person of Obernibesov. This character claims '*ia sozdal mir...ia poet*' ('I created the world...I am a poet') (Kharms, 1978, p. 104), and later on in the play echoes the '*zritel'* ' ('spectator') by giving a judgement on the play's other characters, whom he claims to have created (Kharms, 1978, p. 109). In 'Skazka' the diegetic transgression works in the other direction, as the intradiegetic characters now cross over into our, extradiegetic, world. Here, Lenochka advises Vania that if he wants to read a story about himself he should go out and buy *Chizh*, No. 7, which it so happens was the journal, and edition, in which this story first appeared.[32]

The ironically entitled 'O iavleniiakh i sushchestvovaniiakh No. 2' (Phenomena and Existence, No. 2) contains an example, not of diegetic transgression, but rather of diegetic annihilation. It is not just a character (as in 'Golubaia tetrad' No. 10') which is (de)constructed, but the context *in toto*. The narrator begins by presenting to us Nikolai Ivanovich Serpukhov and his bottle of vodka. As Nikolai is about to take a swig, however, we are told:

> *Teper' prishlo vremia skazat', chto ne tol'ko za spinoi Nikolaia Ivanovicha, no vperedi – tak skazat', pered grud'iu – i voobshche krugom nichego net. Polnoe otsutstvie vsiakogo sushchestvovaniia, ili, kak ostrili kogda-to: otsutstvie vsiakogo prisutstviia.*

(Now the time has come to tell you that not only behind Nikolai Ivanovich's back, but also in front of him – in other words, right in front of his chest – and all around him too, there was nothing at all. There was the total absence of any existence, or, as somebody witty once put it: the absence of any presence.)

(Kharms, 1988, p. 317)

Nikolai, his bottle and all that surround them are deconstructed just as easily as they are constructed.

Such discursive discontinuity has led at least one critic to condemn Kharms for writing texts which 'illustrate the dangers of breaking open the short story and drama too widely' and for causing nothing less than 'the destruction of literature'.[33] On the other hand, it is not uncommon to view literary experimentalism, and particularly the kind in which Kharms was engaged, as constituting a search for what the Russian Formalists called '*literaturnost*' ', or the 'essence of literature'. One of Viktor Shklovsky's most famous pronouncements, and also one of his most important in connection with the Oberiu, is his formulation of the concept of *ostranenie* or 'defamiliarisation' as a quintessential characteristic of art:

> The purpose of art is to impart the sensation of things as they are perceived and not as they are known. The technique of art is to make objects 'unfamiliar', to make forms difficult, to increase the difficulty and length of perception because the process of perception is an aesthetic end in itself and must be prolonged. *Art is a way of experiencing the artfulness of an object; the object is not important.*[34]

As has been seen, the defamiliarising process *(ostranenie)* in Kharms's work largely revolves around the problematising of conventional attitudes towards a whole host of textual 'figures' (which the Formalists referred to as *priemy*, or 'devices'). And the highly unconventional plot models which Kharms uses are examples of 'impeded form' *(zatrudnennaya forma)*. Textual strategies such as these, argued Shklovsky, forced the reader to attend to the whole question of form itself. In this way, Kharms succeeds in undermining conventional attitudes towards the ontological status of literary-fictional discourse, pointing out, as Roman Jakobson puts it, 'that the sign is not identical with its referent'.[35] For, to quote Patricia Waugh:

> To be aware of the sign is thus to be aware of the absence of that to which it apparently refers. ...[The text] thus becomes primarily a

world of words, self-consciously a replacement for, rather than an appurtenance of, the everyday world.

(Waugh, 1984, p. 57)

The Kharmsian universe is very much a 'world of words', and never more so than in a text such as *Elizaveta Bam*. For in this play shifts in context are produced not just, as has already been noted, by considerations of genre, but also, and just as importantly, by the utterances of the characters themselves. The ambience is changed from the melodramatic to the farcical, for example, by Elizaveta telling her two assailants, *'u vas net sovesti'* ('you have no conscience') (Kharms, 1988, p. 177). In many sections of the play, moreover, the context disappears almost entirely, obscured behind the characters' 'poetic' language with its surrealist imagery, zaum'-like verse and quickfire dialogue reminiscent of children's language games (Kharms, 1988, pp. 180, 199 and 202 respectively). This play also presents a 'world of words' in a very literal sense, however, as Ivan Ivanovich, perhaps aware that as a character in a literary-fictional text he is no more 'real' than the *'ryzhii chelovek'* of 'Golubaia tetrad' No. 10' or than Nikolai Ivanovich Serpukhov in 'O iavleniiakh i sushchestvovaniiakh No. 2', declares *'Govoriu, chtoby byt'* ' ('I speak in order to be'; Kharms, 1988, p. 187).

In these and other texts by Kharms, language is 'promoted' within the textual 'system' to the position of what Yuri Tynyanov termed the 'dominant'. As Tynyanov put it, 'a system is not an equal interaction of all elements, but places a group of elements in the foreground – the "dominant" – and thus involves the deformation of the remaining elements'.[36] Furthermore, this 'foregrounding' is achieved in a way which recalls an essential truth concerning all literary-fictional discourse, namely what Patricia Waugh refers to as the 'creation/description paradox'; in her words, 'All literary fiction has to construct a "context" at the same time that it constructs a "text", through entirely *verbal* processes. *Descriptions* of objects in fiction are simultaneously *creations* of that object' (Waugh, 1984, p. 88).

Central to Kharms's metafictional enquiry, then, is the problematisation of the ontological status of literary-fictional discourse. This is perhaps the most important function of the generic indeterminacy and instability in *Elizaveta Bam*, for above all it points to the problematical relationship between language and reality. As Patricia Waugh puts it:

> Each of the parodies of literary styles in th(ese) section(s) presents a direct and problematical relationship between style and content which draws attention to the fact that language is not simply a set of

empty forms filled with meaning, but that it actually dictates and circumscribes what can be said and therefore what can be perceived.
(Waugh, 1984, p. 25)

Language becomes preconstitutive of the world in much the same way as it does in the linguistic philosophy of Ludwig Wittgenstein.[37] The generic headings in *Elizaveta Bam,* the constant foregrounding in the prose texts of the narrator's voice and value scheme, and the closure of many of these works with the emphatic *'vot i vse'* ('that's all') – all these features serve to remind us that we have no immediate *(unmediated)* access to reality, and that, as Wittgenstein puts it: 'One thinks that one is tracing the outline of the thing's nature over and over again, and one is merely tracing round the frame through which we look at it.'[38] More importantly, Kharms, like Wittgenstein, is asking 'What if something *really unheard of* happened?' (Thiher, 1984, p. 33). 'What can one say', as Allen Thiher puts it, paraphrasing Wittgenstein, '[when] language and things go their separate ways?' (Thiher, 1984, p. 33), or when, to quote Kharms, *'rech' svobodnaia ot logicheskikh rusel bezhit po novym putiam, razgranichennaia ot drugikh rechei'* ('a particular discourse, freed from the axes of logic, runs along new paths, cut off from other discourses' ('Sablya' [The Sabre], Kharms, 1988, p. 434)? If, as Wittgenstein argues, 'we live in a world constituted by language games that can only be played as certainties, though future experience could conceivably give them the lie' (Thiher, 1984, p. 29), Kharms's texts show us a world where our language games – and, indeed, our literature – are patently inadequate.

Here as elsewhere, however, Kharms's metafiction points outwards as well as inwards. Writing when he did, Kharms, like so many others, was intensely aware of the very real social effects of any discourse or discursive practice, whether other people's (the state's, or one's neighbour's) or one's own; words literally had the power to 'preconstitute (one's) world' in a very concrete, and frequently tragic, sense. This is nowhere more clearly manifested than in *Elizaveta Bam*. Elizaveta emerges as a victim of discourse in a very real sense; she is arrested on a manifestly trumped-up charge on the strength of her mother's equally absurd denunciation (Kharms, 1988, p. 203). Perhaps surprisingly, the theme of the social nature and effects of language does not recur in Kharms's work of the 1930s until one of his last pieces, 'Vlast' ' (Power), written in 1940. The comic tone which pervades most of this text, as Faol poses a series of ridiculous and largely unanswerable moral questions, is broken at the end, as his 'interlocutor', Myshin, literally pulverises him with just two words:

> – *Khvet!* – *kriknul Myshin, vskakivaia s pola.* – *Sgin'!*
> *I Faol rassypalsia, kak plokhoi sakhar.*

('Shaddup!', shouted Myshin, jumping up off the floor. 'And get out!'
And Faol crumbled, like a pile of bad sugar).

(Kharms, 1988, p. 343)

But if the individual text was considered by Tynyanov and Roman Jakobson to form a 'system' constantly renewing itself, so was the 'text' of literary tradition as a whole. As Roman Jakobson put it: 'Genres which were originally secondary paths, subsidiary variants, now come to the fore, whereas the canonical genres are pushed to the rear.'[39] Many of Kharms's prose texts constitute anecdotes, historically situated in, and therefore particularly relevant to, contemporary Soviet society. They do so, however, in a way which is reminiscent of the minimalist tradition in Russian literature, stretching back through Chekhov and Garshin to Krylov, as well as the much broader, Pan-European folk literature tradition (present, in particular, in the treatment of characters as 'semiotised' textual functions rather than 'mimetic' imitations of 'real' people in the 'real' world).[40] And such 'popular' and 'extra-literary' forms are juxtaposed with more conventional literary modes in texts such as *Elizaveta Bam* and *Komediia goroda Peterburga*. In his discussion of the former, Mikhail Meilakh mentions the inclusion by Kharms of the romance sung by *mamasha* (Elizaveta's 'mummy') on her entrance in the third section, and Ivan Ivanovich's 'nursery rhyme' in section eight. He also alludes to the element of *balagan*, or popular farce, which the play contains, both in the general sense of 'buffoonery', and more specifically as an ancient form of comedy, linked to archaic rituals (Meilakh, 1978, pp. 186 and 245 respectively). Another folkloric element[41] is narrative 'bifurcation', as the plot goes in two directions at once - one 'absurd' (sections two to seventeen), and one 'realist' (sections one, and eighteen to nineteen).[42]

Jakobson also points out, however, that 'changes in the mutual relationship between the individual arts also arise' (Jakobson, 1978, p. 85). Indeed, *Elizaveta Bam* contains significant elements from other art forms, such as the circus,[43] typified when Petr and Ivan 'become' clown-like magicians in the third *kusok*, and music, with the human 'dialogue' punctuated at various times by the sound of a drum, a violin or a piano. By using such forms in *Elizaveta Bam* and elsewhere, Kharms is problematising not only the validity of the rigidly hierarchical distinctions which we tend to make between 'low' and 'high', literary and extra-literary art forms; he is also asking whether conventional genres and art forms are best suited to convey the subject-matter of an age of revolution. As Hugh Maxton puts it, the conclusion to which we, the readers, are pointed, is that 'the great genres, the categories which have marshalled culture for Western *(sic)* humanity these last two thousand years or more, no longer function, or only function in some mutual violation'.[44]

Once again, Kharms's metafiction is characterised by a double thrust, constituting an exploration of the validity of various 'literary' and 'extra-literary' forms of discourse not just in terms of each other, but also in a particular socio-cultural context. This bipolarity, as it were, is particularly characteristic of a tradition usually associated with the novel, namely the 'carnivalesque', as described and analysed by Mikhail Bakhtin.[45] As we have seen, Kharms's works, like carnival literature, display 'a radically new attitude towards the word as the fabric of literature' (Bakhtin, 1972, p. 182), and show us a world where 'laws, rules and constraints which determine the order of everyday, in other words, non-carnival, life, are, for the duration of the carnival, suspended' (Bakhtin, 1972, p. 207), as 'the carnival brings closer, unites, combines and merges the sacred and the profane, the high and the low, the great and the insignificant, the wise and the stupid, and so on' (Bakhtin, 1972, p. 209). Kharms uses his various metafictional strategies less in the modernist attempt to affirm textual closure and 'art-for-art's sake' autonomy, than in order, like Rabelais, to relativise and thereby subvert those discourses dominant in his own society. Just as, in Terry Eagleton's words, carnival 'mocks, materializes and transgresses the metaphysical pieties of the medieval and Renaissance State',[46] so Kharms's work enjoys a similarly dialectical relationship *vis-à-vis* Stalinist ideology, replacing the 'New Soviet Man' with characters, and writers, who are no more than sadistic, mindless buffoons.

And yet Kharms's carnival is perhaps not so much public and utopian, like its Rabelaisian predecessor, as predominantly private and dystopic. On the one hand, *Elizaveta Bam* presents the temporary inversion of the relative social positions of Elizaveta and the two men who arrest her,[47] while a text such as 'Nachalo khoroshego letnego dnia (Simfoniia)' resembles Renaissance carnival by its 'great world-view based on the crowd...which it frees from fear, by bringing the world as close as possible to people, and people as close as possible to each other' (Bakhtin, 1972, p. 273). On the other hand, the Kharmsian character is more often than not an individual profoundly alienated from a society whose mechanisms he fails to understand. And while, as Ann Jefferson reminds us, carnival is 'epitomized by events and activities in which boundaries between bodies, and between bodies and the world, are at their most obscure and eroded: birth, death, copulation, defecation, eating, etc.',[48] these activities rarely take place together in Kharms's work. Indeed, when they do, they are either in the form of relatively private actions ('Reabilitatsiia' or 'Griaznaia lichnost' ' (A Foul Character), with its glutton/murderer anti-hero, Fed'ka (Kharms, 1989, pp. 331–3) or private thoughts, as in 'Menia nazyvaiut kaputsynom' ('They Call Me the Capuchin),[49] where the narrator discusses his sadistic loathing of children.

Whatever the case, these texts serve to question a whole host of conventional presuppositions concerning language, its use, its 'meaning' and its effects – both within the confines of the text and in society as a whole. Like other writers of metafiction, Kharms succeeded in replacing what had become 'a matter of course' with what is 'a matter of discourse'.[50] The 'absurd' and the 'surreal', the nonsensical and the senseless, emerge in his work as the means both to subvert the language of authority and to foreground the authority of language. But these texts, as a result, fell increasingly and inevitably beyond the pale of public 'language games' being played in Kharms's society. Wittgenstein's dismissal of any 'private' language as terminologically impossible was to find a particularly tragic parallel in the Stalinist state's rejection of Kharms's metafictional discourse as ideologically intolerable.

Notes

1. The 'Oberiu' literary manifesto is published in R. Milner–Gulland, ' "Left Art" in Leningrad: The OBERIU Declaration', in *Oxford Slavonic Papers*, New Series, 3 (1970), pp. 65–75, and also in D. Kharms, *Izbrannoe*, ed. G. Gibian (Würzburg, 1974), pp. 287–98. For a summary of the manifesto's main points, see D. Goldstein, 'Zabolotskii and Filonov: The Science of Composition', *Slavic Review*, 33 (1989), pp. 579–91 (particularly pp. 579–81).

    For many years, the 1974 *Izbrannoe* was the fullest collection of Kharms's works in Russian. The official Soviet policy of *glasnost'* led in

1988 to the publication for the first time of a substantial amount of Kharms's 'adult' literature in the Soviet Union: *Polet v nebesa* (Moscow, 1988), edited by A. Aleksandrov. Where possible, subsequent references to works by Kharms will be to this collection and will be indicated in the text as 'Kharms, 1988' with the page reference. (References to works not available in this anthology, but included in Gibian's collection, will be indicated in the text as 'Kharms, 1974', followed by the page reference). Mikhail Meilakh and V. Erl' are currently editing a ten-volume set, to be published in Bremen, and which, it is planned, will contain the complete works. Four volumes from this collection have so far appeared, containing mostly poetry.

2. Unless otherwise indicated, all translations in this chapter are my own.
3. Such a charge was explicitly levelled at the 'Oberiu' group in a fiercely critical article which appeared in the journal *Smena* in April 1930. An indication of the by-now extremely hostile attitude of the Soviet government to artistic experimentation of any kind, this article led directly, and virtually immediately, to the dissolution of the 'Oberiu'. For the full text, see Aleksandr Vvedenskii, *Polnoe sobranie sochinenii*, ed. M. Meilakh, Vol. 2 (Michigan, 1984), pp. 247–9.
4. See A. Gerasimova, 'On tak i ostalsia rebenkom', *Detskaia literatura*, 1988, no. 4, pp. 32–5. Typical of Gerasimova's attitude is her concluding remark: 'For Kharms, childhood was not one element of his existence, but all of it. His contemporaries were right: Kharms got older, but didn't grow up, for in essence he remained a child' (p. 35).
5. It will, I hope, become clear in the course of this chapter that I interpret the term 'metafiction' as referring to a phenomenon which is both textual and social in its ramifications. In other words, I define 'metafiction' as literary-fictional discourse which not only, to quote Patricia Waugh in a recent book, 'lays bare its condition of artifice and thereby explores the problematical relationship between life and fiction', but which also – and this is particularly relevant to Kharms – analyses the dialectical tension between on the one hand the writer, as producer of a certain type of discourse, and on the other his/her society, as the site within which that discourse interrelates with other discourses. See P. Waugh, *Metafiction: The Theory and Practice of Self-Conscious Fiction* (London, 1984), p.5.
6. *Voprosy literatury*, 1987, no. 8, pp. 262–75 (p. 265).
7. Other texts of this kind include *Basnia* ('A Fable', Kharms, 1974, p. 122), *Sonet* ('A Sonnet', Kharms, 1988, pp. 354–6) and *Anekdoty iz zhizni Pushkina* ('Anecdotes from Pushkin's Life', Kharms, 1988, pp. 352–3).
8. The Russian title is my own. The text appears, untitled, in *Sovetskaia kul'tura*, 7 June 1990, p. 10.
9. The writer of the 'letter' thus breaks a number of laws governing successful communication. For a discussion of these laws and of their flouting in experimental literature, see O.G. Revzina and I. I. Revzin, 'Semioticheskii eksperiment na stsene (Narushenie postulata normal'nogo obshcheniia kak dramaturgicheskii priem)', *Trudy po znakovym sistemam*, 5, (1971), pp. 232–54. Ann Shukman has used the Revzins' axioms as a means of approaching Kharms's prose work: 'Toward a Poetics of the

Absurd: The Prose Writings of Daniil Kharms' in *Discontinuous Discourses in Modern Russian Literature*, ed. C. Kelly, M. Makin and D. Shepherd (Basingstoke and London, 1989) pp. 60–72. More and more Kharms scholars, so it would seem, are beginning to examine Kharms's work from the point of view of communication. See J-P Jaccard, 'Daniil Kharms: teatr absurda – real'nyi teatr. Prochtenie p'esy *Elizaveta Bam*', *Russian Literature*, 27 (1990), pp. 21–40.

10. Both versions appear together (although the 'stsenicheskii variant' is, for no apparent reason, reduced to eighteen sections), accompanied by a lengthy introduction by Mikhail Meilakh, in 'O "Elizavete Bam" Daniila Kharmsa', *Stanford Slavic Studies*, 1987, no. 1, pp. 163–246.

11. 'Radiks' was the name of the experimentalist literary group, founded in 1926, of which Kharms and Aleksandr Vvedenskii were both members, and which later evolved into the 'Oberiu'. In his anthology of works by Vvedenskii, Mikhail Meilakh includes an interview with Georgii Katzman, the producer of a 'Radiks' performance, who suggests the significance of the term as part of a search for the 'essence' of theatre:

> '*Radiks' byl zaduman kak 'chistyi teatr', teatr eksperimenta, orientirovannyi ne stol'ko na konechnyi rezul'tat i na zritelia, skol'ko na perezhivanie samini akterami chistogo teatral'nogo deistviia. (Otsiuda, po-vidimomu, i predlozhenie Bakhterevym nazvaniia 'Radiks' – koren' i odnovremenno 'radikal'nyi' teatr).*

> (The term 'Radiks' was intended to mean 'pure theatre', experimental theatre orientated not so much towards the finished product and the audience as towards the feelings of the actors themselves as they took part in activities of a purely theatrical nature (this is apparently what was meant by Bakhterev when he suggested the term 'Radiks' – something which both recaptured the roots of theatre and was itself 'radical').
>
> (Vvedenskii, II, p. 233)

For details of the members and activities of the 'Radiks' group, see I. Bakhterev, 'Kogda my byli molodymi' in *Vospominaniia o N. Zabolotskom*, ed. E. V. Zabolotskaia, A. V. Makedonov and N. N. Zabolotskii (2nd ed., Moscow, 1984), pp. 57–100.

The term *chinarsky* is an adjective formed from the neologism *chinar*, which Kharms and other 'Oberiu' members used to refer to themselves. The origin of this word, which was first coined by Vvedenskii, seems unclear, although one close friend of Kharms and his circle, Ia. S. Druskin, claimed that it came from the Russian *chin*, meaning a 'rank' or an 'official'. See Ia. S. Druskin, 'Chinari', *Avrora*, 1989, no. 6, pp. 103–31, and particularly p. 103.

12. J. Stelleman, 'An analysis of *Elizaveta Bam*', *Russian Literature*, 17 (1985), pp. 319–52.

13. See R. Milner-Gulland, 'Grandsons of Kozma Prutkov: Reflections on Zabolotsky, Oleynikov and their circle', in *Russian and Slavic Literature. Selected Papers in the Humanities from the Banff '74 International*

Conference, ed. R. Freeborn, R. Milner-Gulland and C. A. Ward (Columbus, Ohio, 1974) pp. 313–27.
14. D. Kharms, *Sobranie sochinenii*, ed. M. Meilakh and V. Erl', Vol. 1 (Bremen, 1978), pp. 85–125.
15. See his discussion of the parodic elements of this play, and of Aleksandr Vvedenskii's *Minin i Pozharskii* (Minin and Pozharsky), in 'Tradition in the topsy-turvy world or parody: analysis of two Oberiu plays', *The Slavonic and East European Journal*, 30 (1985), no. 1, pp. 355–66. Ellen Chances analysis Kharms's novella *Starukha* ('The Old Woman') from a similar perspective: 'Daniil Kharms' "Old Woman" Climbs her Family Tree: "Starukha" and the Russian Literary Past', *Russian Literature*, 17 (1985), pp. 353–66.
16. The affinity between Kharms's brand of metafiction and the literary experiments conducted by the French Surrealists is discussed in A. Gallagher's unpublished Ph.D. thesis 'The Surrealist Mode in Twentieth-Century Russian Literature' (University of Kansas, 1975), Chapter 5.
17. The extent to which Kharms was familiar with the views of 'Lef' ('The Left Front of The Arts'), a contemporary group of writers and literary critics working in Moscow at this time, is open to debate. They were proclaiming the irrelevance of the author in the literary process, and, more specifically, in the production of textual meaning, and heralding the age of 'literatura fakta'. Fuller accounts of the group's beliefs are given in an anthology of 'Lef' essays, *Literatura fakta*, ed. N. F. Chuzhak (Moscow, 1929: reprinted Munich, 1972). See in particular Osip Brik, 'Protiv tvorcheskoi lichnosti' (pp. 75–7).
18. This summary of Foucault's attitude towards the 'author' is taken from M. Rose, *Parody/Metafiction: An Analysis of Parody as a Critical Mirror to the Writing and Reception of Fiction* (London, 1979), p. 44. See also Foucault's most famous essay on this subject, published in English as 'What is an Author?' in *Textual Strategies: Perspectives in Post-structuralist Criticism*, ed. J. Harari (London, 1979), pp. 141–60.
19. R. Barthes, 'The Death of the Author', in *Image, Music, Text*, ed. and trans. S. Heath (London, 1977), p. 146.
20. D. Kharms, *Sobranie sochinenii*, Vol. 4 (Bremen, 1988), p. 83.
21. *Iunost'*, 1987, no. 10, p. 94.
22. S. Rimmon-Kenan, *Narrative Fiction: Contemporary Poetics* (London, 1983), p. 81.
23. 'Reabilitatsiia' is contained in D. Kharms, 'Rasskazy' in *Soviet Union / Union Soviétique*, 7 (1980), pp. 228–37 (publication by I. Levin), p. 235.
24. Ibid., p. 234.
25. This is a view similar to that expressed in connection with the *characters* of these texts and the violence which they perpetrate, by Anna Gerasimova in 'OBERIU (Problema smeshnogo)', *Voprosy literatury*, 1988, no. 4, pp. 48–79 (p. 54). See also Anthony Anemone, 'The Anti-World of Daniil Kharms: On The Significance of the Absurd', in *Essays and Materials on Daniil Kharms*, ed. N. Cornwell (forthcoming).
26. D. S. Likhachev and A. M. Panchenko, *Smekhovoi mir drevnei Rusi* (Leningrad, 1976), p. 5.

27. Compare the spectator's comment here with a similarly metafictional outburst in Eugene Ionesco's play *La Cantatrice Chauve* (translated as *The Bald Prima Donna*, London, 1958), when Mrs Martin questions the fire-chief as to the significance of one of his anecdotes:

    Mrs. Martin: Wh-what is the moral?
    Fire-chief: It's for you to discover it!

    (Ionesco, 1958, p. 25)

    For a comparative study of Kharms and Ionesco (and Samuel Beckett), see Jean-Philippe Jaccard's three articles, 'De la réalité du texte. L'absurde chez Daniil Harms', *Cahiers du Monde Russe et Soviétique*, 27 (1985), pp. 269–312; 'Daniil Harms dans le contexte de la littérature russe et européenne', in *Schweizerische Beiträge zum X. Internationalen Slavistenkongress in Sofia, September, 1988*, ed. Peter Brang *(Slavica Helvetica,* 28) (Bern, 1988), pp. 145–69); and 'Daniil Kharms: teatr absurda – real'nyi teatr. Prochtenie p'esy *Elizaveta Bam*' (see note 9 above).
28. The term 'diegese' refers to the spatio-temporal context in which the 'story' is said to take place. 'Intradiegetic' thus signifies the 'world' in which the characters of a text are given as existing, while 'extradiegetic' is used to describe the ontological level on which the act of narration occurs. For a fuller account of these terms see G. Genette, *Figures III* (Paris, 1972), pp. 238–9; partial English translation, *Narrative Discourse* (Oxford, 1980). For the sake of simplicity in this paper, I am extending the 'extradiegetic' realm to include the 'real' world, in which a text is produced and received, although Genette is careful to omit this world from his discussion.
29. The terms are Linda Hutcheon's, and come from her book *Narcissistic Narrative: The Metafictional Paradox* (London, 1984), p. 46.
30. *Russkaya mysl'*, 3 January 1985, p. 8.
31. B. Tomashevskii, *Teoriia literatury* (Moscow and Leningrad, 1931), p. 154. The English translation is taken from B. Tomashevskii, 'Thematics', in *Russian Formalist Criticism: Four Essays*, ed. and trans. L. Lemon and M. Reis (Lincoln, 1965), pp. 61–95 (p. 90).
32. *Chizh* and *Ezh* were the names of children's journals for which Kharms wrote throughout the 1930s. A comprehensive list of Kharms's publications for children is given in J. P. Jaccard, 'Daniil Harms: Bibliographie', *Cahiers du Monde Russe et Soviétique*, XXVI, 3–4 (1985), pp. 493–522 (pp. 499–502).
33. E. Chances, 'Čexov and Xarms: Story/Anti-Story', *Russian Language Journal*, 123–4 (1982), pp. 181–92 (p. 190).
34. V. Shklovskii, 'Iskusstvo kak priem', in *O teorii prozy* (Moscow, 1984), p. 15. The English translation is taken from V. Shklovsky, 'Art as Technique' in Lemon and Reis (eds), 1965, pp. 3–24 (p. 12). The exact nature of the Oberiu – Opoyaz relationship has yet to be explored. The extent to which Kharms was consciously putting Shklovsky's – and the other Formalists' – literary theories into practice is, of course, impossible to ascertain (not to say largely irrelevant, given the Formalists' views on the role of the author in the literary process). Kharms and Shklovsky

certainly knew of each other's existence; Shklovsky apparently attended an 'Oberiu' evening, while Kharms twice made plans for Shklovsky (along with, on the first occasion, Tynyanov and Eikhenbaum) to collaborate with the 'Oberiuty' on *avant-garde* literary reviews (although these were never published). For details of these projects, see A. Vvedenskii, *Polnoe sobranie sochinenii*, Vol. 1 (Michigan, 1980), pp. xviii and xxiii; and Vol. 2 (Michigan, 1984), pp. 236–7. Shklovsky played a role (albeit a relatively minor one) in the 'rediscovery' of Kharms and his work by the Soviet public: 'O tsvetnykh snakh', *Literaturnaia gazeta*, 22 November 1967, p. 16.

35. R. Jakobson, 'Čo je poesie?', in *Volne Smery*, 30 (1933–34), pp. 229–39; quoted in V. Erlich, *Russian Formalism: History, Doctrine* (New Haven and London, 1981), p. 181.

36. Iu. Tynianov, 'O literaturnoi evoliutsii', in *Arkhaisty i novatory* (Leningrad, 1929), pp. 30–47. The English translation is taken from Iu. Tynyanov, 'On Literary Evolution', in *Readings in Russian Poetics: Formalist and Structuralist Views*, ed. L. Matejka and K. Pomorska (Michigan, 1978), pp. 66–78 (p. 72).

37. My discussion of Wittgenstein's linguistic philosophy is partly inspired by Allen Thiher's comments in *Words in Reflection: Modern Language Theory and Postmodern Fiction* (Chicago, 1984), and in particular Chapter 1. Surprisingly, virtually no one has yet linked the names of Kharms and Wittgenstein. The only critic to have done so is Robin Milner-Gulland: see his review of A. Stone-Nakhimovsky, *Laughter in the Void: An Introduction to the Writings of Daniil Kharms and Aleksandr Vvedenskii* (Vienna, 1982), published as ' "Kovarnye stikhi": Notes on Daniil Kharms and Aleksandr Vvedensky', *Essays in Poetics*, 9 (1984), pp. 16–37, and particularly p. 33.

Interestingly, Wittgenstein's views on language are in some ways close to the linguistic theories espoused by a close associate of the Oberiu, L. S. Lipavskii. He held that the 'world' in which each individual existed was constituted primarily by his/her language. For details of Lipavskii, his philosophy and his influence on the 'Oberiuty', see Ia. S. Druskin, 1989, pp. 113–15. During the 1930s, Lipavskii held regular meetings, which were frequently attended by Kharms and the other members of the group, at which discussions of a general intellectual nature took place, Druskin notes (p. 115) that, of all the Oberiuty, Kharms expressed the most interest in Lipavskii's views on language. In particular, Lipavskii's concept of the 'vestnik', meaning a messenger from the world of divine logos, appears in Kharms's prose text *O tom, kak menya posetili vestniki* ('A Tale About How I was Visited by Messengers', Kharms, 1988, pp. 503–4).

38. Quoted from the abridged version of Wittgenstein's *Philosophical Investigations*, contained in *Deconstruction in Context*, ed. M. C. Taylor (Chicago, 1986), p. 232.

39. R. Jakobson, 'The Dominant', translated from the Czech by H. Eagle, in *Readings in Russian Poetics*, ed. L. Matejka and K. Pomorska (Michigan, 1978), pp. 82–7 (p. 85).

40. For a discussion of the subordination of 'mimesis' to 'semiosis' in folk

literature, see P. Bogatyrev, 'Semiotics in the Folk Theatre', published in English translation in *Semiotics of Art: Prague School Contributions*, ed. L. Matejka and I. R. Titunik (Cambridge, Mass., 1976), pp. 33–50.

41. For a (brief) discussion of this element of the folkloric tradition in Kharms's work see V. Sazhin, 'Literaturnye i fol'klornye traditsii v tvorchestve Daniila Kharmsa' in *Literaturnyi protsess: razvitie russkoi kul'tury XVIII–XX vekov* (Tallinn, 1985), pp. 57–61.

42. Shklovsky points out the importance of narrative 'bifurcation' (i.e. the recurrence of the same episode in the text) in the ballad or folk song in his essay, 'Svyaz' priemov siuzhetoslozheniia s obshchimi priemami stilia' in *Poetika: sborniki po teorii poeticheskogo iazyka* (Petrograd, 1919).

43. The integration of circus elements into theatrical performances was widespread in the Soviet Union of the 1920s, and particularly in the agit-prop spectacles of troupes such as the 'Siniaia Bluza'. For information on this group, see F. Deak, 'Sinyaya Bluza', *The Drama Review* (Russian Issue), 17 (1) (1973), pp. 36–46.

44. H. Maxton, 'Kharms and Myles: An afterword', in D. Kharms, *The Plummeting Old Women*, ed. and trans. N. Cornwell (Dublin, 1989), pp. 93–100 (p.96).

45. Bakhtin discusses the 'carnivalesque' principally in two works, namely *Problemy poetika Dostoevskogo*, 3rd edn, Moscow, 1972) and *Tvorchestvo Fransua Rable i narodanaia kul'tura srednevekovia i Renessansa* (Moscow, 1965). The extent to which, as Bakhtin puts it, 'in the narrowly formalist, literary parody of the modern era the link with the carnivalesque world view has almost totally been lost' (Bakhtin, 1972, p. 217) is, unfortunately, beyond the scope of this paper. I am in agreement, however, with Linda Hutcheon when she argues that 'despite Bakhtin's rejection of modern parody, there are close links between what he called carnivalesque parody and the authorised transgression of parodic texts today'. See her book, *The Theory of Parody: The Teachings of Twentieth-century Art Forms* (London, 1984), p. 26.

46. T. Eagleton, 'Wittgenstein's Friends', *New Left Review*, 135 (1982), pp. 64–90 (p. 79).

47. This inversion of the relative social position of these characters is never more apparent than in the third *kusok*, where Ivan Ivanovich begs Elizaveta to be allowed to go home; *Esli pozvolite. Elizaveta Tarakanovna, ia poidu luchshe domoi,... Vy uzh prostite menia. Ia, Elizaveta Mikhailovna, domoi poidu'* ('If you don't mind, Elizaveta Cockroachovna, I think I'd better go home. ... Please excuse me. Elizaveta Mikhailovna, I shall go home now') (Kharms, 1988, p. 181).

Significantly, perhaps, this inversion is maintained in the text only as long as 'realism' is absent either from the section headings or from the text itself (in other words, sections one, two, eighteen and nineteen). Moreover, in the penultimate heading, 'Realisticheskii sukho-ofitsial'nyi' (Realistic, dully-official'), art which is 'realist' is identified with the overtly unethical 'official' language of the Stalinist state and its agents (see Meilakh, 1987, p. 240).

48. A. Jefferson, 'Bodymatters: Self and Other in Bakhtin, Sartre and Barthes', in *Bakhtin and Cultural Theory,* ed. K. Hirschkop and D. Shepherd (Manchester. 1989), p. 166.
49. Text untitled in Kharms's manuscript. *Soviet Union / Union Soviétique,* 7 (1980), pp. 232–3.
50. These terms are taken from S. Stewart, *Nonsense: Aspects of Intertextuality in Folklore* and *Literature* (London, 1979), p. 19.

10 Pilate and Pilatism in Recent Russian Literature
Margaret Ziolkowski

'Then it is an affair that does not concern me, and I wash my hands of it,' said Nunzio Sacca, going through the motions of washing his hands as he spoke.
'I'm glad to hear you express yourself in such Biblical fashion,' said Spina. 'It's obvious your religious education wasn't wasted.'
Ignazio Silone, *Bread and Wine*

In recent decades, Russian writers have made effective use of Pontius Pilate, as a character, reference or allusion, in a wide variety of works published abroad and in the Soviet Union. Undoubtedly the best known is Mikhail Bulgakov's satirical fantasy *Master i Margarita* (The Master and Margarita), finally published in 1966–67, which altered forever Soviet literary appreciation of the sometimes enigmatic encounter between Jesus and Pilate. It would now require a deliberate obtuseness on the part of a Soviet author wishing to treat the figure of Pilate at any length to ignore Bulgakov's portrayal of the psychological, social and political factors that enter into Pilate's desire, but ultimate refusal to help Jesus escape execution. The cynical question 'What is truth?' has long been virtually synonymous with Pilate's name. To this expression of amoral relativism, Bulgakov has added the provocative notion that '[cowardice] is the most terrible vice' (735).[1]

Bulgakov's highly original treatment has received much attention. The ethical implications of Pilate's behaviour command the interest of Soviet intellectuals even without such encouragement, however. Indeed there exists another tradition of using the figure of the Procurator, independent of the influence of Bulgakov's masterpiece. The extent and nature of the impact of Bulgakov's assessment of Pilate on writers like Chingiz Aitmatov and Iurii Dombrovskii form part of the subject of this chapter. An equally important concern is the recurrence in several literary works produced in recent decades of the image of Pilate or motifs associated with his ostentatiously disengaged stance, namely, his infamous handwashing. Such references provide a convenient shorthand for abnegation of ethical responsibility and reflect the peculiar congeniality of Pilate within a Soviet milieu. This is especially true of works set in the Stalin era and concerned with the lingering influence of Stalinism. Within this corpus Pilate functions as one of several potent recurring images employed to suggest the socio-psychological damage inflicted by Stalin on the Soviet populace.

Bulgakov's Pilate is torn by the competing demands of political concerns, aptly symbolised by the odious head of Tiberius that he imagines when the issue of *lèse-majesté* is raised in connection with Jesus's purported crimes, and his suspicion that Jesus is actually innocent, the victim of Sanhedrin desires for his destruction. Relying heavily on the biblical scholar S. G. F. Brandon's discussion of the ways in which the Gospels portray the Procurator's psychology, the Bulgakov specialist Andrew Barratt refers to this recognition by Pilate as the 'Markan hypothesis'; this theory, which is actually implicit in all four Gospels, apparently originated with Mark (200).[2] It accounts for Pilate's initial reluctance to uphold the decision of the Jewish authorities, a reluctance he suppresses in order to maintain political face. Barratt convincingly posits the influence on *The Master and Margarita* of a 'Johannine hypothesis' as well, that is, the idea hinted at in the fourth Gospel that Pilate reacted not only to an intellectual sense that Jesus had been falsely accused, but also responded on an emotional level to his charisma (200). The interaction between these two complementary motives makes Bulgakov's Procurator a credible and moving figure.[3] His cowardice is the more painful for representing not only a concession to political expediency, but also a betrayal of personal feeling. No attempts to assuage his conscience, whether by arranging the death of Judas or by trying to come to the aid of Matthew Levi, can erase Pilate's sense of failure; his cowardice becomes his obsession.

For Soviet as well as many Western readers, Bulgakov's condemnation of moral cowardice in the person of the Procurator of Judea suggested a direct applicability to the novel's other socio-graphical locus, Moscow of the 1930s, Stalinist Russia. Bulgakov himself may, as Konstantin Simonov claims, eschew 'superficial historical analogies', considering them 'literary cheapness', but many of his interpreters are less restrained.[4] In a well-known and influential essay on the novel written in 1968, the Soviet critic Vladimir Lakshin asserted that the interaction between Pilate and Ieshua Ga-Notsri touches on 'the same problem of good and evil, of the weakness and power of the human will that underlie the story of Woland's Moscow adventures' (264).[5] Of Pilate's lack of evil intentions towards Ieshua, Lakshin observes that

Bulgakov is nonetheless merciless in his condemnation because of his awareness that it is not those few people actively pursuing evil who are so dangerous, but those who because of their faintheartedness and cowardice become the blind instruments of evil (268). Lakshin makes a subtle distinction between fear and cowardice, defining cowardice as 'fear multiplied by baseness, an attempt to preserve peace and well-being by compromising one's conscience' (276). In the context of his article, this concept is by implication eminently applicable to life under Stalin. Comparing the Moscow and Jerusalem sections of the novel, Lakshin draws a parallel between the interaction of Pilate and Ieshua, on the one hand, and that of the opportunistic critic Latunskii and the Master, on the other. While Lakshin acknowledges that Latunskii is 'far lower and pettier' (304) than Pilate, his comparison is nonetheless suggestive, for it is indicative of the tendency of Soviet liberal critics, discussed at some length by Barratt, to view the story of Pilate as an example of the process by which tyranny is facilitated and his cowardice as an implicit commentary on the behaviour of many of those who lived during the Stalin era.[6] The émigré critic Leonid Rzhevskii formulates this idea even more explicitly when he defines 'Pilate's sin' as 'the grave sin of betrayal, of tolerance of evil out of fear for one's personal well-being'. Rzhevskii goes on to suggest that Bulgakov intended the term 'Pilatism' *(pilatchina)*, used in *The Master and Margarita* as a sneering reference to the Master's novel, to signify 'the cowardice and treachery prevalent among people in a country of police surveillance and investigation'.[7]

An interpretation of Pilate's behaviour that underscores connections with Soviet existence has undoubtedly often proved congenial to Soviet intellectuals as well as readers abroad. One indication of the continuing appeal of such an approach is found in Chingiz Aitmatov's recent novel *Plakha* (The Place of the Skull, 1986), where the influence of Bulgakov's Procurator is clearly felt, but which offers a more circumscribed view of his character. Aitmatov's own somewhat obscure appraisal of the relationship between his Biblical characters and those of Bulgakov emphasises the direct dependence of his interpretation on recent historical developments:

Of course I thought about Bulgakov in the sense that Pontius Pilate and Jesus the Nazarene – these are the same characters and they are in the same situation. But...since the time that this meeting found a reflection in Bulgakov a certain amount of history has passed and we live in a somewhat different temporal dimension. I felt like introducing something new that we are getting to know today, and, in part, to speak about the global vulnerability of the human world as such.[8]

Aitmatov's most extensive original contribution to the dialogue between Pilate and Jesus is a consideration of the meaning of the Last Judgement and the Second Coming, a discussion whose anachronistic features are acknowledged by the character supposedly responsible for this version of the encounter, the former seminarian Avdii Kallistratov. The primary import of Jesus's discourse is that the Second Coming will take place if men begin to live righteously, to abandon 'the evil of lust for power with which all are infected' (155).[9] The necessity for such a radical reassessment of existential priorities is the theme of many of Aitmatov's works. However, this kind of thinking has little impact on Pilate, who is unwavering in his certainty that the power of Rome is supreme and that this is as it should be.

Aitmatov's Procurator bears a pronounced superficial resemblance to Bulgakov's. Cynical but intelligent, he is reluctant to give immediate approval to the Sanhedrin death sentence. Insistent on maintaining, or at least appearing to maintain, his morally uncommitted stance, however, he rationalises his ill-defined doubts regarding Jesus's guilt as a desire for complete understanding of the latter's political motives. His wife's note begging him not to sanction Jesus's execution, a detail borrowed from Matthew 27:19, implicitly provides another externally-motivated reason for Pilate's attempts to sway Jesus in his convictions; the Procurator cannot acknowledge the possibility of his own sympathy for Jesus.

The source of Pilate's doubts regarding Jesus's guilt would seem to lie in that same 'Markan hypothesis' that plays an important role in *The Master and Margarita* and elsewhere. 'Who are you, that the Roman emperor should beware of you? – some unknown wanderer, a doubtful prophet, a market-place loudmouth, which the land of Judea is chock-full of' (142), observes Aitmatov's Pilate. His contemptuous assessment reveals a sense that the sentence against Jesus is of unwarranted magnitude. But when Jesus resists his efforts to convince him to recant, Pilate concludes that he is wasting his time and declares that he washes his hands of the affair. He then feels a certain relief, a conviction that Jesus's impending death is the self-styled prophet's own responsibility. Rationalisation succeeds rationalisation, as Pilate decides that perhaps Jesus had indeed had grandiose political ambitions.

To the extent that Aitmatov's Pilate is suspicious of the Jewish authorities and doubts Jesus's guilt, trying instead to convince him to help lessen the severity of his punishment, there is a certain similarity with Bulgakov's Procurator.[10] There are, however, fundamental differences between the two characters. These stem largely from the relative unimportance of the 'Johannine hypothesis' in Aitmatov's account. Aitmatov's Pilate is sympathetic to Jesus and intrigued by his views, particularly on the question of the Last Judgement, and part of him applauds Jesus's refusal to recant and beg for mercy, all of which suggests at least some responsiveness to the force of Jesus's personality. Yet the startling and intensely emotional reaction to Jesus's clairvoyant and commanding spirituality that characterises Bulgakov's Pilate is lacking in Aitmatov's character, for whom Jesus's charisma is essentially alien. How complete Pilate's lack of comprehension is becomes apparent at the end of his meeting with Jesus, when he is flattered by the latter's suggestion that the Procurator will find a place in history forever. The only chink in his complacency occurs when he observes a large bird that has been circling over the palace all morning fly off after Jesus as he heads towards Golgotha. Unable to appreciate true spiritual integrity, this Pilate can only respond to portents.

Aitmatov's lesser emphasis on the 'Johannine hypothesis' has suggestive implications as regards Soviet liberal understanding of the figure of Pilate updated to incorporate present-day realities. Avdii Kallistratov expresses an explicitly contemporised view of Pilate when he thinks about how 'the shade of Pilate...has not disappeared even to this day. (After all there are potential Pilates even now)' (164). From Aitmatov's account of the encounter between Pilate and Jesus, it would appear that this potentiality consists of a willingness to ignore the probable innocence of victims in favour of self-serving, power-orientated considerations. This interpretation of Pilate concedes little if any spiritual sensitivity to the Procurator and lends itself well to applicability to Soviet existence, for it reduces the encounter between victim and victimiser to a largely external level, minimising the possibility of psychological attraction to the victim on the part of the victimiser. Thus diminished in complexity, Pilate is both easier to condemn and simpler to adduce as a reference point for contemporary abuses. Significantly, Pilate and Jesus appear in *The Place of the Skull* immediately after an analogous confrontation between Avdii and the drugrunner Grishan, who resembles Pilate in his relativistic apprehension of righteousness, his unshakable belief in temporal power, and his ultimate willingness tacitly to sanction murder.[11] Grishan far exceeds the Procurator in his cynicism and viciousness, however.

The Master and Margarita and *The Place of the Skull* contain the most extensive treatments of the figure of Pilate found in Russian literary works published in the past few decades. The notorious handwasher has evoked consistent interest, however, and there are several other works that contain references to Pilate and, in some instances, brief discussion of his significance. Many of these are set in the Stalin era, a coincidence which implies that the type of behaviour exemplified by Pilate may be perceived as peculiarly relevant to that period, even when its apparent relevance has not been suggested by *The Master and Margarita*. The reasons for this in turn often reflect a view of Pilate much narrower in scope than Bulgakov's.

Two pertinent and well-known underground works published abroad several years before *The Master and Margarita* are satirical pieces by, respectively, Andrei Siniavskii and his later co-defendant Iulii Daniel', *Sud idet* (The Trial Begins, 1959) and 'Govorit Moskva' (This is Moscow Speaking, 1960–61). *The Trial Begins,* set on the eve of Stalin's death in 1953, boasts several unsympathetic characters, the most unscrupulous of whom is the defence lawyer Iurii Karlinskii. Karlinskii's ethical position is familiarly relativistic; the idealistic teenager Seriozha reports him as saying that what matters is one's point of view: 'For some, what's just is the opposite for others' (203).[12] When Seriozha's friend Katia comes to him with a notebook describing their plans for reforming society, Karlinskii amuses himself by exposing their ideas as 'Trotskyism'. Simultaneously, however, he has no desire for contact with subversive elements and hopes that Seriozha will subsequently show more caution and avoid implicating him; this fear of authority is, of course, also a familiar phenomenon where evocation of 'Pilatism' is concerned. Meanwhile, completely undone by Karlinskii's rhetoric and fearing that he will denounce Seriozha, Katia decides to go to school authorities to clarify the situation. This leads to Seriozha's arrest. Unaware that her own actions are responsible, however, and convinced that Karlinskii must have betrayed her friend, Katia leaves him an angry note: 'You have treacherously denounced Sergei Vladimirovich, but all the same he is not a Trotskyite, but an honest revolutionary, while you are a coward and a scoundrel' (260). Karlinskii is undismayed by this accusation, which is justified in general, if not specific terms, and after he puts the note aside, the narrator observes: 'Then, like Pontius Pilate, Iurii washed his hands. He did not feel like remembering Seriozha and Katia. Probably Pontius Pilate thought little about Jesus Christ when he went to have his wash. Perhaps Pontius also had a purpose, unknown to the Evangelists' (260).

Karlinskii's similarity with Pilate lies in his knowledge that Seriozha is innocent of any crime of which he may have been accused and his simultaneous refusal to involve himself, to concern himself with Seriozha's fate. Like Pilate's, Karlinskii's handwashing is symbolic of indifference, avoidance of responsibility, and not a little cowardice. There is no suggestion of any kind of sympathy for his teenage victims on the part of the selfish lawyer. Instead, as the reference to Pilate underscores here, Karlinskii is an example of complete moral cynicism, the inevitable product of a society obsessed with purposes and ends to the exclusion of morality.

Although Daniel"s satirical fantasy 'This is Moscow Speaking' is set in 1960, it also implicitly concerns the lingering consequences of Stalinism. The story revolves around the announcement of a Public Murder Day, a legally sanctioned opportunity for virtually any Soviet citizen to kill another. The narrator, Tolia, a still youthful war veteran, retains idealistic feelings about the inception of the Soviet Union and about Lenin in particular. He is angered when one of his friends suggests that the Decree is a logical outgrowth of socialist doctrine, a simple codification of longstanding attitudes. Soon afterwards, though, disgust at his fearful plans for spending Public Murder Day in hiding drives Tolia to confront his own questionable attitudes: 'Then what was I worth, with all my splendid enthusiasm for exposure, for scorn, with my revolting detached position? A Pontius Pilate, daily betraying his own soul - what was I worth?' (45)[13] As elsewhere, Pilate in this context becomes a metaphor for cowardly moral compromise. In Tolia's eyes detachment is suspect, a synonym for betrayal. Unlike Karlinskii, complacent in his 'Pilatism', Tolia is shocked by self-analysis into going out on Public Murder Day with vague plans for offering his fellow citizens an alternative vision of existence. By the end of 'This is Moscow Speaking' Tolia has adopted an ethical philosophy that stands in direct opposition to the indifference exhibited by Pilate: 'This is your world, your life, and you are a cell, a particle of it. You must not allow yourself to be intimidated. You must answer for yourself, and in this way you are answerable for others' (61).

Before its publication in 1966, *The Master and Margarita* was known only to a small circle.[14] The references to Pilate in *The Trial Begins* and 'This is Moscow Speaking' do not suggest an awareness of Bulgakov's character on the part of their authors, but instead a more stereotyped understanding of the Procurator's significance derived from popular views of him as the personification of cowardly moral indifference. It is this popular understanding of Pilate which may account, for example, for the writer Fedor Abramov being nicknamed 'little Pilate' (Pilatushka) in the postwar period or, more recently, for an interview on psychiatric prisons being entitled 'Inkvizitory i pilaty' ('Inquisitors and Pilates').[15] In both *The Trial Begins* and 'This is Moscow Speaking', 'Pilatism' appears linked to the phenomenon of Stalinism, which is perceived by Siniavskii and Daniel' as a comprehensive socio-political system that encourages relinquishment of responsibility and devotion to selfish concerns.

The pernicious relationship between Stalinism and 'Pilatism' is also the subject of Varlam Shalamov's short story, 'Prokurator Iudei' (The Procurator of Judea, 1978). Influenced by Anatole France's story of the same name published in 1891, Shalamov uses the image of Pilate in a slightly different way from Siniavskii and Daniel'. France's story describes a meeting between Pilate and a Roman friend some years after the former's tenure in Jerusalem. Expressing violent distaste for the Jews, this Pilate recalls the parodies of justice in which he was forced to participate:

> A hundred times, at least, have I known them, mustered, rich and poor together, all united under their priests, make a furious onslaught on my ivory chair,...all to demand of me – nay to exact from me – the death sentence on some unfortunate whose guilt I failed to perceive, and about whom I could only pronounce that he was as mad as his accusers... .At the outset of my term of office I endeavored to persuade them to hear reason; I attempted to snatch their miserable victims from death. But this show of mildness only irritated them the more...(20–21).[16]

Yet though he remembers such scenes, Pilate cannot recall Jesus. When his interlocutor asks about him, Pilate can only answer: 'Jesus – of Nazareth? I cannot call him to mind' (25). France's story ends with this comment, and the reader is left to ponder the irony of Pilate's forgetfulness. Did repeated participation in miscarriages of justice dull the memory of particulars, or were the events involving Jesus so painful that Pilate deliberately suppressed the recollection of them? Shalamov's story suggests that it may have been the latter. Shalamov's 'Procurator of Judea' concerns not Pilate, but the surgeon Kubantsev, who comes from frontline service to head the surgical division of a hospital for prisoners on Kolyma. On his first day, in the winter of 1947, a ship arrives filled with three thousand victims of severe frostbite, prisoners sprayed with water when they staged a shipboard uprising. Kubantsev cannot come to grips with the situation and hands over direction of operations to someone else. In order to function in such circumstances subsequently, the surgeon's psychological recourse is to obliterate the horror from his memory: 'It was necessary to forget all this, and Kubantsev, a disciplined and strongwilled person, did just that. He forced himself to forget' (613).[17] Seventeen years later he can remember everything about his experience on Kolyma except the ship with its wretched load. The narrator concludes the story by drawing an analogy with France's Pilate: 'Anatole France has a story "The Procurator of Judea". There Pontius Pilate cannot remember Christ after seventeen years' (614). The reference suggests that when forced to be a party to vicious crimes against humanity, people of normal sympathies and intelligence react by suppressing their knowledge of evil, for otherwise they might lose their mental equilibrium. In this instance, Pilate represents deliberate coarsening of the spirit, a psychological mechanism once again implicitly related to the specific conditions of Stalinism.

The indifference of Pilate, his refusal to concern himself with Jesus's fate, is symbolically linked in the New Testament to the Procurator's washing his hands. His unconvincing demonstration is intended to show that his conscience is clean. As a metaphor for abnegation of responsibility, the handwashing motif is widely familiar, and explicit reference to Pilate is not necessary to make its import clear.[18] In Aitmatov's play *Voskhozhdenie na Fudziiamu* (Ascent of Mount Fuji, 1975), which deals largely with the question of which of a group of friends betrayed another friend during the war, the issue of moral responsibility is pointedly evoked when one of the characters objects to the suggestion that they dispense with intimate revelations: 'So, I display my soul before you, but you – so good, so pure – wash your hands?' (29).[19] In Anatolii Rybakov's *Deti Arbata* (Children of the Arbat, 1987), a young woman is criticised for her lack of political vigilance in regard to her fellow student, the virtuous Sasha Pankratov: 'You washed your hands, you wanted to secure yourself' (36).[20] In this instance, the use of the motif is ironic, for in fact the student is attempting to 'secure' herself by *not* defending Pankratov against accusations of subversion; she has made the decision to wash her hands of him.

The examples above refer to metaphorical use of the handwashing motif. In another work concerned with repression under Stalin, Iurii Trifonov's semi-autobiographical *Ischeznovenie* (The Disappearance, 1987), the motif is exploited in literal and original fashion, but with similar significance. After the search of the apartment of an arrestee, one of the NKVD agents wants to wash his hands and asks for soap:

> Sergei took him to the bathroom. His hands didn't wash clean because they were soiled with oil paint. Sergei brought a bottle of turpentine. He did this involuntarily, not out of obligingness, but simply because he wanted them to leave somewhat more quickly. While [the agent] was rubbing his hands with the turpentine, lathering and rinsing them under the faucet, Sergei looked at his unpretentious ... face (82).[21]

Symbolically, the agent is attempting to wash away his share in the responsibility for the travesty of justice in which he has just participated.

A similar scene is described in *Children of the Arbat*, when Sasha Pankratov is arrested in early 1934:

> while the [GPU] representative washed his hands, [Sasha's mother] stood in the door of the bathroom with a towel in her hands and held it out with a pitiful, ingratiating smile: perhaps this person would lighten the lot of her son there....
>
> The representative dried his hands, went out into the corridor, made a phone call...Then...he leaned against the door with the unconcerned face of a person who has finished his business (80–1).

Here, too, the handwashing provides a symbolic corollary to the detachment exhibited by the GPU operative. In both *Children of the Arbat* and *The Disappearance* the act of handwashing evokes the moral evasiveness traditionally associated with Pilate, even though the handwashers themselves are presumably unaware of the symbolic implications of their behaviour.

The influence of Bulgakov and the ascription of 'Pilatistic' behaviour to literary characters found in works dealing with the Stalin era coalesce in one of the most sophisticated treatments of the Great Terror, Iurii Dombrovskii's *Fakul'tet nenuzhnykh veshchei* (The Department of Unnecessary Things, 1978), recently published in the Soviet Union for the first time.[22] Dombrovskii worked on the novel between 1965 and 1976; *The Master and Margarita*, it will be remembered, appeared in 1966–67.[23] As in his earlier novel, *Khranitel' drevnostei* (The Keeper of Antiquities, 1964), the protagonist is the Alma-Ata museum curator Georgii Zybin. The plot of *The Department of Unnecessary Things* revolves around Zybin's arrest in 1937, his lengthy interrogation by the NKVD, and his eventual, and surprising, release. On another level, the novel constitutes an extended philosophical analysis of Stalinism.

Two other important characters in *The Department of Unnecessary*

Things are the archaeologist Volodia Kornilov and the former priest Father Andrei. In the course of their rambling and inebriated conversations, the two touch at some length on the significance of the story of Jesus in terms closely linked to contemporary socio-political phenomena. One of the issues they discuss is that of forgiveness, a process Kornilov has difficulty understanding. In considering Jesus's apostles, Kornilov comments sarcastically on how many of them failed their leader (he has in mind Judas, Peter and Thomas), speaking of this in deliberately contemporised terms: 'Just think what kind of company he gathered for himself...Twenty-five percent defective products *[brak]*. Any director of cadres would be removed for such a selection' (224).[24] Kornilov's impression of Pilate is similarly harsh and likewise expressed with reference to Soviet categories:

> and what do you do with Pilate? A judge, washing his hands? Who even passed a death sentence, and is supposedly not guilty of the death. Because if the community howls 'crucify, crucify!', then what remains for the judge, it's true, but to crucify? So what should we do with this president of a military tribunal? Forgive him, too? For his decency? He didn't simply crucify, he said, but washed his hands beforehand? He didn't want to, he said, but he submitted to the community. Ah, what a mitigating circumstance! So will he enter into the Kingdom of God or not? (224–5)

Kornilov is contemptuous of Pilate for what he perceives as his mealy-mouthed accommodation to public pressure. Father Andrei disagrees, however. He believes that Pilate should be forgiven, arguing that Pilate's moral squeamishness is a positive phenomenon because it represents the first step towards the development of a sense of morality.

Father Andrei, it subsequently appears, is very much interested in Pilate. During his next conversation with Kornilov, Andrei begins to speak of the procurator immediately after Kornilov has confessed to showing the local NKVD representatives Andrei's manuscript about Jesus. Father Andrei begins his discourse on Pilate by pointing out that there may be diametrically opposed interpretations of his behaviour. He quotes Kornilov as an example and reiterates the latter's use of the metaphor for the president of a military tribunal, thus underscoring Pilate's potential as an analogue for contemporary phenomena. After a lengthy digression on Jesus and the witnesses against him, Father Andrei returns to Pilate. He cites the opinion of an academic with whom he once spoke, which, like Kornilov's appraisal, is couched in terms applicable to the present-day situation:

we are rolling in such Pilates. He's a typical average bureaucrat of the times of empire. Stern, but not cruel, crafty, and knowledgeable about the world. In small and indisputable matters – just and even principled; in matters on a larger scale – evasive and indecisive. And in everything else – very, very crafty. Therefore, although he even understands the truth, at the least fogginess he begins to twist, he washes his hands, so to speak. (269)

The academic's view, though slightly more charitable than Kornilov's, is also a variant of traditional and widespread assumptions about Pilate's essential lack of moral fibre.

Father Andrei's point of view is somewhat different, however. Andrei makes much of Pilate's hatred of the Jews. He also suggests that Pilate had a good grasp of Jesus's philosophy and that his opposition to political upheavals and emphasis on internal, psychological revolution was very much to Pilate's taste, as was Jesus's apparent antipathy to Jewish authority; Jesus, Pilate felt, could be useful to Rome. Finally, according to Andrei, Pilate did not wish to be a passive tool in the hands of Jewish religious authority. All these reasons, however, yielded in the face of the threat of political consequences.

In the midst of his speculations about Pilate, Father Andrei digresses on the dramatic potential of the story of Jesus and offers as an example a scene between Pilate and Jesus which shifts into the Procurator's confrontation with the crowd over which prisoner should be released in honour of Passover. Andrei refers in a general way to the Evangelists as the inspiration for his own account, but even a cursory reading of his dramatised version reveals that it is largely a condensation, often nearly verbatim, of passages from John. The famous question about truth is included, as is the accusation that Pilate is no friend of Caesar's if he releases Jesus. Indeed, Andrei's interpretation of Pilate as a whole consistently reflects the greatest dependence on John, particularly in terms of Pilate's appreciation of Jesus's potential as an iconoclastic religious leader.

The influence of Bulgakov's portrayal of the encounter between Pilate and Jesus is most evident in *The Department of Unnecessary Things* in Andrei's great reliance on John's more thoughtful treatment of the Procurator, which is also apparent in *The Master and Margarita*, and his extensive attention to the reasons for Pilate's antipathy to the Jews.[25] As in Bulgakov's novel, in Dombrovskii's work Pilate emerges as a far more complex personality than the cynical and insensitive coward of time-honoured tradition. Like Bulgakov's Pilate, Dombrovskii's Procurator does, of course, ultimately succumb to cowardice for fear of political consequences, but only after sincere attempts both to comprehend Jesus's personality and motives and to release him. Dombrovskii's Pilate is no epigone, however. He differs most clearly from Bulgakov's character in that his intuitive appreciation of Jesus, though far superior to that of Aitmatov's Procurator, does not lead to a personal, emotional response to the prisoner. Thus, while operative to the extent that Pilate does recognise Jesus's charisma, the implications of the 'Johannine hypothesis' are not fully exploited by Dombrovskii.

An equally important difference between *The Master and Margarita* and *The Department of Unnecessary Things* is that in Dombrovskii's novel the relevance of Pilate's experience to Soviet existence in the 1930s is not simply implied, but explicitly stated. On the one hand, this is the logical culmination of the deliberately provocative analogies suggested between Biblical and contemporary events throughout Kornilov's conversations with Andrei. It is also once again reflective of Soviet liberal perceptions of Pilate as, in a sense, an eminently Stalinist type. Father Andrei most directly enunciates the applicability of Pilate to the present. His careful study of the personality of the historical Procurator lends greater credibility to his assertion, at the conclusion of his discourse, that the NKVD agents are modern-day Pilates:

> you say they summoned you and appropriated my manuscript from you....because they don't want to crucify me. So, you were speaking there with the same Pilates. With the same unfortunate Pilates, on whom absolutely nothing depends. With murderers and butchers in the name of an alien god! With poor Judas, whom it's not even possible to forgive, because there isn't anything [to forgive him for]! For it's not they who are all guilty, but those nonentities who sit behind seven walls and send them messages in cipher: 'Seize, judge, execute.' (274)

When Kornilov disingenuously asks him to identify these nonentities, Andrei characterises them as 'the ruddy dwarf and the half-witted Moses' (274), a clear reference to Nikolai Ezhov, the head of the NKVD, and Stalin. Andrei's designation of Stalin as a kind of Moses further enriches the Biblical parallel, pointing to the pseudo-religiosity of Communist faith. Kornilov's refusal to understand elicits a final desperate reaction from Andrei: 'However many times I tell this story, no one understands anything about it... .But you know, it's simple. Very simple. But because of it one either dies or betrays!' (274). Thus, in Andrei's conception, contemporary realities create innumerable Pilates and Jesuses. Yet being a Pilate means only that one is a tool, a puppet, in the hands of those few evil geniuses who actually retain political control. Andrei's interpretation of Pilate suggests that cowardice is not tantamount to responsibility and that only a very few are actually culpable.

Andrei's seductive logic is shortly undermined, however, by the revelation that he has scurrilously denounced Kornilov for anti-Soviet remarks, believing, Kornilov realises, that he has 'sold him out' (285). His sympathy for the likes of Pilate and Judas now appears coloured by personal considerations; in playing down their responsibility, he minimises his own.[26] Yet while this may cast doubts on the generosity of Andrei's interpretations of the behaviour of Biblical characters, it does not invalidate the suggested relevance of the experience of these characters to the Soviet situation. This is borne out by subsequent references to Pilate in *The Department of Unnecessary Things*.

Other references to Pilate occur in the conversations the incarcerated Zybin has with his temporary cellmate Georgii Kalandarashvili, a longtime prisoner and acquaintance of Stalin. Kalandarashvili recounts a discussion he had with a certain NKVD official and former friend, during which he told the latter: 'the trouble is that our argument is never-ending, it's a question as old as the world – what is truth? Christ, as you remember, didn't answer Pilate' (357). When his friend asks what Kalandarashvili would respond, he answers: 'White is white, and black is black' (357). His reply constitutes a refusal to accept the relativistic world-view implied by Pilate's question. His friend, though, insists on the difficulty of distinguishing between black and white, on their changeability depending on circumstances, a truly Pilatistic point of view.

Kalandarashvili refers again to Pilate when Zybin asks him about the role of conscience: 'Well, and what about conscience....What kind of conception is it?...it's almost Pilate's question: "What is truth?" ' (364). The old Georgian uses references to Pushkin and Saltykov-Shchedrin to illustrate the idea that conscience is a fluid notion, dependent on individual belief. All the characters in *The Department of Unnecessary Things* must make a choice. In his actions, Zybin adheres to the idea that it is possible to distinguish between black and white, while Kornilov is submerged in a morass of equivocations. While the question of the degree of responsibility remains controversial, Father Andrei's division of people into Pilates and Jesuses, into those who compromise and those who retain their integrity, holds true for the fictional world of Dombrovskii.

By implying that such a clear-cut division between good and evil may exist, *The Department of Unnecessary Things* serves as an example of how ultimately limited the impact of Bulgakov's apprehension of Pilate on later Russian literature has been. The existence of the Jerusalem chapters of *The Master and Margarita* encourages extensive literary attention to the figure of the Procurator, as may have occurred in the cases of Dombrovskii and Aitmatov, but the poignancy and subtlety of Bulgakov's portrayal are lacking in other works. One reason for this is that the depth of Pilate's responsiveness to Jesus is lessened in works like *The Place of the Skull* and *The Department of Unnecessary Things* and the major focus remains the destructive influence of political considerations on the workings of justice. The most obvious function performed by *The Master and Margarita* has been to suggest broadening the perspective of an already existing popular conception of Pilate through the use of historical details which elucidate the pressures under which the Procurator operated. In *The Department of Unnecessary Things,* this in turn undermines the image of Pilate as a cynical opportunist, pointing instead to the possibility that he was less an executioner than a tool. In *The Place of the Skull*, historical details reinforce a sense that human behaviour is often dominated by power-oriented considerations that lead to the suppression of genuinely compassionate feelings.

Within the corpus of recent Russian literature, Pilate appears in the form of a character, reference or passing allusion most often in works concerned with the Stalin era or the lingering consequences of Stalinism. In some instances, specifically in *The Department of Unnecessary Things,* the appropriateness of references to Pilate in discussion of these subjects may have been suggested by the example of *The Master and Margarita,* but in general it is more likely that other factors were involved. Isolated references to Pilate, or allusions to the handwashing so closely associated with him, tend to ignore the possibility that he was in any sense himself a victim and to concentrate instead on features derived from nebulous popular conceptions of the Procurator that emphasise his cynicism, cowardice, and indifference. For many writers, these traits contain a ready-made applicability to description of the Stalin era and the psychological legacy of Stalinism. This may often have less to do with literary example than with cultural stereotyping; in liberal Soviet circles, where the works discussed in this chapter often originate, interpretations of the Stalin era frequently tend towards highly schematised conceptions of victims and victimisers.[27] The Pilate of popular tradition easily corroborates such a world-view, offering in addition the advantage of widespread recognisability. If this is the case, the likelihood of the appearance of similar allusions in as yet unpublished Soviet literary portrayals of the Stalin era seems almost inevitable, while the recurrence of perspectives as original and compassionate as Bulgakov's is unlikely. Damned for two millenia by popular opinion, the Pilate imagined by Soviet authors seems largely doomed to resemble nothing so much as the kind of corrupt intellectual mediocrity embodied in Bulgakov's Latunskii, not his Procurator.

Notes

1. Mikhail Bulgakov, *Romany: Belaia gvardiia, Teatral'nyi roman, Master i Margarita* (Leningrad, 1973). Unless otherwise noted, all translations are my own. In his study of the Jerusalem chapters of *The Master and Margarita*, A. Zerkalov convincingly argues that these words represent the sole direct address to the reader by Bulgakov within the novel. See *Evangelie Mikhaila Bulgakova* (Ann Arbor, Michigan, 1984), p. 156.
2. Andrew Barratt, *Between Two Worlds: A Critical Introduction to The Master and Margarita* (Oxford, 1987). Brandon's discussion of Pilate in the Book of Mark is found in *The Trial of Jesus of Nazareth* (New York, 1968), pp. 79–106.
3. The term *prefect* is actually more accurate than *procurator,* but I have retained *procurator* because it is the term often employed by the Russian authors whom I discuss. Cf. C. K. Barrett, *The Gospel According to John*, 2nd edn (Philadelphia, 1978), p. 533.
4. Konstantin Simonov, 'O trekh romanakh Mikhaila Bulgakova', in Bulgakov, *Romany,* p. 9.
5. Vladimir Lakshin, 'Mikhail Bulgakov's *The Master and Margarita'*, tr. Carol A. Palmer, in Victor Erlich, ed., *Twentieth-Century Russian Criticism* (New Haven, Connecticut, 1975). Lakshin's essay first appeared in *Novyi mir,* 1968, no. 6, pp.284–311.
6. Cf. Barratt, *Between Two Worlds,* pp. 29, 96.
7. L. Rzhevskii, 'Pilatov grekh: O tainopisi v romane M. Bulgakova "Master i Margarita" ', *Novyi zhurnal,* 1968, no. 90, pp. 79–80.
8. Chingiz Aitmatov, 'Tsena-zhizn' ', *Literaturnaia gazeta,* 13 August 1986, p. 4. Elsewhere Aitmatov suggests that Bulgakov's Pilate 'moves Jesus into the shade somewhat' and that his own intention was 'to return Jesus to the centre'. See Chingiz Aitmatov, 'Kak slovo nashe otzovetsia' (interview by N. Anastas'ev), *Druzhba narodov,* 1987, no. 2, p. 237.
9. Chingiz Aitmatov, *Plakha* (Moscow, 1987).
10. On points of similarity between Bulgakov's and Aitmatov's Pilates, see, for example, A. I. Pavlovskii, 'O romane Chingiza Aitmatova *Plakha*', *Russkaia literatura,* 1988, no. 1, p. 112.

11. Comparisons between the Pilate/Jesus and Grishan/Avdii encounters have been made by both Soviet and Western scholars. See, for example, N. N. Shneidman, *Soviet Literature in the 1980s: Decade of Transition* (Toronto, 1989), p. 204; and Aleksandr Kosorukov, 'Plakha – novyi mif ili novaia real'nost'?, *Nash sovremennik*, 1988, no. 8, p. 146. Ironically, Aitmatov himself denies having wished to create such an analogy. See Aitmatov, 'Kak slovo nashe otzovetsia', p. 236.
12. Andrei Siniavskii [Abram Terts], *Sud idet*, in his *Fantasticheskie povesti* (New York, 1967).
13. Iulii Daniel' [Nikolai Arzhak], *Govorit Moskva* (Washington, 1962).
14. In her study of Bulgakov, Ellendea Proffer comments: 'After Bulgakov's death [his wife Elena Sergeevna] was careful not to let anyone outside of her own circle know about his manuscripts – and she managed to keep *The Master and Margarita* from circulating widely even in the 1960s, the Golden Age of *samizdat* when virtually everything came out of the drawers.' See *Bulgakov: Life and Work* (Ann Arbor, Michigan, 1984), p. 504.
15. On Abramov, see Carl R. and Ellendea Proffer, 'Introduction' to Fyodor Abramov, *Two Winters and Three Summers*, trans. D. B. Powers and Doris C. Powers (Ann Arbor, Michigan, 1984), p. vii. The Proffers raise the question: 'Can a bad man – an executioner, at the very least, a Pilate – write a good novel?' (viii). 'Inkvisitory i pilaty', an interview with Viktor Fainberg, appeared in *Posev*, 31 (1975), pp. 7–13.
16. *Golden Tales of Anatole France* (New York, 1927).
17. Varlam Shalamov, 'Prokurator Iudei', in his *Kolymskie rasskazy*, 2nd edn (Paris, 1982).
18. A curious example of the use of this motif occurs in Venedikt Erofeev's *Moskva-Petushki* (Moscow-Petushki, 1973), in which the alcoholic narrator twice compares himself to Pilate in the context of a drunken fantasy.
19. Chingiz Aitmatov and Kaltai Mukhamedzhanov, *Voskhoshdenie na Fudziiamu* (Moscow, 1973).
20. Anatolii Rybakov, *Deti Arbata* (Moscow, 1978).
21. Iurii Trifonov, *Ischeznovenie*, *Druzhba narodov*, 1987, no. 1.
22. *Novyi mir*, 1988, nos 8–11.
23. Cf. Marianne Gourg, 'Dombrovskij commentateur de la Légende du Grand Inquisiteur dans la Faculté de l'Inutile', *Dostoevsky Studies* 8 (1987), p. 168.
24. Iurii Dombrovskii, *Fakul'tet nenuzhnykh veshchei* (Paris, 1978).
25. On some oblique references to Bulgakov in *The Department of Unnecessary Things*, see Gourg, 'Dombrovskij commentateur', p. 162.
26. On this point, cf. Aleksei Zverev, ' "Glubokii kolodets svobody...": Nad stranitsami Iuriia Dombrovskogo', *Literaturnoe obozrenie*, 1989, no. 4, p. 19. Zverev is particularly insistent that portraits of Judas and Pilate delineated by informers are unreliable.
27. Anna Akhmatova, for example, spoke of the rehabilitations of the late 1950s in the following way: 'Two Russias will look each other in the eye – those who imprisoned, and those whom they imprisoned.' See Lidiia Chukovskaia, 'Iz knigi *Zapiski ob Anne Akhmatovoi*', in *Pamiati A.*

Akhmatovoi (Paris, 1974), p. 188. More recently, Roy Medvedev declared in a roundtable discussion conducted by *Moskovskie novosti:* 'One cannot consider the victims of repression only those who were in the camps or perished. In principle the victims of repression were the entire people' (*Moskovskie novosti*, 12 February 1989, p. 9).

Index of Names

Notes: (1) 'n' after a page number indicates that a name appears once or more in the endnotes on that page; (2) Russian names have been transliterated according to the US Library of Congress transliteration table, irrespective of their spelling in the text.

Abramov, V.   3, 108, 110, 119n, 120n, 171, 180n
Abuladze, T.   93, 103n
Adamovich, A.   4, 7
Afanas'ev, Iu.   92–3, 103n
Afanas'ev, V.   99
Agranovich, S.   74n
Agurskii, M.   120
Aitmatov, C.   4, 5, 6, 13, 65–74 *passim*, 77, 81, 164, 166–8, 172, 178, 179n, 180
Akhmatova. A.   1, 9, 10, 94, 103n, 136n, 180n
Aksakov, I.   117
Aksakov, K.   117
Aksakov, S.   117
Aksenov, V.   32, 117n, 121n
Aleksandrov, A.   157n
Allworth, E.   119n
Amlinskii, V.   94, 103n
Anastas'ev, N.   7, 179n
Anenome, A.   159n
Anninskii, L.   14, 63, 73n, 74n
Antonov, S.   92, 94, 101, 103n
Aristotle   34, 48, 60n, 87n
Arutiunov, L.   6, 16n
Arzhak, N. *see* Daniel', Iu.
Aseev, S.   12
Astaf'ev, V.   1–15 *passim*, 77, 79, 81, 88n, 109, 112, 116, 120n
Augustine   59n, 60n
Averintsev, S.   74n

Babaevskii, S.   114
Bakhterev, I.   138, 158n
Bakhtin, M.   36, 40, 49, 51, 58n, 61n, 155, 156, 162n
Baklanov, G.   93, 99, 103n
Barber, J.   104n
Barratt, A.   165, 166, 179n

Barrett, C.K.   179n
Barthes, R.   142, 159n
Bastos, A.R.   5, 6
Bek, A.   93, 97, 103n
Belaia, G.   118n, 119n, 121n
Belinskii, V.   78, 88n
Belov, V.   1–13 *passim*, 94, 98, 104n, 108–20 *passim*
Bely, A.   10
Benjamin, W.   62n
Beria, L.   95
Bergson, H.   36, 37, 58, 58n
Bocharov, A.   114, 119n
Bogatyrev, P.   162n
Bondarev, Iu.   115
Botticelli   88n
Brandon, S.G.F.   165, 179n
Brang, P.   160n
Brecht, B.   28
Brezhnev, L.   90, 91, 101
Brik, O.   159n
Brodskii, I.   99, 120n, 122–37 *passim*
Brooks, P.   48
Bukharin, N.   95
Bulgakov, M.   1, 5, 9, 10, 18, 85, 88, 164–79 *passim*
Bunin, I.   76
Bykov, V.   4, 9

Carroll, L.   38, 60n
Cassirer, E.   55, 62n
Cavafy   128
Chaikovskii, P.   60n
Chalmaev, V.   114
Chances, E.   159n, 160n
Chebrikov, V.   90, 103n
Chekhov, A.   4, 154
Christie, I.   102n
Chukovskaia, L.   53, 180n
Chuzhak, N.   159n

183

Index of Names

Clark, K. 66–7, 74n
Coe, R. 120n
Cohen, R. 120n
Cohen, S. 93, 103n
Conquest, R. 93, 98, 103n
Cornwell, N. 159n
Crane, S. 75

Daniel', Iu. 169, 170, 171, 180n
Danilov, V. 98, 104n
Davies, R.W. 102n, 104n
Davis, F. 111–12, 120n
Deak, F. 162n
Dejevsky, M. 102n
Denisieva, I. 61n
Deshevov, V. 26
Dombrovskii, Iu. 164, 173–8, 180n
Dorosh, E. 119n
Dostoevskii, F. 10, 60n, 79
Druskin, Ia. 158n, 161n
Drutse, I. 6
Dudintsev, V. 94, 103n
Dunlop, J. 104n

Eagleton, T. 155, 162n
Eder, R. 137n
Eidel'man, N. 116, 120n
Eikhenbaum, B. 161n
Eizenshtein, S. 23, 26–7, 30, 34n
Ekimov, B. 108
Emel'ianov, L. 9
Emerson, C. 58n, 59n, 61n
Epshtein, M. 67, 73n, 74n
Eremina, L. 105n
Ere', V. 157n, 159n
Erlich, V. 161n
Erofeev, V. 180n
Ezerskaia, B. 137n
Ezhov, N. 95

Fainberg, V. 180n
Farino, J. 122, 135n
Farrell, J. 75
Faulkner, W. 6, 7
Filipov, B. 33n
Filonov, P. 23
Foucault, M. 142, 159n
France, A. 171, 172
Freeborn, R. 159n
Freud, S. 60n
Furmanov, D. 29

Gallagher, A. 159n
Gardner, J. 13, 17n
Garshin, V. 154

Genette, G. 39, 42, 45, 52, 60n, 61n, 160n
Genis, A. 62n, 119n
Gerasimov, I. 93, 103n
Gerasimova, A. 157n, 159n
Gibian, G. 119n, 157n
Gilis, F. 119n
Gillespie, D. 104n
Ginzburg, L. 11, 17n
Glad, J. 137n
Goethe 58n
Goldshtein, D. 156n
Goncourt brothers 75
Gor, G. 34b
Gorbachev, M. 11, 89–103 *passim*, 117
Gorbachev, V. 114
Gorbanevskaia, N. 137n
Gorbenko, A. 19
Gor'kii, M. 10, 31–2, 35n
Gorshenin, A. 119n
Goscilo, H. 60n
Gourg, M. 180n
Graffy, J. 102n
Granin, D. 94, 104n
Greenwood, E.B. 48, 61n
Grigorovich, D. 78
Grossman, V. 1, 2, 9, 92, 95, 103n, 104n
Gumilev, N. 136n

Harari, J. 159n
Haugh, R. 104n
Heidegger, M. 62n
Hirschkop, K. 163n
Hoffman, E.T.A. 61n
Holquist, M. 59n
Hosking, G. 102n, 111, 114, 120n
Husserl, E. 40, 59n
Hutcheon, L. 147–8, 160n, 162n

Iampol'skii, B. 94, 104n
Ibragimova, A. 74n
Ilev, S. 70, 74n
Ionesco, E. 160n
Ionin, L. 93, 103n
Iskander, F. 4
Iukina, E. 67, 73n, 74n
Ivanova, N. 74n

Jaccard, J.-P. 158n, 160n
Jakobson, R. 48, 61n, 62n, 154, 161n
Jefferson, A. 156, 163n

Kaganovich, L. 95

Index of Names

Kaledin, S. 76–87 *passim*
Kamenev, L. 98
Kant, I. 51, 59n
Kariakin, Iu. 114
Katsman, G. 158n
Kazakov, Iu. 108
Keller, B. 121n
Kelly, C. 158n
Kermode, F. 39, 40, 59, 60n
Kharms, D. 10, 138–62 *passim*
Khentova, S. 34n, 35n
Khrushchev, N. 89, 91
Khvatov, A. 119n
Kinarskii 137n
Kirshon, V. 34n
Knorin, V. 32n
Korobova, E. 136n
Korotich, V. 99
Kosorukov, A. 74n, 180n
Kozhinov, V. 104n, 114
Krauss, R. 120n
Krivulin, V. 136n
Krupin, V. 108, 115
Krylov, I. 154
Kubilius, V. 63, 73n
Kublanovskii, Iu. 125, 136n
Kuniaev, S. 115
Kuznetsova, N. 104n

Laqueur, W. 102n
Lakshin, V. 121n, 165–6, 179n
Latsis, A. 104n
Latynina, A. 101, 105n
Leibniz 54
Lemon, L. 160n, 161n
Lenin, V.I. 11, 95–6, 101
Leskov, N. 4
Levin, B. 138
Lewis, P. 119n
Leyda, J. 34n
Libedinskii, Iu. 29, 30, 34n
Lichutin, V. 108–19 *passim*
Lifson, M.R. 59n, 60n
Ligachev, E. 90, 103n
Likhachev, D. 90, 117, 146, 159n
Lipavskii, L. 161–2n
Likhonosov, V. 115
Liubomudrov, M. 121n
Lobanov, M. 114
Lodge, D. 61n
London, J. 75
Losev, A. 5, 73n
Losev, L. 124, 125, 132, 135n, 136n, 137n
Lotman, Iu. 76, 88n

Lunacharskii, A. 18, 21, 33n
Lur'e, S. 136n
L'vov, N. 19

McCarthy, M. 37
Maiakovskii, V. 10
Makarenko, A. 81
Makedonov, A. 158n
Makin, M. 158n
Mamardashvili, M. 15
Man, P.de 61n
Mandel'shtam, O. 9, 10, 24, 53
Maramzin, A. 135n, 137n
Marinchik, P. 19, 32n, 33n
Marquez, G. García 6
Marsh, R. 103n, 104n
Matejka, L. 161n, 162n
Matevosian, G. 5, 6, 7
Maxton, H. 155, 162n
Medvedev, R. 93, 98, 103n, 181n
Meerson-Aksenov, M. 120n
Meierkhol'd, V. 21, 23, 25, 30, 33n
Meilakh, M. 142, 154, 157n, 158n, 159n, 162n
Meletinskii, E. 64, 73n, 74n
Metcalfe, A. 34n
Milner-Gulland, R. 156n, 158n, 159n, 161n
Mironova, B. 32n, 33n
Mirza-Akhmedova, P. 74n
Mokul'skii, S. 34n
Monas, S. 120n
Morson, S. 58n, 61n
Mozhaev, B. 4, 92–104 *passim*, 108, 111
Muir, E. 37, 59n
Mukhamedzhanov, K. 180n

Nabokov, V. 37, 99, 59n, 61n
Naiman, A. 123, 135n
Nepomnyashchy, C.T. 119n
Nicholson, M. 104n
Nietzsche, F. 55
Nikolaeva, G. 114
Nivat, G. 135n
Nosov, E. 5
Nove, A. 102n, 104n
Nuikin, A. 74n

Oja, M. 62n
Okudzhava, B. 4
Ostrovskii, A. 115
Ovechkin, V. 106, 119n

Panchenko, T. 70, 73n, 74n, 146, 159n
Panferov, F. 32

Parshchikov, A. 134, 137n
Parthé, K. 118n
Pasternak, B. 1, 9, 10, 99, 105n
Paton, S. 74
Pavlovskii, A. 179
Pel'she, R. 21, 33n
Pertsovskii, V. 3, 33n
Petrik, A. 119n, 120n
Petrov, N. 29, 32n, 34n
Petrushevskaia, L. 76–88 passim
Pil'niak, B. 18
Piotrovskii, A. 23–34 passim
Piskunov, B. 74n
Piskunova, S. 74n
Platonov, A. 99, 105n
Poliakov, Iu. 92
Polukhina, V. 136n
Pomorska, K. 161n
Popov, E. 76–88 passim
Popov, G. 93, 103n
Pristavkin, A. 92, 94, 103n
Proffer, C. 180n
Proffer, E. 180n
Proskurin 115, 116
Proust, M. 42, 53
Prutkov, K. 141
Pushkin, A. 51

Radiants, N. 32n
Radlov, S. 33n
Rafalovich, V. 32n
Rasputin, V. 1, 4, 7, 8, 15, 77, 81, 107–21 passim
Razgon, L. 92, 95, 103n
Razumovskaia, L. 78, 79, 88n
Rein, E. 136n, 137n
Reis, M. 160n
Rezvin, I. 157n
Rezvina, O. 157n
Richards, I.A. 61n
Ricoeur, P. 36, 37, 40, 55, 58n, 59n, 60n, 62n
Rimmon-Kenan, S. 145, 159n
Romm, S. 34n
Rose, M. 142, 159n
Rousseau, J.-J. 37
Rubtsov, N. 119n
Rybakov, A. 91–104 passim, 172, 180n
Rzhevskii, L. 166, 179n

Sazhin, V. 162n
Sedakova, O. 128, 136n, 137n
Seleznev, G. 114
Shafarevich, I. 115, 120n
Shalamov, V. 53, 62n, 71–2, 180n

Shapiro, J. 105n
Shatrov, M. 91–103 passim
Shepherd, D. 158n, 163n
Shipler, D. 120n
Shishkova, R. 62n
Shklovskii, V. 151, 160n, 162n
Shneidman, N. 180n
Shostakovich, D. 23–31 passim
Shragin, B. 120n
Shukman, A. 157n
Shukshin, V. 3–14 passim, 80, 119n
Sidorova, K. 104n
Simonov, K. 92, 103n, 179n
Siniavskii, A. 105n, 169–70, 171, 180
Sokolovskii, M. 19–34 passim
Sollertinskii, I. 34n
Soloukhin, V. 110, 112, 119n, 121n
Solov'ev, V. 33n
Solzhenitsyn, A. 53, 62, 95–6, 97, 98, 101, 104n, 109, 115, 119n, 120n
Spring, D. 104n
Stalin/Stalinism 2, 9, 89–102 passim, 165–79 passim
Stanislavskii, K. 27, 31, 34n
Starikova, E. 114
Stelleman, J. 140, 158n
Stewart, S. 163n
Stimpson, C.R. 120n
Stone-Nakhimovsky, A. 161n
Strizhalova, L. 104n
Sumerkin, A. 159n

Taylor, M. 161n
Tendriakov, V. 92, 103n, 108, 110, 113, 119n, 120n
Tertz, A. see Siniavskii, A.
Tevosian, I. 93
Thiher, A. 153, 161n
Titunik, T. 162n
Tiutchev, F. 47, 61n
Todorov, T. 47
Tolmachev, D. 32n
Tolstaia, T. 36–62 passim, 85, 88n, 121n
Tolstoi, L. 4, 10, 37
Tomashevskii, B. 149, 160n
Trifonov, Iu. 4, 11, 36, 58n, 94, 104n, 172–3, 180n
Trotskii, L. 98
Tseitlin, A. 77, 88n
Tsvetov, G. 119n, 120n
Turgenev, I. 115, 118n
Turner, J. 97, 104n
Tvardovskii, A. 9, 11, 94, 103n
Tynianov, Iu. 152, 154, 161n

Index of Names

Ueland, C.   59n
Urban, A.   103n
Urnov, D.   5
Uspenskii, E.   10
Uspenskii, G.   4
Utkin, I.   10

Vaginov, K.   138
Vail', P.   62n, 119n
Velikanov, E.   105n
Vil'chek, L.   118n, 119n
Villon, F.   60n
Vishavskii, A.   141
Voinovich, V.   121n
Volkogonov, D.   93, 103n
Voronov, V.   119n
Vvedenskii, A.   138, 157n, 158n, 159n, 161n

Wachtel, A.B.   59n
Ward, C.   158n
Waugh, P.   142, 152–3, 157n
Weststeijn, W.   135n

Wheatcroft, S.   98, 102n, 104n
White, H.   60n
White, J.   64, 73n
Witte, G.   119n
Wittgenstein, L.   153, 161n
Wolf, C.   62n

Yarmolinsky, A.   118

Zabolotskaia, E.   158n
Zabolotskii, N.   138, 158n
Zalygin, S.   3, 95, 104n
Zamiatin, E.   18, 99
Zerkalov, A.   179n
Zhdanov, A.   10
Zhigulin, A.   92, 95, 103n
Zinov'ev, G.   98
Zola, E.   75, 77, 87n, 88n
Zolian, S.   135n
Zolotusskii, I.   7, 13, 114
Zoshchenko, M.   10, 25
Zverev, A.   180n